*Happy Trails!*

*Don*

# THE FREEWAY

Dori DeCamillis

# THE FREEWAY

*Two Young Artists In Love,*
*On The Road In Search Of Home*

Library of Congress Number:          00-191429
ISBN #:          Hardcover          0-7388-2768-1
                 Softcover          1-59109-268-X

This book was printed in the United States of America.

*For Joe.*

*Our deepest gratitude goes out to all the people mentioned in this book who helped us find the road, stay on it, and ultimately find our home.*

*In memory of our beloved Elga Green.*

## AUTHOR'S NOTE

*The Freeway* is a chronological, comprehensive record of the three years we lived on the road, between 1991 and 1994. From the beginning, this book was intended to tell most of the stories of our life on the road so we wouldn't forget them and so others could enjoy them. Some of the book is inspired by our sparse journal writings from that time, but most is conjured from memory years later.

# PART 1

## The Hood

### June 10, 1991  Boulder, Colorado

My best friend Katie asked me today why we want to leave.
I gave the usual answer, that we need to find a way to make a
living from our art and that Colorado isn't the place to do it.
Thinking about it tonight, though, I know it's more complicated
than that. Our life has been hell lately. Every bad thing that I
would never want to happen to me or anyone else has
happened to Joe and me in the past year. (Or has it been two?)

Dori graduates from college, moves in with her mother, her
anorexia worsens, she makes art 16 hours a day, and goes
mental. Dori and Joe get married. IRS puts lien on D and J's
property, so they work three jobs apiece for six months to pay
back IRS. Joe falls asleep at the wheel and totals car after
working several 23-hour days, so they buy new car on credit. D
and J get in fistfight over money, go to jail for one night.

Henceforth, fighting stops.

D and J, physically exhausted from paying off IRS, stop
working and live off credit cards. Dori's anorexia results in
messed up reproductive system, has emergency surgery on
baseball sized ovarian cysts. No medical insurance.

Henceforth, Dori starts eating.

D and J decide to buy motor home and leave Colorado.

(These events are too horrific to explain in detail now.
Maybe later when I want to face it all).

I have changed swiftly from an optimist to a person who walks down the street wondering not if, but when the sky is going to fall on her head. I am ashamed of our financial stupidity and our craziness. But there must be some spark of hope in us. Somewhere away from here we hope to find a way to become rich and famous from our art. It would be the only way, given the skills we have, to get out of this massive debt we've acquired.

Katie knows about all these terrible things. It's hard to believe she still associates with me. We've been friends since second grade and I always tell her everything, but today was the first time I've mentioned anything to her about going away. She had to find out after I excitedly told her about Lucy, the beautiful motor home that Joe discovered yesterday.

He came running down into our basement apartment yelling, "I found it! I found it!" Joe is usually calm and economical with words, so I knew that something outrageous lay ahead. He blabbered on almost incoherently about the perfect motor home, insisting I drop everything to go look at it.

For weeks we had searched in vain for a recreational vehicle. We'd seen and smelled converted milk trucks, boxy Winnebagos, pickups with homemade wooden camper shells shake-shingled and towering out the back—nothing remotely right.

He dragged me out to our car and we sped us off to see this spectacle, whatever it was. Moments later, in a field of weeds next to a junky house, there sat the RV of our dreams. (Our dream is to live somewhere in this motor home to save ourselves the cost of rent and enable us to get out of debt sooner).

She looked like a giant loaf of white bread with a sloping teardrop-shaped rear end. Apparent years of neglect had left her original white paint job a dismal gray, and a peek into the filthy windows revealed shredded vomit-green curtains barely concealing the dusty interior, which looked stuffed with old tires. Long grass grew up through her wheel wells and engine.

Fortunately we are artists with overactive imaginations. Ordinary humans would never have glanced at this pile of rotting metal. But through it all we pictured a shiny, pure white 1950s style motor home with a red tire mounted in front and shimmering hubcaps.

A homemade For Sale sign taped to the door said, *1970 Ultra Van, $6,000 OBO*, along with a phone number to call, so we raced home to call it. We considered stopping at the nearest pay phone lest some other desperate romantics steal our dream machine.

Our spirits were dashed when we were forced to leave a message, but we spent hours here at home going over our plans to fix her up and how great she'll look and where we'll park her. We've named her Lucy. Lucille Ball would love that motor home.

### June 15, 1991

We own Lucy. We finally reached Vaughn Fosmo, the owner of the coach, who, after inviting us over to see Lucy again, was very surprised to see us arrive minutes after he set the phone down. He was a quiet man, wearing much more than his forty-something years under his long hair and baggy overalls. He would mutter quietly, rambling off all the mechanical information we could ever want to know about the coach, sometimes stopping his monologue to stare for a few seconds, then start up on another subject. As we are completely inept at auto mechanics anyway, we barely understood a word he said. He eventually explained that his mind was a bit fuzzy from years of working with the toxic dust of some metal or other.

After a few days of going back and forth on the price, we have finally settled on $4,000 in our never-to-be-spent emergency savings fund. Our motor home purchase could be a screaming deal or a complete rip-off. We are both thrilled and scared at owning, in full, our first piece of private property bigger than a stereo or a ten-speed.

Tonight Lucy sleeps alone at the Table Mesa Apartments paved parking lot across the street from where we live. They charge us $10 a month even though Lucy is parked in two of 94 open spaces that are never used.

### June 16, 1991

We call our basement apartment "The Stank Shack". Each huge room has one tiny window that only opens a crack right against the ceiling. This evening we walked over to admire Lucy after housepainting in the hot sun all day. Her wretched smell reminded us of our basement home. She is actually stinkier than the Stank Shack, and we are looking forward to gutting her creepy insides soon. She smells like a wet dog. After Vaughn Fosmo removed all the tires, trash, and rusty tools, we found Lucy to have orange hexagon-patterned carpet that is filled with holes, grease, and gravy stains. The front seats are covered in faded orange upholstery with cigarette burns and crumbling foam spilling out of rips. Although we are excited about making major changes, I have no idea when we will have the time.

### June 31, 1991

Now that we have the vehicle, we need the journey. We've been discussing ideas of where to travel and how to make a living. Every day at work, painting houses, we rake through the pros and cons of various itineraries while I trim the windows and Joe hangs from our rickety ladder, rolling some boring color onto someone else's house. California seems to be our first choice for a try at art stardom with its rich people and tender climate. Joe went to college in Los Angeles for a few years and loved it; I decided it was paradise when my family vacationed there during my teenage years. Living in a motor home could only be possible in a warm place anyway.

### July 4, 1991

We've officially decided upon California, because we can't think of any place better, considering our circumstances. What better reason to make a life-altering choice?

We visit Lucy nightly to remove strange remnants of Vaughn Fosmo's inventiveness. Knobs, hooks, bolts, holes; we call them Vaughn Gizmos. They are attached to Lucy's insides in profusion and have no apparent use other than a potential place to attach something else in the future. It has been an unending task to try to extract them all. Each time we think we have located the last one, we find a half dozen more hidden in another corner.

### July 6, 1991

I'm exhausted. Joe and I are lying in our bed, cussing about our sore feet, sore hands, and dirty bodies. We have been painting houses by day and ripping out Lucy's innards by night. Joe has always had a strong stomach, able to keep his lunch down while witnessing or cleaning the most foul of substances. But our work today had him flying out the camper door, gagging and spitting. We were pulling up the hexagon carpet. As the stuff peeled back, the mildewed, crumbly foam that lay underneath flew in all directions, and particles of it floated in the air and into our nose, eyes, and mouth.

The cupboard shelves are covered with a thin black layer of goo topped with dust. The curtains have to be removed very carefully to prevent them from disintegrating into the air like some ancient Egyptian artifact. I personally will go nowhere near the toilet.

## July 8, 1991

Through Vaughn Fosmo and the Ultra Van manual, Joe and I are becoming educated about Lucy's past.

A BRIEF HISTORY OF THE ULTRA VAN (This is important stuff)

In 1960, the first Ultra Van Motor Home was designed and hand-built by an aircraft engineer named David Peterson of Oakland, California. A total of 380 Ultra Vans were built, mostly in Hutchinson, Kansas, in a former World War II airplane hangar until the year 1970, when the company went out of business. Due to the mass production of other motor homes, the hand-built Ultras were relatively expensive, and the company could not stay afloat.

All Ultra Vans were built from General Motor parts, the earlier coaches from parts of the Chevy Corvair—a beautiful car, air-cooled instead of water-cooled, with the engine in the back. Corvair production discontinued after the car was labeled "dangerous at any speed" by consumer advocate Ralph Nader in the 1960s. After the death of the Corvair, the last fifty Ultra Vans were equipped with the powerful but weighty 307 cubic inch Chevy V-8 engine, which would have made the vehicle into a potential hot rod motor home had it not been for the coach's Corvette suspension in the rear, unable to support the heavy engine along with a motor home. This design flaw is one of the main troubles for "V-8 owners" (that's us) who have to service our rear bearings (somewhat of a pain in the butt) every 10,000 miles.

For the purpose of keeping Ultra Vans alive, the *Ultra Van Manual* was written by Len and Edie Ryerson, in response to the destruction by fire of the Ultra hangar with all Ultra records inside. The book required years of painstaking effort to

research and includes every detail of Ultra maintenance and
repairs one could consider, from cleaning the walls to taking
apart the transmission. (SPECIAL NOTE: The entire four-inch-
thick book is typed on a *manual* typewriter!!!) This book is an
absolute must for the Ultra owner.

Ultra Van owners must keep in touch, in order to keep their
coaches on the road. The vehicles are now at least twenty years
old, some thirty, and repairs are tricky because of the unique
construction, some rare parts, and design flaws that were never
quite worked out. For contact with other Ultra fanatics, there
are two clubs—The Ultra Motor Van Motor Coach Club, Inc.
and Group Ultra Van, both with a president, vice-president,
secretary-treasurer, and newsletter editor. Each has their own
newsletter with helpful Ultra "tech tips", bits of silly advice,
stories of Ultra owners, photos of Ultra Vans, letters from coach
owners and such. Some of the articles are pretty dry, such as
"The History of the SafeGuard Ignition Retard System" or
"Causes and Cures for Engine Knock." One club even
distributes the *Ultra Van Motor Coach Directory*, which lists all
Ultra owners, their coach number (ours is 538), their address
and phone. Most owners welcome a visit from other traveling
Ultra people, provided forty-eight hours notice is given. Rallies,
or big get-togethers for coach-owners, happen nearly every
month of the year in some part of the country, and can include
potlucks, tech sessions, crafts "for the ladies", skits, raffles, and
election of officers.

To demonstrate the seriousness of the Ultra World, here is a
quote from "Ultra Postscripts" in the *Ultra Van Motor Coach Club,
Inc. Newsletter*:

"My brother, Larry, says, "I FEEL myself all over every
morning when I wake up. If I'm WARM I know that I'm alive;
then I get up."

**August 20, 1991   Weeks later**

After many grueling nights and weekends of spitting out
her old interior and carefully piecing together a new one, Lucy
is a goddess. Black and white tiled floor, red gingham curtains,
aqua appliances, and blue denim seats have replaced the
previous putridity. The only remains of the old look are the
brown wood-grain walls and cabinets. However, as any RV
owner can attest, looks aren't everything. Being artists, we've
put aesthetics first and empowered Lucy with a gleaming
facade but have not even tinkered with her ability to function.

Tomorrow we are attempting the bold experiment—putting the key in the ignition.

## August 21, 1991

We put the key in and turned. Lucy wouldn't start. Last week we found a note attached to our windshield wiper. It said, *I own an Ultra. Call me. Christy Barden.* So we did and found out that Christy is a man with an Irish name and is coming over to look at our coach tomorrow. Maybe he can help us start Lucy.

## August 22, 1991

Today in the Table Mesa parking lot after lunch, we met Christy, a guy in his fifties who prides himself on his ability to make others think he is a bit weird. He did not hesitate to offer us help with our start-up problem. After an hour or two of testing solenoid, starter, battery, fuel pump, and more, he finally asked, "You put gas in it, didn't you?"

We added gas. Lucy started.

## August 23, 1991

Today we attempted our first test drive. Lucy started, but our first expectant press on the gas pedal gave no response. Some deductive reasoning on Joe's part led to the addition of transmission fluid. I was behind the wheel when we tested his hypothesis, and we cheered wildly when Lucy began to move across the parking lot. Seconds later, when I pressed the brake pedal and received no indication of slowing whatsoever, a different kind of bedlam ensued. I panicked, screaming profanities about our inevitable crash into a parked car and suggested we bail into the bushes. Joe, the Iceman, calmly suggested I steer Lucy through the parking lot until she glided to a stop, which I did.

Liquid seemed to be the answer to all of our mechanical problems thus far (gas and transmission fluid), so our next try was brake fluid. It worked. I think we are in real trouble if anything involving solids should cause a problem.

## August 24, 1991

Joe and I seem to get along better and better these days. Last year our relationship was close to ruin, but recent peacekeeping efforts have been more than fruitful. We are

quick to compromise or see the other's point of view, petrified
that we might start fighting about some inane triviality. It has
made our summer a joy in comparison to previous times. We're
little love buddies.

"I'm going to King  Soopers to get some fruit, honey."

"Oh, let me go with you."

"But it's just across the street."

"I'll miss you."

"O.K. We can pick out grapefruit together."

I just wish our money situation  was as sweet as our attitude
toward each other. We've renovated Lucy with the lowest
amount of funds possible, but our outrageous debts have seen
no improvement. House painting sustains us, but it sure doesn't
get us ahead. Our only hope is to become rich and famous
artists in California. We talk incessantly about our big dreams
while we work together each day. And when we're not talking
about them, we're thinking them.

### August 29, 1991

We painted Lucy's exterior today in Christy Barden's
backyard. As we are the masters of cut-rate refurbishing, we
managed to accomplish the job for next to nothing. A couple
coats of white tractor paint sprayed on with our house-sprayer
transformed Lucy into a milky, radiant, hi-gloss beauty. A red
tire cover, custom made last week and placed in front between
her two headlights, formed the nose of her giant happy face.

Christy was on the scene taking photos of our every action
and facial gesture for Ultra Van posterity. I don't think he
expected a couple of kids in a dusty field to yield such a
smooth, shiny product.

### September 1, 1991

We've been so busy it has taken us a month to finish one
lousy painting. I hardly see how we can become rich and
famous artists without any art. As soon as we get settled in Los
Angeles, we can get down to the business of creativity. My
impatience accumulates daily.

Ours has been a career of many compliments but few sales.
Up until last year, we were always involved in some gimmick
or scheme to get attention in the art world. Finally, after a
heinous failure of a show at a gallery in Denver last year, we
changed our artistic purpose. We had spent a full year toiling
over this hugely elaborate conceptual installation with

thousands of tiny details only to receive some pats on the back. We promptly took the show home and destroyed the entire mass by punching, kicking, and crushing it to pieces in the Stank Shack backyard and stuffing it into trash cans.

We decided that we no longer had any interest in being intellectual, cutting edge, or even clever. Our artistic purpose became to make money from our art. So now we make paintings for "ordinary people". In college I painted large, expressionistic, colorful canvases of house interiors and they were well received by "ordinary" family and friends. In our first official attempt at collaboration, we've reverted back to that theme, and are painting smaller, more controlled interiors, still with bright colors, always empty of objects or people. A local gallery, Dunbar Morss, has sold a couple pieces, but as always, compliments vastly outweigh the dollars they bring in.

Our collaboration happened without much forethought or analysis. Before we were married, Joe started helping me in the studio—sanding canvases and frames, loading stuff. When we first got married I taught him how to paint, for fun. I was amazed at how quickly he picked it up and developed into a talented painter. By the time we came up with the idea of returning to interiors, we decided to try a painting together. Without much effort, we seemed to be able to discuss what we wanted to achieve and set out doing it. In no time we were working together as one entity. We'd work on the same piece at the same time, tackling opposite ends of the piece until our paintbrushes would clack together.

I love collaborating because if I have difficulty with an area or idea, I can hand it to Joe and say, "See what you can do with this." We never have problems with artist's block. We never feel isolated or misunderstood like many artists. And a nice fringe benefit: We make art twice as fast.

**September 2, 1991**

Today I looked up Elga (pronounced El-gee) and Hilda Green, perfect strangers, members of the Ultra Van Motor Coach Club, residents of Los Angeles. Ages: over seventy. I called for suggestions on places to park and live in a motor home in Los Angeles and was treated like an old friend the minute I uttered the Ultra word. They both spoke on the phone simultaneously, eager to help, and unselfishly offered to

investigate our request. I am to call them back in one week to
see what they've come up with.

### September 9, 1991

I am shocked. I called Elga and Hilda back today and found
that this past week, they drove around the L.A. vicinity looking
for accommodations just for us! Strangers! They found
absolutely nothing, but to add to their magnanimity, they
offered their own driveway until we find something else!

It gets even more amazing.

We will be arriving in L.A. around September 20. They will
be traveling when we get there and won't return until late
October.

"Just stay in our driveway until we get back." Hilda said.

"Are you sure you trust us?" I asked.

"You have a kind voice and you own an Ultra. What more
do we need? Go ahead and get water from our hose, and on
the side of the house, you'll find a sewer outlet for your
holding tank."

"What will the neighbors say?" I worried.

"You don't have to worry about them. I should tell you it's
not a very nice neighborhood."

"What do you mean?"

"Well, it's just not a very nice neighborhood. It's fine for us
but it might bother you."

"Oh, I'm sure it will be fine," I quickly replied, positive that
the deal was already too sweet for anything to upset it.

After my most enthusiastic thank yous and well-wishes, we
said our see-you-in-Octobers and hung up. I bounced around
the living room like a pogo stick while giving Joe the good
news.

### September 12, 1991

We had a gargantuan yard sale this past weekend. We love
to attend big cheap yard sales, so we treated Boulder to an
extra big cheap one. That's exactly what our signs said: BIG
CHEAP YARD SALE. We divided the yard into fourths: the
nickel section, the dime section, the quarter section, and the
over a dollar section. People swarmed in and cleaned us out of
everything but the goo-covered or broken stuff by 1:00 p.m.

YARD SALE HAPPENINGS:

a) A large Korean family, ages ranging from one month to 102 years, spent an hour trying to talk prices down on everything we had, including the nickel stuff. I finally told them to leave because I was ready to bonk them with my 25¢ set of crockware.

b) I got choked up when I sold my entire vintage apron collection for $1.00. It won't fit in the Ultra, and we can't save everything, so out it goes.

c) A lady and her daughter nearly fainted from shock that I was selling my Pierre Cardin luggage set for 50¢. They bought it, obviously.

d) We phoned a junk man at day's end to come take the leftovers. He stuffed his beat-up station wagon until it had a four-foot tower of junk on top and things spilling out the windows.

e) We made $350 (that's a lot of change), enough to get us to L.A., we hope.

## September 13, 1991

We put the belongings we couldn't part with in a storage space in Arvada, Colorado. I didn't miss much of the things we sold at the yard sale (aprons not included) but I was sad to lock up our best stuff and leave it. Who knows when we'll be retrieving it? Our plan is to pick it up in six months, when we settle down.

We bought a super heavy-duty fancy shiny everything-proof lock so we will feel safer. As we drove away, I proudly watched it gleam in the sunshine, knowing our things would be secure.

Lucy and the Ford Probe are ready to travel.

## September 15, 1991

Goodbye Boulder. Goodbye all you flaky granola hippies. Goodbye beautiful mountains. Goodbye yucky snow. Goodbye Stank Shack.

We've lived here over ten years, put ourselves through college here and between the two of us, we've worked at nearly every one of the many restaurants in town. We met and fell in love here, have broken our limbs here, lost our virginities here, and I couldn't be more excited about leaving. It must be the right time to move on.

We're packed, our stuff is stored, all loose ends tied, and we're taking off. One of us will drive Lucy, the other; the Probe. Hopefully I will be Master of the Probe most of the time.

## September 20, 1991   Zion National Park, Utah

I feel so lucky. It's night, and I almost always write at night. I just got back from the campground bathroom where I cleaned up, since Lucy has no running water yet. As I walked toward our little camp in the dark, I beamed with pride at the sight of our cute Minnie Mouse Mobile lit up with the glow of candles that shone through our gingham curtains. Earlier, before dark, some German campers in the neighboring site took pictures of our set-up. Surely the photo will be the highlight of their United States vacation scrapbook. I hid because my lipstick had worn off. No one takes my picture without lipstick.

So far the trip has been smooth. Lucy can't travel faster than 55 mph, so our driving days were long, but Utah, the most amazing state in the Union, kept incredible scenery before our eyes. One adventurous incident resulted from Lucy's wiggly suspension. Joe was driving Lucy and I was following in the Probe, witnessing Lucy's back end swerving down the highway, sometimes off onto the shoulder. Terrified that Joe was falling asleep at the wheel, I'd blare the horn and yell out the window to try to keep him awake. Each time we'd stop, I'd be a white-knuckled, nervous wreck.

"What's going on?" I'd yell once we got together.

"What do you mean?" he'd calmly say.

"I thought you were falling asleep at the wheel. Didn't you hear me honking and screaming?"

"No. I was just enjoying the scenery. Lucy's back-heavy so the tail kind of wags the dog, I guess."

"I feel like I'm going to have a heart attack."

"Well, relax, honey. I'm O.K."

But the next time we'd take off, I'd be sure he was drifting off. I'd start my hollering all over again. By mid-Utah I finally got used to it.

The other problem with Lucy became apparent when we pulled off the freeway onto an exit ramp, hoping to find a bathroom at the tiny gas station there. As I slowed down to drive alongside Lucy, I peered over at Joe who had a look of consternation on his face. I was puzzled until he smiled and lifted the steering wheel up in the air over his head. He veered off toward the edge of the road, but stopped just before going over the edge. As usual, I ranted about our inevitable doom while Joe got his toolbox out and fixed it.

## September 21, 1991

We climbed to the top of Angel's Landing today. The five-mile hike ends with a crawl across a thin rock bridge with a 1500-foot drop on both sides. At the end of the narrow bridge is Angel's Landing, a flat rock approximately 20 feet in diameter, surrounded on all sides by the 1500-foot drop and subject to gusty breezes. The view is obviously spectacular, but not many hikers were attempting it due to their fear of heights.

We enjoyed the view not nearly as much as we delighted in the several tiny chipmunks that were on the rock, eating out of our hands and crawling on us, wanting to be stroked. Manly Joe almost killed one of the poor little guys when it scurried up his back while he was bending over. The frightening beast scared poor Joe, who stood up suddenly. The chipmunk flew off, landing inches from the edge of the cliff, nearly producing the world's flattest roadkill. Then the chipmunk came right back over for more love.

Lying in Lucy's bed now with warm, dry air puffing the curtains and the murmur of fellow campers drifting in, I feel more relaxed than I have in months. I'm glad we're taking advantage of a cost-free good time; I'm sure Los Angeles is low on free adventures.

## September 23, 1991   Las Vegas, Nevada

Wooooooo! Here we are at Bob Stupak's Vegas World, lying in our air-conditioned room with purple and silver abstract expressionist wallpaper and a bed set of black lacquer with silver trim. I only care about the cool air.

We arrived at 6:00 this evening to a temperature of 115 degrees. It's September, for God's sake. On the freeway to here, poor Joe had to chug up the desert hills at 30 mph with the heater on full blast to take heat away from the engine and keep Lucy from overheating. I was in the Probe enjoying my cruise control and air conditioning.

We're ecstatic that we previously signed up for Bob's incredible Vegas Vacation offer. In the mail a few months ago, we received one of those "free" vacation packages for only $200. We paid then, and arrived today to receive our $200 in gambling tokens, a beautiful Zsa Zsa Gabor diamond pendant, and a try at the million-dollar jackpot. We will also receive a free meal each day in the "Skylab Lounge" where an actual-size replica of a rocket hangs above the dining room.

## September 24, 1991

We arose early this morning—a habit acquired in the newspaper delivery business and never abandoned—to get in on the $1.99 all-you-can-eat buffet at Circus Circus. Of course, none of the food was good, but we stuffed ourselves anyway to avoid eating lunch later, which costs money. At 9:00 a.m. we had $40 to our name, a sum too small to get us to Los Angeles. Lucy's gas mileage is about eight to ten miles to the gallon, which is good for a motor home but costly nevertheless. We could only hope Bob Stupak's tokens would produce some fruitful results.

We spent the morning using our gratuitous $200 in slot tokens and after keeping all the winnings, came up with $38. Then we devised an ingenious plan for some guaranteed money. The remaining $200 in tokens was designated for roulette use only. So on each bet we placed a token on red and a token on black, guaranteeing us $100 cash. These tokens are given out to visitors with the assumption that anyone coming to Vegas for a vacation is here to gamble and hence, lose all of their money. If they had sneaky people like us coming through all the time, they'd go out of business.

We did decide to splurge a little bit, however, and gamble $10 just in case Fate was on our side. We took our cash to other casinos to see if their slots were a little more liberal, so each casino on the strip ended up taking one of our dollars. We ended up at Caesar's Palace. We walked past the toga-clad cocktail waitresses, and Joe pulled out a quarter.

"What are you doing?" I asked.

"I'm going to try a slot," he replied absently.

"But we already spent our ten dollars."

"It's just a quarter."

"But it's a quarter we need."

"This slot could make us some money."

"This slot could take our quarter."

"Please," he begged.

"All right. But I'm going to lose sleep over that quarter after it's gone," I grumbled.

He put our quarter in and suddenly quarters started shooting and clanging out the bottom. We made $5.

"Aren't you happy? Aren't you glad I made us do that?" he beamed.

"We could just as easily be crying right now, so don't do that again," I warned. Secretly, inside I was gleeful, but I didn't want to encourage another rampant display of decadence. Joe kept nudging me the rest of the day saying, "Eh? Five dollars, eh? Eh?"

Our favorite Casino Hotel on the Strip was the Mirage where we spent a full hour gazing at a big fish tank and another half-hour watching Zeigfried and Roy's famous white tigers playing in their zoo-like fake pond behind glass. We were strongly tempted to spend $1.50 each to pet a dolphin by the pool area, but $3.00 is a hell of a lot of money.

We took a quick trip off the Strip into downtown and were disappointed to find only more big Casinos with a jillion slot machines but were elated to run into a movie set in the middle of the street outside the Golden Nugget. Nicholas Cage was starring in *Honeymoon in Vegas*, and we photographed him picking something out of his eye.

Our dinner at the Skylab Lounge was as discouraging as our Circus Circus breakfast, but it was free and close to our room. We are hitting the hay at 5:00 this evening so we can wake at 2:00 a.m. to drive through the desert in cool air to avoid overheating.

## September 25, 1991  Torrance, California

We drove through the night. Joe was perfectly wide-awake in the Ultra Van, he told me this morning, while I on the other hand had to yell songs in the Probe to keep myself awake. "Ghost Riders in the Sky." "American Pie." "Some Enchanted Evening." "Lucy in the Sky with Diamonds." By the time I resorted to "Sweet Caroline," my throat was sore and the sun was coming up.

Our directions from Elga and Hilda were detailed and direct; we had no problem finding Torrance, California, just inland from Redondo Beach. However, I was certain we must have misunderstood something along the way as we drove into less inviting territory. When Hilda had said "not a very nice neighborhood," I pictured the run-down neighborhoods of Boulder, Colorado, which are a very different thing than the bad neighborhoods of Los Angeles. As we pulled onto the thin street that was to be our new home, I immediately burst into tears. Graffiti covered the small run-down houses, stop signs, and even cars. The street was littered, and the nicest homes had dirt front yards and chain-link fences. Some teenagers yelled Spanish words at me (cowering in the Probe at this point) and I don't think they were, "Welcome to the neighborhood."

The Greens' house is two-tone pink (top half: dingy pink; bottom half: fresh, bright pink). Its well-manicured front yard makes it a bit of an oasis in the midst of this frightening place of human desolation. We parked our vehicles in the driveway as instructed, finding only a few feet left over on either side of Lucy, since the house next door sits right up against the Green's driveway. Before I had time to start crying again, we needed to get food. An interrogation of the neighbors produced no help in finding a grocery store.

"Can you tell us where we can find a grocery store?"

"No speak English."

"Donde esta el mercado?" stuttered Joe.

"Balue Time blah, blah, blah," he said too fast, seeing that Joe knew some Spanish.

"On what street?" Joe asked in choppy Spanish.

"Blah, Blah, Blah," the man said, pointing.

I asked Joe for a translation.

"That way."

We meandered around, found food, and came back to our new home to sulk. We've only been here three hours and we've heard four gunshots.

### September 28, 1991

Yesterday we drove the Probe up to Venice Beach, where Joe's very good friend from college, Jake Heggie, lives. Besides wanting to visit, we thought he might have some ideas on a safer place to park Lucy and reside. I'd never met Jake but found him to be handsome, goofy like us, and an extraordinarily gifted classical composer. He played a few of his new pieces on the piano for us, and I caught myself momentarily forgetting about our monstrous problems. I was mesmerized. For a few hours, we spoke of art, lost loves, and the weirdos of Venice Beach.

He has no idea where we could live in our motor home and probably thinks we are nuts for attempting such a lame idea. But we left his house glad to have visited and relieved to know someone in Los Angeles speaks English besides us.

On our way home down the Pacific Coast Highway, we stopped at a Chicken Thing

Grill for a cheap dinner. As I was ordering, I set the keys to the Probe down on the counter, only to find them missing twenty seconds later. There were very few people in the restaurant, but we still couldn't be sure who had taken them.

"Did you see anyone take my keys?" I asked the teenaged, male, Latino order-taker.

"I didn't take them! It wasn't me! I don't know what you're talking about!" he said guiltily.

"Well, could you help us find them?" I said, getting annoyed.

"I don't know what happened to them. I didn't see anything. I'll look but I didn't take them, I'll tell you that."

"Nobody said you did," Joe replied with a death stare.

Now that we knew who the culprit was, we realized we must try to get a locksmith as soon as possible. We couldn't accuse the guy. We couldn't beat him up. And we knew he wasn't handing over the keys. The worst part was that the Probe was the only car in the lot. Two hours later, after dark, a locksmith arrived to find Joe and I sitting on the curb in front of the car. We couldn't venture anywhere without risking the ownership of our Probe, so our butts were numb from the cement. The locksmith took an hour to get the door open and another hour trying to get a key made for the ignition.

Finally, after stripping the ignition hole and leaving scratches all around it, he gave up and told us to call a tow truck. "Welcome to L.A.," he said.

Midnight found me and Joe lying in our  fully-reclined Probe seats, waiting for a tow, cussing and questioning our loser-existence on Earth. "It's a sign," I said. "We should never have come out here." At 1:00 a.m. the tow man pulled up, telling us it was too late to tow us all the way back to Torrance and that we'd have to wait until morning. He offered us a free place to stay—the car-impound lot. "Welcome to L.A.," he said.

The car impound lot had a small mechanic's lounge where we were instructed to make ourselves comfortable. We invoked mountains of pity from the tow truck drivers coming and going as we tried to get some sleep on a green plaid diesel-fuel-soaked couch. After hearing about our stolen keys, they all said, "Welcome to L.A."

This morning we were towed back to our pitiful home. We sat in the cab of the tow truck, and when we pulled onto our street the driver said, "Oh. You live in the Hood."

**October 2, 1991**

We've been poring over the want ads for three days and have each applied for jobs at seven restaurants. We are desperate to find a place that will hire both of us, considering our fear of being separated for more than five minutes.

We have no phone, so we drive to a nearby phone booth to make inquiries. Yesterday, returning from a crappy, smelly phone booth where we were told, "That position's been filled," we drove past a particularly wicked residence five houses down the street from our driveway/home. Three teenagers approached us in our Probe, flipped us the bird, and called us fucking pigs, as we passed.

Since we have moved to Los Angeles, I cry two hours a day and Joe sits and stares.

**October 7, 1991**

Ah! Employment! Joe and Dori  DeCamillis are now proud members of the Rolling Hills Country Club Staff. I've never felt happier or more grateful to have a restaurant job, my joy solely motivated by fear of starvation.

When we went in for our interview, we knew our clean-cut appearance, our no less than twenty-eight years combined restaurant experience, and our offer to work all holidays and weekends would give us a good chance at the job, not to mention the offered salary: $7.00 per hour. Not many self-respecting waiters and waitresses would take an hourly wage that amounts to a fraction of the money tips could bring in, but by the time we saw this ad in the paper, we literally had no money left.

After our interview, at which we were told, "We'll call you," we realized how badly we wanted that job. The Country Club is no more than a mile from our home, and the manager was more than willing to hire us together. In an act of desperation, we raced to a phone booth and boldly told Gina, the manager, "It's now or never." We lied about another restaurant that wanted to hire us, telling her we'd have to take the other offer unless she gave us the jobs that moment. Thank God she did. She even agreed to let us have a week off in November so we could travel back to Colorado for that little art show we had agreed to do at Dunbar Morss Gallery.

We start tomorrow but we don't get paid for two weeks. Although we receive one free shift meal, it's not enough food to sustain us. The restaurant policy book states that in emergency situations we are allowed to ask for an advance, but we're refusing to do so, because we don't want the managers to think we are losers. We'll probably starve, but when they find us lying dead in the Hood, on the linoleum floor of a 1970 motor home, they'll still be able to say, "At least they have their pride."

## October 10, 1991

After going to bed on a belly full of stale corn chips the other night, we decided food is an important thing. The next day we dug out Joe's coveted collection of baseball and other sports' cards that he'd saved since he was a kid, which was packed at the bottom of one of Lucy's many storage compartments. We still aren't sure why we brought it along. We're glad we did, though, because we had to sell something to buy food, and I can't imagine anyone wanting to buy our pots and pans or our shoes.

The collection wasn't in mint condition, but it had some prizes: a Roger Staubach rookie, a good Joe Namath, and a Lew Alcinder (who later became Kareem Abdul Jabar). Joe was berating himself for the childhood abandon he'd displayed back in the 70s when we pulled out his O.J. Simpson rookie card, made worthless by a ball point pen. Joe had given O.J. a two foot high afro and a handlebar mustache.

After begging three different card shops to purchase the shoebox full of old sports stars, we finally found a nut who felt sorry for us. We were told by everyone the collection wasn't worth anything because it wasn't mint, but this guy gave us $30 for it after hearing we were hungry.

## October 15, 1991

A car was set fire down the street from us a few days ago and has yet to be hauled away. I thought burning cars were only found in really bad neighborhoods. The gunshots can still be heard at a steady two to three per hour.

"I think that one was a car backfiring," Joe lied to me this morning.

"You always say that. It's either a backfire, a tire blowout, or a firecracker. Do you think I was born yesterday?"

"I'm just trying to cheer you up."

"You're nice. Maybe you could come up with a new sound effect that might fool me."

"How about if I say it's one of my farts?"

If I could only count the number of times in a day Joe mentions his penis and his farts. I guess it's better than talking about the stack of bills we owe.

## October 16, 1991

Lucy's water pump still isn't working. We probably need a new one but can't afford it, so we've been washing the dishes and ourselves with the Green's garden hose in the backyard. I complain about it frequently since the cold water doesn't get things very clean, and it would be so nice to have a hot shower. If only we had running water, I would be supremely happy.

## October 21, 1991

Elga and Hilda came home today and greeted us with open arms. They are a sweet-looking old couple. While Joe and Elga unloaded the couple's conversion van of three months of traveling gear, Hilda and I sat in their living room and got acquainted. It's funny; we've been here a month and have never seen the inside of the house.

After telling me that I'm too skinny, one of Hilda's first questions was, "What do you think of the neighborhood?" to which I replied, "We're getting used to it." She went on to explain that she and Elga had lived in the house for forty years. When they first moved into the area, their street was a dirt road and their only neighbor was a chicken farmer. Gradually over the years things changed as things do and they couldn't see any reason to leave the house, now that they were both seventy-five. "How about fear of an early violent death," I thought to myself. She said they'd only been broken into once, which is pretty lucky for anyone living in Los Angeles in any neighborhood. She also explained that the two-tone pink exterior paint job came about when Elga covered half of the house with new paint to hide vandalous graffiti.

Hilda generously offered to let us take showers in the house whenever we wanted to, which made me want to call the Pope and recommend her for sainthood. After the boys finished their unpacking, Elga offered to help us fix our water pump when he settled in more. Joe and I are lying in bed now, stunned at the goodness of humankind.

## October 22, 1991

Our job at the Rolling Hills Country Club has proved to be the light in our dim existence with its regular hours, pristine environment, and easy work. They are vastly overstaffed, leaving much less work for each individual, and an actual team spirit pervades without the competition for tables and tips.

Joe and I wait tables in the clubhouse, atop a hill overlooking the city of Los Angeles, where, through walls of glass, we see the perfect greens of the first hole, the shining pro shop, the driving green, and usually a brown haze of a city beyond.

The members of the Club are far and away the most courteous customers either of us have ever waited on, probably made happy by lack of financial hardship. The club initiation fee alone is more than Joe and I have made in our twenty-eight years combined restaurant service.

Our first day on the job, the general manager, Greg, lined up several of the employees to introduce them to us. We met Jaime, Jose, Carlos, Pedro, Jesus, Angel, Juan, Miguel, Marcos, and Skipper. Why a Mexican was named Skipper remained a mystery to us until today when Gina told me that Skipper's actual name is Gilberto. When he was hired, Gina asked Gilberto what name he'd like on his nametag and he gave, in his Mexican accent, the American name Gilbert, sounding more like "Geeper."

"My name eess Geeper," he repeated.

"Skipper?" Gina asked twice.

"Si," he answered.

Not all of the employees at RHCC are Mexicans. We have also met Mab, a fifty-something bleached blonde waitress/bartender with a Southern accent, who would look much more at home in a truck stop. A quick interrogation revealed that she had indeed worked at truck stops in the past and was quite proud of the fact. She seems to have endeared herself to the club members and employees with her salty sense of humor and refusal to act the least bit refined. Suzy, a tiny fifty-something Japanese-American woman works behind the bar, and so far I haven't understood a word she has said. Her super-high voice combines with an indecipherable accent, sounding much like a nail being pulled out of a board. She is so sweet and obviously eager to help me; I feel terrible for just staring at her when she asks me a question. Lou and Norma are also 50-something women who are very devoted to their waitress jobs, and other than a couple younger women waitresses and several WASP valet boys, the rest of the thirty or forty restaurant employees are Mexicans. We're looking forward to working with a restaurant staff that varies from the usual twenty or thirty-something heavy partying crowd.

**October 23, 1991**

Finally, payday is here. The $30 from the baseball cards and the free meals at work  were sufficient to keep us from dying, but we were by no means well-nourished. We ate lots of carrots because a) they're only 10¢ a pound here, b) they sort of fill us up, and c) we like them. We thought our paycheck would cheer us up considerably, but it doesn't amount to enough to pay even half of our many monstrous bills, which now come to the Green's mailbox. I drive to a nearby crud-covered phone booth to promise the hospital and the credit card companies a payment soon and come home crying knowing we can't possibly make all the payments.

Our art seems like a distant memory already. Since we left Colorado, our demeanor has not been conducive to creativity.

**October 24, 1991**

Another birthday has passed for Joe, and I, without a cent to spend on him, picked a fight this morning out of frustration. The argument was patched before it could build any momentum at all, but I felt terrible that I couldn't make his day special.

We drove the fifteen minutes to Redondo Beach, as we have been doing each evening for the past week to partake in the sand and the ocean. It is the only free entertainment here. As usual, its beauty and vastness only served to deepen our melancholy. We sadly remembered the California vision we day-dreamed about back in the Colorado winter—of frolicking on the shore, selling artwork to fancy movie stars, and paying off our debt within a year. We see absolutely no way out of our financial prison.

To add to our troubles, this morning we went to the bank to open a checking account with our new paycheck so we could pay bills and eat. The account-opener lady was a cold-hearted woman and told us that we couldn't open a checking account without a California Driver's License and that no bank would cash our check. Fraud here is a daily occurrence, we were told, and there is no exception to these rules.

So we drove over to the DMV, where we waited in a four-hour line with persons of all faiths and nationalities, to take our driver's test. The test was full of trick questions. Joe did O.K. but I missed passing by one question. The gruff Test Man said, "All right. I'll give you that one since it's such a tricky question." I would be there still had he not let me slip by. The final tragic event of our DMV visit was realized after we had out photos taken and were told, "O.K! Those licenses will be sent to you by mail in four to six weeks." We shuffled out the door, dejected, wondering how we were going to eat for the next month. Our only choice was to beg.

We sped back to the bank before it closed, summoned our grouchy lady friend, and told her our situation. It was not out of mercy that she suggested an idea, but of desire to rid   herself of us. She took our check stubs and called the Country Club to vouch for our employment and good standing, whereby we were awarded the monumental and coveted status of Checking Account Owners.

"Welcome to L.A.," I said to Joe.

**November 1, 1991**
Yesterday we spent from dawn to late night carving and painting two pumpkins. The Country Club had a Halloween pumpkin-carving contest for the employees with a $50 first prize and a $25 second prize. Figuring the competition to be minimal, we invested a full day on a gamble—not one of my favorite things to do. There was also a costume contest with similar prize money, but with our limited supply of materials we decided our time would be better spent focusing on something we could win.

Last night's pumpkin contest did display strong work, including the cornucopia pumpkin sporting a zucchini nose and baby squash eyeballs, as well as the serial-killer victim pumpkin which was hacked to pieces. But we exited the victors—Joe with his carefully dug-out relief face painted in scary colors, and me with my painted golf-theme pumpkin, with faithfully rendered golf balls for eyes, the 18th hole for a nose, and two crossed putters for a mouth, all on a putting-green background.

As for the costume contest, Joe wore a sailor hat and shirt, and borrowed Skipper's nametag, while I was a cowgirl. We never could have competed with the costume contest winners, which included Angel dressed as Don King, and the blond-haired, blue-eyed valet boy named Chip, dressed as a Rastafarian. Miguel, a sweet, shy, giggly guy, had the enviable job of lying in the makeshift coffin at the club entrance, dressed as Dracula, and sitting up as guests entered the un-spooky spook house. Halfway through the evening, he stopped his routine, sound asleep with his arms crossed over his chest and bloody fangs poking out of his snoring mouth.

The Country Club is still the oasis in the midst of our disturbing life.

## November 6, 1991

We still haven't lifted a paintbrush.

## November 7, 1991

Our work-a-day lifestyle has kept us from creating, leaving us drained and dry, but we are acquiring a plethora of information about our neighborhood that is, if nothing else, culturally educational.

Angel, the cocky and sometimes volatile Mexican waiter, has become a close ally. Underneath his antagonistic exterior lies the heart of a lamb, and he has been informing Joe and me of the lurking dangers of our neighborhood.

Spray-painted on houses, fences, cars, stop signs, and buildings all around our house are the letters E.S.T., standing for East Side Torrance, the resident gang, of which Angel was once a member. He said there are 300-400 members in the gang, and over half will be in prison or dead by the age of nineteen.

"What do you do in a gang?" I asked Angel one day.

"Oh, you know, hang out, sell drugs, do drive-by shootings," he said casually.

I got up close and whispered, "Did you sell drugs?"

"Hell no! I don't do that stuff".

"Did you do any drive-by shootings?" I asked even more timidly.

"Yeah, sure."

"Did you kill anyone?"

He smiled and said as he walked off, "I don't know. I didn't hang around long enough to find out."

Daily, I ask more questions of Angel, eager to become educated in the ways of the street, if only from a distance. One day he showed me a scar on his stomach where a rival gang member had plunged a pencil during school.

When I told him of the teenagers down the street and their fucking pig comment he said, "You better watch out, they think you're cops. Three cops have been killed in the past year no more than two blocks from your house. That house, where those gang members yelled at you, is one of the main hangouts of the E.S.T. gang. I wouldn't go by there if I were you, homegirl."

We don't. After Angel's little warning, we drive all the way around the block to avoid being seen by those evil-doers.

Elga recently told us the story of a drive-by shooting that took place last year from a bicycle. A thirteen-year-old kid was proudly riding his bike that was decorated with streamers and flowers for a local Cinqo de Mayo celebration. Some other kids his age, loitering a few houses down from the Greens, yelled and made fun of him. He promptly went home, got his gun, and rode back to his enemy's territory where he fired shots into the group before speeding off.

After the police arrived, the boy-murderer had changed his clothes, intending to disguise himself, and walked innocently up to the crime scene to survey the damage. He was immediately recognized by the two victim's friends and taken into custody.

Joe and I don't quite know how to feel about our neighborhood now. It seems we've become used to it, and out of an inability to afford a change, we pretend that we are in a protective bubble, safe from the perils that surround us.

## November 8, 1991

Half of the employees at the Country Club hate us now. It was just revealed that the week we need to return to Colorado for our art show is the same week everyone wants off for Thanksgiving. One of them, Lulu, has worked at the Club for eleven years and can't have her requested vacation, thanks to our audacity. We receive gnarly looks and cutting comments as we go about our duties, and the only response we can reasonably return is none. Gina told us, "They'll get over it."

At least, when we leave, we'll be away from it for a week. Financially, this trip probably isn't the most lucrative thing we could do, but we have a stupid policy to always try anything when it comes to our art. Today we realized we have only two weeks before our big journey. I guess this would be a good time to start painting.

**November 10, 1991**
Elga fixed our water pump with Joe's help. Praise be to Our Lord Almighty in Heaven Above the Earth. We have water.

**November 15, 1991**
This week has been nuts. We work all day and paint all evening. The intense colors of our interiors seem to brighten our spirits once we get started. Today Joe finished a 30 by 24 inch painting of a grass-green staircase with orange light pouring into window at the top. We called it Leprechaun and Creamsicle after the colors it might match on one of those paint store color cards. The one I'm working on is called Hollywood and Vine—an empty flaming red room with a lime green lamp shining on an easy chair of the same color. While we're working on them we think of nothing but the enjoyment of paint and wild color. When we're done we inevitably say, "Let's hope it sells."
Once in a while, we'll take a break to go inside for television with Hilda or Elga. Hilda watches her hi-tech, fancy TV in their cozy TV room, sitting on a soft La-Z-Boy and flicking her remote. Elga views his tiny old TV from a rickety kitchen chair in the back of the garage, with a pair of pliers to turn channels. Yet, we usually end up watching with Elga, since Hilda's favorite programs are the news, *Matlock*, and other detective/lawyer/shoot-em-up shows. Elga watches intelligent and tasteful programs such as *Studs*, the dating game for horny, crude, scantily-clad Los Angelites, or movies such as *Tremors*, in which Kevin Bacon and Reba McIntyre are chased through the desert by underground-dwelling monsters with giant tentacles. Hilda says our fare is much too raunchy for her. Her shows give me nightmares, especially the news.

**November 29, 1991**
We're leaving for Colorado tomorrow, with ten new paintings stuffed into the trunk of our Probe, big hopes for a raging success of a show, and even bigger doubts and worries.

It seems we have continually invested money, time, and soul into our art career with little or no financial reward, and yet we press forward as if we still believe all the pep talks and positive reinforcement we used to thrive on. I feel crazy, but happy to get away from the smog for a few days.

**November 31, 1991**

I'm lying in Katie's bedroom in Boulder, Colorado, staring at the faded Andrew Wyeth poster I gave her years ago for her birthday. Our trip from L.A. was a straight-through drive with a two-hour nap in the car somewhere in Southern Colorado about 4:00 a.m. this morning. When we stopped, it was snowing like mad (a deadly condition when driving a Ford Probe) and the freezing weather produced not a wink of real sleep for me, but Joe managed to pass out for a precious hour of snoring. I stared out the window at the stupid snowflakes, recalling the long conversation we'd had through California, Arizona, and New Mexico. We reminisced about how we met each other in college and what ensued...

Joe and I met in college at the ages of nineteen and nineteen, respectively. I was in a clothing store shopping with a friend, when I saw a dark-haired, blue-eyed, tan, Italian, well-dressed mirage walk down the sidewalk past the store window. I waited for him to pass, with my eyes locked on him, ran out the door to see his behind as he disappeared around the corner, and bolted back into the store asking, "Who was that?"

That fateful question was easily answered by my good friend, Marci Turk who, at a school with a population of 25,000, knew everybody, replied, "That's Joe DeCamillis. I used to go out with his brother Mike."

"Can you introduce him to me?"

"Sure. He always goes to Eddie's Mexican Cafe on Monday nights. Now we can finally get you a fake I.D. so you can meet him." Marci had been trying to talk me into getting a fake I.D. for months, but I was too chicken.

"O.K. let's do it." I said without hesitation.

Eddie's was the crowded, frat and sorority cheap drink hangout on Monday night. A place I ended up frequently in later college days. I had no trouble getting in on my first night, passing as a twenty-four-year-old named Margaret.

By the time I saw Joe, I had had one too many giant rum punch umbrella drinks (one was enough) and I boldly told Marci to put in a good word for me, not realizing how many rum drinks she'd consumed.

"You see that girl over there in the long blond hair?" she asked him. "She thinks you're gorgeous and she wants you."

Marci returned to our table, smiling, and repeated to me the message she'd given Joe. I put my face in my hands to hide, whispering to her and our friend, Crazy Allison, that I had to leave. When I put my hands down, Joe was standing by our table and said, "Hi."

I never believed in love at first sight before that night, but Joe and I were smitten as we slurred our first conversation over that table, and were inseparable for months afterward. I knew within a week that he would be the man I would marry.

After a year of dating, Joe left Boulder to go to UCLA and our relationship was relegated to "good friends" while we dated other people. But our obvious love connection always seemed to get in the way of our other relationship prospects, and eventually, Joe came back to Boulder.

At this time I lived with my mother, whom I had moved in with after graduating from college. Shortly after this move, all of the obsessions I had been harboring during college—an eating disorder, workaholism, and over-achievism—came to a head. (I was well aware of all the reasons one ends up with these problems—crazy childhood, etc. One can read all about it in any self-help book. But knowing about it doesn't make it go away). Anyway, at his time I had some sort of megalomania mental attack, in which I thought I knew everything and was convinced everyone around me should adore me. The fact that Joe asked me to marry him during this time shocks me now. I was so controlling! I must have forced myself to seem sane enough to marry.

After the wedding, my wackiness subsided somewhat but manifested itself in less obvious ways. I was certain about Joe's and my future in the happily ever after. Our first year of marriage didn't disappoint us; we used all the willpower of newlyweds to do everything right, with our hard work at jobs and on our art, keeping overly fit, and other self-righteous endeavors. But things changed. We began arguing, usually about money, and work seemed to come between us all the time, especially art. The pressure of always trying to look like the perfect couple on the outside made everything in our life tense. Arguments turned to nasty fights and eventually every day felt like a bad dream. I couldn't imagine how things could get worse but they did. Much worse.

I better sleep now.  More on misery later.

## December 1, 1991

Our show at the Dunbar Morss Gallery opened last night, and I'm glad we came. We sold two paintings, their sales amounting to two weeks of Country Club paychecks for the both of us. What a wonderful life we would have if our paintings sold all the time!

Several of our Boulder friends came to support us at the gallery. After the show, we went out to the Walnut Brewery with Patty and Dan Tomlin and Katie, all childhood friends from my hometown of Steamboat Springs who had ended up settling in Boulder. The hot topic of the evening was whether or not birds have penises—a mystery question I came up with in high school while witnessing two birds procreating. The penis question then dawned on me after a few minutes of observation, and I've been posing the query to anyone with the slightest scientific leanings ever since. Dan Tomlin, an elementary school science teacher, was the victim of my quest for information. After howls of laughter from everyone, numerous speculatory suggestions of possible answers, and crude remarks from the men, there are still no new insights to the penis question. It's remarkable that very few people know the answers to nature's simplest questions.

We leave tomorrow morning. I am dreading such a long drive so soon after we just undertook it. Katie generously gave me $30 for an early Christmas present so we could afford a hotel room in Arizona instead of freezing in our car seats again. She's something.

## December 2, 1991

It's actually nice to be "home" again. I missed Elga and Hilda and Studs and the Mexicans at the Country Club and the palm trees.

No matter where you go in L.A., even in our neighborhood, there are palm trees. They conjure visions of tropical vacations and shaded boulevards for blonde girls with sunglasses and '57 convertible T-birds. As I lie staring out Lucy's rear window, with a view only of a palm treetop and semi-blue sky, these dreamy images help me to forget what is actually under this palm tree. It grows in the yard of an extended family of Mexicans where at least fourteen people reside in a tiny two bedroom home. Several broken, dirty toys lie around its base and sometimes a couple of old men sit near it drinking beer.

As palm trees afford little shade, the neighborhood beer-drinking hangout is usually in Elga and Hilda's front yard, under a small but very shady tree—the only real shade on our street. Daily, five or six gray-haired men bring their six-packs and spend the afternoon relaxing on the Green's fresh grass. Hilda says she doesn't mind unless they leave their cans, in which case she runs out and yells at them (in English) to pick them up. They seldom forget to take their beer cans with them because they would hate to lose their shade privileges.

### December 3, 1991

Another paycheck that barely covers half of our bills. I feel trapped in one of those TV vertigo spirals with laughing dollar signs spinning around me saying, "You'll never get out!" I don't see how we ever will. We work a lot at the Country Club to take our minds off of it, but I still feel so demoralized and hopeless.

### December 4, 1991

Between gunshots, we have become accustomed to the sound of the ice cream truck, which drifts through our neighborhood all too frequently. Its song is one of those annoying ones that sticks in your brain for days, like Disney's "It's a Small World". Just when we've drummed it out of our heads by singing a different annoying song, the ice cream man comes along again and reprograms us. Joe tries to get under my skin at the Country Club by do-do-doing it in my ear as he passes by.

We would really hate the ice cream truck if it weren't for the way it looks. At first we couldn't tell if it was an ice cream truck or an illegal drug-mobile, with its dented half-rusted exterior and old half-peeled 70s bumper stickers covering the sides. The words, SLOW WATCH FOR KIDS CAUTION, are spray-painted on the front. It usually stops for long periods of time in front of the dumpiest houses on the street. The ice cream man gets out and leans on his hood to talk in Spanish to a crowd of gang-aged youths. But closer inspection has revealed that he does indeed sell ice cream to kids. I wish we could afford a creamsicle once in a while.

## December 5, 1991

We went down to that depressing ocean again. It didn't solve any of our financial problems, as I had hoped it would. Our conversation was less than stimulating.

"I'm depressed."

"Me too."

"What are we going to do?"

"I don't know."

"We say this everyday."

"I know."

"I'm so worried that I'm going to get sick."

"I already am."

"Really?"

"No."

## December 6, 1991

This afternoon, after work, I was sitting at Lucy's little kitchen table, staring and crying about our money problems while Joe worked on Ultra Van fix-it problems in the Green's garage. I heard voices coming from the house next door and tried to control my sobs in order to better listen to the goings on. The house was literally three feet from my sitting position. I figured I'd rather hear them than have them hear me.

In English, with a heavy Mexican accent, a mother instructed her little boy.

"Hail Mary, full of grace, the Lord is with Thee. Blessed art thou amongst women and blessed is the fruit of thy womb Jesus."

A little voice said slowly, "Hail Mary..."

"HAIL MARY, FULL OF GRACE!" the mother yelled.

"Hail Mary, full of grace..." Three seconds of silence.

"THE LORD IS WITH THEE! Start again!"

"Hail Mary..." the boy whimpered.

"Hail Mary, full of grace, the Lord is with thee! Again!" she screamed.

"Hail Mary, full of grace...then what?"

"HAIL MARY, FULL OF GRACE THE LORD IS WITH THEE!"

By now, the boy was half crying.

"Hail Mary full of grace, the Lord is with thee," he finally got out.

"Blessed art thou," the mother said impatiently.

"Hail Mary, full of grace..."

Silence.

"THE LORD IS WITH THEE!" she screamed again.

My tears of money problems were long gone, and I shuffled back to the garage to see what   Elga and Joe were doing.

## December 7, 1991

In the midst of the lunch rush at the Country Club, one of the waitresses who had earlier heard me complaining of our money woes had an interesting suggestion. As I passed by with a giant tray of hot plates, she whispered, "Why don't you just go bankrupt?"

I thought she was joking so I smiled quickly and told her I'd talk to her about it later. After all the club members had retreated to the golf course, I pulled her aside and asked, "Have you done it?"

"Sure," she said, "Twice."

"I thought you could only do it once," I said in disbelief.

"Oh no. It only lasts seven years. After seven years it's wiped off your record. I just waited seven years and did it again. I can never buy a house but I don't want one anyway."

I stared at her, pondering in silence for a few seconds until I whispered, "Don't you feel guilty?"

As this novel idea occurred to her, she replied, "I guess I should."

Mab, drying glasses behind the bar, overheard our discussion and piped in, "I've done it, too. Best thing there is. One day you're up to your eyeballs in shit, the next you're debt-free. And you don't have to worry about losing credit, neither. As soon as you do it, credit card companies send you applications up the yin-yang because they know you can't go bankrupt for another seven years. You should do it."

"But I'd feel so guilty," I said. "All these people loaned us money and we'd just say, ' Sorry, screw you.' My family would think I was the devil. My Dad would just as soon I murder someone as go bankrupt."

"Why don't you ask him for money?"  Mab asked.

"Oh God no," I said. "We may be desperate but we're not that stupid. We put ourselves through college without help, and we sure aren't going into debt with families now, especially with as much as we owe. If I think the pressure is bad now, I'd hate to know what it would feel like owing our families a ton of money. They couldn't even put a dent in the debt anyway. It's one thing to ask for a little help once in a while (and we have) but it's another to expect a total bail-out. Sheesh. Family relations are hard enough without that kind of strain."

"Well, what choice do you have then?"

After years of crushing debt with no foreseeable solution, I imagined the prospect of a new start, another chance to do it again, the right way. It seemed much too good to be true so I quickly dismissed it.

After work, I brought up the idea to Joe.

"I don't see that we have any other choice," he said. "We don't have experience at anything that brings in good money. Even if we could make four times what we make now, we'd only be able to pay off past debt. We'd still have to find more money for toothpaste and toilet paper. But I never would have thought of this if someone else hadn't brought it up."

"We can't though. It isn't right."

"Dori, what else are we going to do?"

"We'll feel guilty forever."

"So. At least we'll be able to eat."

"Let's let it sink in a little bit. The idea has just been brought up and I'm severely traumatized."

So here we are, lying on Lucy's bed after a silent dinner of Ragu spaghetti. I'm writing, and Joe's staring at the fake wood ceiling that's two and a half feet away from our bodies. Occasional tears drip on my paper as I imagine the devil's pitchfork poking me in the butt. I can't believe this is happening to us.

### December 8, 1991

This is the first time I've felt brave enough to write in detail about the sad events that occurred after our first year of pretend happiness in marriage. In this time of financial crisis, I need to face the wretched guilt over the mistakes that got us here.

We'd always spent money with no regard for the future, particularly on our art career. Although we almost never made money from art, we were sure that if we just tried harder or put more into it, we'd hit the jackpot one day. Money and fame would be instant, and lasting. This inevitable overnight success was always just around the corner, therefore spending money on frivolous things was perfectly reasonable. We always had some lame excuse.

Being self-employed house painters and artists, we were required to pay estimated taxes throughout the year, a fact we were ignorant of at that time. The IRS had ended up with nothing, even on April 15th. By October, they squeezed their unforgiving vice. We received an explicit letter from the IRS stating that our home, car and belongings would be confiscated in thirty days if we didn't pay $5,000 immediately.

I remember the day Joe phoned an IRS representative to set up a payment plan. He put the receiver down, walked over to me and said, "We need to get a couple more jobs apiece." They had arranged for us to pay $1,000 a month for five months. Considering we never ever had a cent left over after paying bills and buying art supplies, this was a huge sum. We began an excruciating regime that still hurts to think about. We would rise at 4:30 a.m. to deliver newspapers—as many as two people can throw before 7:00. We'd suck down breakfast and start painting houses at 8:00. That particular winter we spent our days painting a mental hospital a soft shade of pink. (We felt fate had sent us to the proper place.) At the end of the day, we'd rush home to eat dinner and then speed off to a late night of high-speed pizza delivery. I only lasted two weeks at Domino's. I was so exhausted I was sure I would fall over and die at any given moment. But Joe kept on working, usually until 2:30 or 3:30 in the morning. I felt like a sadist rousing him an hour later for our paper route.

Through the winter we continued this nutty existence. I watched Joe lose weight, his eyes hollow and his skin yellow. I, too, lost even more weight. My ongoing anorexia heightened until I refused to eat fat at all and sugar of any kind, including ordinary fruit juice. I exercised every day, sometimes twice, if I feared one of my tiny meals was going to make me gain weight. At 5' 11" and 117 pounds, I was still trying to get skinnier. Joe and I looked terrible and felt it, too. We fought constantly. One night, before Joe went to his pizza job, a heated argument over something stupid escalated until I punched him, hard, on his back (smart move) and hit one of his shoulder blades. I knew immediately I'd broken my hand but waited until Joe returned home after midnight to tell him. I was so obsessed about art that I used scissors with the broken hand for hours, knowing that if I went to a doctor, I wouldn't be able to make art, because of the cast. As it turned out I never got a cast since we decided we couldn't afford the $600 quoted by the doctor at the emergency room. I painted the mental hospital with my left hand for two months.

One night, very late, while Joe was delivering pizza, the phone rang.

"I had an accident," Joe's scratchy, exhausted voice said. "I fell asleep at the wheel."

"Are you OK?" I asked frantically.

"I'm fine but the Subaru's not." After a few seconds of dejected silence, he added, "It's totaled."

I drove to the site of the accident and found Joe in front of a large business, half-asleep, standing by the car. He'd run over a sprinkler system valve and a small tree. Both were crushed, just like the car.

Still in denial about money problems, we bought an unpractical sports car, a Ford Probe—on credit. We finally paid off the IRS, but were so weak from fatigue, we could barely work, especially Joe. We began living off credit cards. Financial pressures and our pretense that our problems really weren't that bad, caused tension to build more than ever.

Our frequent fights became more intense as we still tried to push ourselves at everything. We made art most of the day. I continued over-exercising and eating a fat and sugar deprived diet, which Joe was forced to adhere to at home because I allowed none of these dreaded foods past our threshold. We both stayed emaciated and grouchy. This time-bomb lifestyle bottled up until one horrible evening, the single worst event of my life

We were both working on a new art project, bickering as usual. Hostilities escalated until we came to blows, and I called 911. We both spent the night in jail. This was the final event that brought me to my senses. As I lay in my little cell, crying all night and watching the sun come up, I realized that nothing I had done in my life up to this point had gotten me anywhere. Look where I had ended up. I would have vowed to change everything at that very moment if I'd known how to change at all. My problem had been that I was always trying to control everything. It certainly hadn't worked. I'd turned into a maniac.

Joe and I quit fighting after that. A small argument would start building steam and be squelched before it could lead to anything. I can say, for myself, that I was scared sick to allow anything to come between us. We had experienced the repercussions of our own stubbornness and self-righteousness—a painful lesson. In any case, we reaped the benefits of one of life's growth opportunities.

The final chapter of the sordid tale will have to unfold later. Hilda is calling me in the house to help set the table. She has invited us inside for dinner tonight!

## December 9, 1991

Today we went to our bankruptcy appointment. Yesterday at work, the assistant manager of the Country Club restaurant, Marco, assured us that bankruptcy was a simple, painless process that nearly everyone he knew had gone through. He seemed to think we'd be crazy not to do it. California is a very different place than Colorado, I am thinking.

We got the name of Attorney Assisted Legal Services from a bus stop bench on Crenshaw Boulevard. It advertised the cheapest way to go bankrupt in Southern California, so we looked them up. We've been told to watch out for those places—that getting a lawyer would be a better idea. "Maybe getting a lawyer would cost more than the debts we're trying to get rid of," Joe said.

I was in tears throughout our visit with Paul, the Attorney Assisted bankruptcy man, which procured us a fee discount. We are required to declare our motor home our "homestead" in order to keep it. This declaration costs $100, which has been discounted to $0, thanks to my bawl-baby tactics. I wish I could summon this kind of sadness at will.

Paul told us that the minute we declare bankruptcy, we will receive no more harassing letters or phone calls, that legally, our creditors are required to leave us alone. His first job is to call and tell them of our intentions, after which we will be free of our obligation to pay any of them. Then he will have all the myriad of papers prepared while we wait for our court date where we will be officially relieved of our debt. Now that we are actually diving into this cesspool of shame, I am beginning to see that it might be for the best, although a shitty best, at that.

We still eat carrots by the truckload.

## December 13, 1991

We have opted to work every day during the Christmas holidays to keep our minds off our regrets. The extra money won't hurt either. This season brings Country Club banquets by the dozens, so there is plenty of work available. We actually enjoy working, because the Mexicans treat work as a place to socialize and joke around, no matter how busy they are. We tend to fall in with this attitude when we are around them, resulting in more laughing than complaining about money or work. We have spent many late nights cleaning up after drunken office parties or drunken weddings, as well as many long afternoons bussing the tables of cute, rich, old women after they've opened their solid silver party favors at their various senior club annual Christmas luncheons. And it's always fun.

The only species of people we hate to wait on are Realtors. Every time they rent out the Country Club for one of their events, we are treated like peons. They dress flashy, yell instead of speaking, get slobbering drunk, hang all over each other, and try to steal the centerpieces. Realtor-men are the only ones that have consistently made sexual remarks to me. Many nasty Spanish words fly around the kitchen on Realtor-party nights. I have picked up on all of them.

The only other major generalization I can make about banquet guest peculiarities relates to money. The richer they are, the better they treat the wait staff. This is always true, across-the-board. The less money they have, the more they like to make themselves feel big by abusing the hired help.

## December 15, 1991

A CONVERSATION FROM WORK, TODAY

Kevin, the cook: What's wrong with your hands?
Dori: What do you mean?
Kevin: They're orange.
Dori: They are?
Kevin: Look. (Shows his hands and turns over Jose's hands.)
Dori: Wow. I guess they are kind of orange.
Kevin: Kind of?! You look like an oompa loompa. (Jose looks puzzled, not understanding oompa loompa.)
Dori: It must be from all the carrots we eat.
Kevin: What does that have to do with it?

Dori: The beta-carotene turns your skin orange, especially your hands.

Kevin: I've never heard of that.

Dori: It's true.

Kevin: You're lying. You must use some kind of orange dyes in your artwork.

Dori: I wouldn't know what to do with an orange dye if it bit my butt. I'm telling you,
it's the carrots.

Kevin: (Calls in Greg the manager, six waiters and Joe, who has equally orange hands.) Look at their hands.

Chorus: They're orange! What's wrong with you?

Joe: It must be the carrots.

Dori: That's what I told Kevin, but he doesn't believe me.

Kevin: You guys are so full of it.

Chorus: Yeah, right. Carrots. Who would eat that many carrots anyway?

No one believed us.

### December 26, 1991

We worked the Christmas Eve Club Dinner, spent Christmas Day with Elga, Hilda and their kids and grandkids and great-grandkids, and slept through a grizzly murder right outside the camper, Christmas night. Hilda gave us all the gory details this morning.

Late Christmas night, after everyone was asleep, Hilda heard a screeching sound outside, like metal scraping. She donned her robe and went out onto the front porch where she saw a man lying in the middle of the street under his fallen motorcycle, moaning and gurgling and calling for help. Hilda called 911 but the man had stopped his death-cries by the time she got back outside. The police came to cart the body away, questioned the neighbors, and left. Apparently, the man had been shot in the back while driving down the street.

This morning after Hilda told us what we had missed, we drove to the nearby Pollo Loco for a Los Angeles Times, to see what information we could find on the incident. There was nothing. The local South Bay paper had a short paragraph near the last page. The man had been drinking in a local bar when he realized that someone had stolen his leather jacket. He assumed it was one of the E.S.T. members—the ones with their hang-out a few doors down from our place—and went there to investigate. An argument ensued after which he drove off in a huff, only to be blasted in the back with a shotgun. The murderer is still at large.

Joe and I saw a dark puddle in the street, the size of a bathroom throw rug. It was blood.

I think it's a bad sign that we slept through this.

## December 30, 1991

One of the popular traditions in this neighborhood is the festive Burning of the Christmas Tree in the middle of the street. Every day we drive down an obstacle course of burning or already-burnt Christmas trees, set afire by the usual hoodlums, we suspect. I can't decide whether to laugh or be afraid.

This bankruptcy thing is sinking in. I feel even more guilt than ever because I should still be feeling terrible. Instead, I have now gone a record two days without weeping. I have forgotten how it feels not to wonder where my next meal or hospital payment is coming from. The pressure has been lifted so abruptly, that I find my mind reaching for worrisome thoughts, or comfortably settling into an unnamed anxiety, until I alert myself that I don't need to be there. Our court date has been set for February 4, 1992. I know I'll be apprehensive until then.

We've decided to give up the Probe. The payments aren't large, but in order to give ourselves a completely new start, we need to rid ourselves of all the debt we can. We will have it "voluntarily repossessed." I hate to see it go, as it somehow gives us a hint of aristocracy in the midst of our semi-destitute lifestyle.

## January 1, 1992

We worked the Members Only New Year's Eve banquet, an extravagant affair complete with a live pop band and rented dance floor; a banquet table larger than Lucy; a giant ice sculpture of a mermaid (her nipples were the first thing to melt away, much to the delight of the Mexicans); and the unveiling of the new $50,000 cutlery service Greg had ordered from England. A grand time was had by all the members and their guests.

The drunkest of the drunks finally finished trickling out by 1:00 a.m., at which time we slaves were finally allowed to eat.

We knew we'd probably watch the sun come up while carting champagne glasses back to the kitchen or picking confetti out of the carpet, so we naturally began an unannounced party of our own.

The pop band ate with us and began breaking down their set-up as we began the massive task of cleaning up. Discarded party favors lay scattered about the place and the Mexicans immediately started a rousing chorus with the horns, kazoos, and other noisemakers. Joe joined in, and although tooting toy instruments may not sound like a manly endeavor, the fun swiftly turned into a racket competition. Joe would blast his horn until his cheeks had red veins. Then Jose and Jaime would answer back with riotous blows on their noisemakers: the ones with the paper spiral that extends out. This went on until several of the cheap toys had exploded from the pressure. I was the contest cheerleader, giving joyful laughter for encouragement.

The pop band members totally ignored the juvenile exhibition, which made the guys want to capture their attention all the more. In answer to their blatant disregard, Jaime put horns in each of his nostrils and four in his mouth and began blowing them all at once to the beat of the piped-in   Muzak, and following the female lead singer as she carried away her band paraphernalia, raising his arm in imitation of an elephant. Even with six paper trumpets blown in her ear by a crazy man, she pretended he didn't exist. I felt sorry for the woman; she obviously just wanted to go home after a long night of singing, but I couldn't contain myself. I was literally on the floor.

We slept most of today. Hilda received one of her usual leftover centerpieces from the previous nights festivities. If we had space, I would have saved that bouquet in a memory box. I have a hard time staying up past 11:00 and I'm usually not much of a drinker, so I'd never had so much fun on New Year's Eve.

**January 2, 1992**

I have come to the conclusion that this is a weird world. I called our entire list of creditors today to make sure they had received the message about the upcoming bankruptcy. Each person who assisted me was shocked that I called to clear up the matter. They were overly gracious and sympathetic about our situation and sorry they couldn't help in some way. A quote from the lady at Citibank: "You poor dear. This must be terrible for you. I wish you all the luck in the future. You take care of yourself." I was altogether dumbfounded over my special treatment, after expecting to be berated. Finally, I asked the woman from the bank at which the Probe was financed, "Why is everyone being so nice to me?"

She replied, "You see, in almost no cases do the repossessee or defaulted borrower call to admit their guilt, or make sure the accounts have been settled. Most people are disagreeable, if not hostile, even when they are free of obligation to pay. When we have to repossess a car, we usually have to hire a private detective to find the car, and then pay a repo man to steal it. By then the car is nearly destroyed anyway. It costs us sometimes more money to reclaim the car than it's worth! It is very rare to have someone call us who is willing to cooperate and make it easy on us."

For once in this process, I don't feel like scum.

The repo man will be flying here from Colorado, one week from today. We had better find another car.

## January 3, 1992

While watching Lawrence Welk reruns in the garage last night, we confessed our situation and our impending need of a new vehicle to Elga. Hilda already knows about the bankruptcy. She overheard me crying on the phone one day, trying to work out some details with Attorney Assisted Paul. After I got off the phone, I spilled our story on her sympathetic ears, and although I know she and Elga have not borrowed a thin dime in their entire seventy-five years, she did not lecture or give the slightest hint of disapproval. Elga was also compassionate and suggested we get in touch with his son, Lee, who has an old car he might want to sell us.

We met Lee and his friend, Bruce, at a Christmas party a few weeks ago. We spent the evening engrossed in conversation with Lee, a refined, middle-aged gentleman, and Bruce, his handsome, younger friend. They live with Bruce's progressive mother, Ginny, up in West Hollywood.

We called Lee about the car today. He seemed to like the idea of selling their old 1966 Plymouth Valiant, but warned us that it might need a new transmission. The only way he says he can sell us the car in good conscience is to offer it for $200. Even if we have to buy a new transmission, its total cost would be equivalent to two Probe payments, so we agreed to buy it without seeing it.

Lee said the car's name is Betty.

## January 4, 1992

We drove up to West Hollywood to inspect our cherry new machine. Betty isn't a beauty. She's two-toned: primer gray and rust. But she runs. And she has the coveted Slant 6 engine so popular to motorheads. The car has only 75,000 miles on the odometer and was owned by a little old woman, for the first 70,000. Ginny, another old woman, has driven Betty for the last 5,000 miles. Betty has good Karma.

We drove Betty behind the Probe for the twenty miles back to Torrance with little transmission trouble. She jerks when she shifts gears (she's an automatic), but it's nothing that seems like an emergency; we'll have her examined soon. The Green's driveway looks like a perpetual party with two Ultra Vans, their conversion van, Elga's tool van, their little compact car, the Probe, and now Betty.

## January 8, 1992

Joe worked today and I did not. At work, Gina, Mab, and Paco were teasing Joe about being sad when I'm not with him. They've been joking lately about the fact that we're miserable when we're not together. They think it's cute that we're so in love and can't bear to be apart. I don't even notice it. Times have changed since the basement brawl days.

## January 10, 1992

The repo man came today. A cab deposited him in front of the Green's, at which time Hilda came out scolding him for what, I don't know. I apologized to him, explaining that she's protective of us and doesn't like people who come to take our things.

He was surprised to find the Probe in spotless, near-new condition, and even more surprised to find us apologizing for the inconvenience of having to fly from Colorado. He stared at us, dumbfounded, and stated that in all his years of recovering vehicles he had never met anyone as cooperative as us. I'm not sure if that is a huge compliment, considering his usual associates, but it sounded nice.

As we watched him drive the Probe away, Joe asked, "Are you sad?"

"I thought I would be. But no, I'm actually relieved."

"Me too."

"Is there something wrong with us?"

"Probably."

## January 20, 1992

As our court date draws near, my apprehension builds and my mind conjures scenarios of indignant creditors appearing on the scene to pound the table and rant at us, calling us ne'er-do-wells. I've asked a few bankruptcy-veterans from work if this is likely to happen, to which they reply with a laugh. I am small potatoes, they say. Joe and I owe practically nothing compared to most offenders. This helps me dismiss my fears, if temporarily.

No problems with Betty so far.

## February 4, 1992   THE BIG DAY

It's over! I am alive!

Our court time was 10:00 a.m., in the big Los Angeles courthouse downtown. All of my expectations about the official procedure were completely wrong. We entered the courtroom, a low-ceilinged, fluorescent lit, carpeted room with pew-like seats for the financially ruined to find hundreds of other bankrupt buddies going through the same process. There were wealthy, flashy sorts; a few seemingly trashy couples; a spattering of shady, twitchy characters; but mostly, average people like us. I wondered how long the process would take with all these cases.

Joe stared quietly around the room, while I experienced a flashback of the final events that led to our financial ruin...

After our night in the slammer, we continued to charge on our credit cards, like idiots. Money was something we'd just think about later, we said. We were too shaken up from all the crud that had befallen us so far. Then suddenly, I was stricken one morning with unbearable abdominal pain. Joe rushed me to the hospital and I spent the day undergoing numerous X-rays and pelvic exams and finally, an ultrasound. The doctors found a sea of various size ovarian cysts that required surgery immediately. It didn't help matters when a nurse injected me with a shot of Morphine while I waited for my surgeon to arrive. I launched into a screaming and kicking fit, as if I were on a bad acid trip. I didn't come down until hours later when I was anesthetized for the operating room hours later, and only Joe's soothing whispers in my ear kept me from trying to escape the hospital.

After surgery, the doctor explained that he found over twenty cysts—two the size of baseballs—all bleeding and rupturing in my pelvic area. He also told me that he had found virtually no fat in my body. He told me that I was either anorexic or bulimic. I ignored his plea for me to get help then, but subconsciously something sunk in because I began gaining weight after that. I knew had tried to control my health with every ounce of my will, and had failed. Somehow, giving up that control helped me to start becoming healthier.

The financial part of the story can be summed up in two words: no insurance. The hospital sent us bills totaling $10,000. Now our demise was in full view. I missed a month and a half of income as I recovered from my operation. This was about the time we started looking for a motor home. Our reasoning, I am embarrassed to have already reported, was that we would never be able to keep up with our bills as house painters or newspaper carriers, so we were counting on our art career to suddenly take off and save us from poverty. The motor home would save us money on rent while we pursued this ambition. Our present situation is proof of the errant preposterousness of that idea.

A judge entered at 10:00 a.m., followed by two fellows with large stacks of manila envelopes and files, containing our lives' financial histories. "I hope he doesn't tell the whole world what financial dorks we are," Joe whispered to me. The judge explained that as he called our names, we were to approach the bench, be seated in front of him, answer yes or no to three simple questions, and leave. It would then be over. Joe and I looked at each other, smiled, and squeezed hands. It didn't sound too bad so far.

After an hour and a half of "Yes, Yes, Yes" from every person that stepped up to the judge, we were finally third in line for our turn. A mean-looking, ugly man was on deck, with his creepy son, both shifting their beady black eyes.

"You have a creditor here to protest your bankruptcy," the judge said to the dirty duo when they were up to bat.

"Oh yeah?" The father was doing the talking, apparently.

"Please state your grievance," the judge told a businessman across the table.

"You borrowed $2 million from me less than a year ago, showing assets in your gas stations of well over that amount. What happened to your businesses?" the moneylender asked accusingly.

"They're gone," the father grumbled.

"Gone. Gone. Where have they gone?"

"Let's just say they were taken away from me."

"By whom?"

"I'm not at liberty to say," he said while peering around the room.

"Why can't you tell me?"

"The mob. Someone could be in this building right now, waiting for me."

The judge and the businessman glanced at each other, both smirking, but obviously frustrated. They questioned him further, seeking to reason him into some straight answers, but to no avail. Eventually they gave up and let him leave. Joe and I were so entranced by the thug's testimony, we gratefully forgot about our own turn at the stand for a few minutes, and in comparing ourselves to them, temporarily upgraded our self-image to upstanding, responsible citizens.

Our testimony whipped effortlessly by, leaving us, minutes later, stupefied and debt-free on the courthouse steps. Now, back in the Hood, it's night. Joe's asleep in the back. I'm writing by the light of our dim camper bulbs, and warming my feet next to the cheap space heater we broke down and bought last week. We don't own many things, but they seem so very valuable to me now. I feel so grateful to have a new start. I never want to borrow money again, or have a credit card.

### February 14, 1992

Joe comes across to most people as easy-going and reserved, calm in stressful situations, and blessed with common sense and a good listening ear. Yes, he is all of these things. But little is the general public aware of the warrior beast that resides in his heart (or sometimes colon.) Joe will let no one stop him from getting what he wants. My mother pointed it out years ago, during a card game after a Christmas dinner when Joe and I were first dating.

"Watch him," she said, taking me aside. "He's quiet but there's a reason for it. He's concentrating. I've never seen anyone so determined to win in my life. He's analyzing and calculating and concentrating. I'll bet you he wins more games than anyone."

"Oh Mom," I said, blaming her over-sensitive astrologically-trained mind for playing tricks on her. Joe did win most of the games that night, but I couldn't succumb to the idea of my mild-mannered husband hosting a fiery will until I observed him over the years. He is fiercely competitive and stubborn, but never reveals it in an obvious manner.

He was the third child in a family with six children, and took on the roll of the invisible kid. His two older brothers received copious attention for their athletic skills, artistic abilities, and good looks, while Joe, even though just as talented and beautiful, preferred to remain anonymous rather than join in the family carousel of battling for rank. Inwardly, however, he wished all of the attention on himself, and became an expert at winning in later life from all his practice at standing back and watching while others wasted their energy fighting and strutting their stuff. Today during our shift lunch break at the Country Club, confirmed all I've ever come to realize about my mate's inner monster. Angel had picked a fight with a banquet guest the night before, for looking at him funny.

"What were you thinking?" I asked him, "That guy was twice your size!"

Angel flatly replied, "He wanted to fight, he was cocky, so I told him to meet me outside. What's the big deal?"

"He could have killed you!"

"No way, homegirl. Just because they're big doesn't mean they can fight."

"So how do you know whether they can fight or not?"

"By looking at them."

"What do you see?"

"A look in their eye, the way they look at you. The cocky-looking ones are the first to go down."

"Aren't you cocky?"

"I know what I can handle, cocky assholes don't."

"So you wouldn't take on just anybody?"

"Hell no. I wouldn't take on Joe, for instance."

"Joe? Why not?"

"He's one of those guys who's easy to get along with, doesn't cause any trouble, a good guy. But he's got that look that says 'No one better mess with me'. I've seen guys like him before. You push him far enough, he'll go crazy on you. And when that happens, God help whoever's in the way."

"And you know all this about Joe, just by looking at him?"

"I know what I'm talking about. When you're in a gang, you learn who you can fight and who not to mess with. I'm alive; that says something."

Marco had just sat down to join us and heard the last part of our discussion about Joe. "Angel's right about Joe," he said.

So my theories have been confirmed by indisputable experts, although the test subject himself, when confronted with the results, replied with a bashful smile, "I don't know what they're talking about."

## February 15, 1992

I'm not sure I like Los Angeles for a place to live. Anytime we need to run errands, even a small grocery run less than a mile from our driveway/home, we end up sitting in traffic for a half-hour—minimum. Every menial task outside the home becomes a treacherous, time-consuming journey wrought with long stop lights, long lines, high prices, and throngs of other frustrated, hurried people. In its defense, this city's inhabitants are uncommonly friendly and have unsurpassed driving skills (for obvious reasons), but the sheer volume of people makes every day a fight for ground to stand on. We don't take our frequent jaunts to Redondo Beach much anymore, because we've grown tired of fighting traffic on the drive down Sepulveda. Some days I yearn for the country.

We've been talking about discovering some of California's many tourist attractions, since we live here now and are "running in the black" for the first time. This weekend we are planning a day at Huntington Gardens in Pasadena. It's some rich, dead guy's mansion and grounds that are open to the public. There's nothing like an eyeful of opulence to make you feel the pain of living in the Hood.

SPECIAL NOTES:
1)  Now that we can afford it, we have graduated from our hoggish consumption of carrots. We'll eat any vegetable

that can be grown, except for carrots. I hope I never eat
another carrot as long as I live.

2) Betty is still performing well, but we're having her jerky
transmission looked at tomorrow. Here's praying for a good
check-up.

### February 16, 1992

Two big news breakthroughs in one day! First, Betty's
transmission is fine. She just needed a servicing which ran us
only $35. I was so relieved I didn't notice Joe rip farts for half
the day.

Second, I got a promotion. Greg offered me a receptionist
position, because I am "popular with the members, have a
sunny disposition, and show up on time." I will be grateful to
have a break from carrying twelve dinners on one tray and
being on my feet all day, even though the pay is the same.
When I mentioned to Greg that I couldn't type, he said, "We'll
pay for you to learn how." I feel so special. Of course this
means I'll be working eight-to-five, Monday through
Friday—something I vowed would never happen. I guess being
a bankrupt bonehead allows me to stoop to new lows.

### February 17, 1992

We are finally commencing to enjoy our life, basking in the
subtle nuances and pleasures of the banal. Up until now, our
L.A. experience has been one long, horror movie, peppered
with plenty of ironic comedy. We are eagerly jumping into an
easier, softer haystack, hoping that we land on something
besides the pitchfork of catastrophe for the first time in years.

Our excursion to Pasadena was an inspiration beyond
words, but I will try to write about it anyway. The mansion of
Somebody Huntington, which housed a splendid art collection,
including Gainesborough's *Blue Boy*, and a rare book room with
such novelties as first editions of Mark Twain, a *Gutenberg Bible*,
and original writings of Shakespeare and Lincoln, was only an
appetizer for the main course in the gardens. Acres of
flawlessly landscaped flora were in full bloom. We wandered
for hours through cactus gardens, Japanese gardens, European
gardens, rose gardens, replicas of Roman temples, and strolled
beneath vine-covered trellises, engulfing weeping willows, and
fresh-scented eucalyptus. Our favorites, in the end, were the
cactus gardens, with their crazy profusion of twisted shoots,

and gnarly, spiny shrubbery that reminded us of the best *Star Trek* sets.

Now that we're back in the camper, overhearing gun shots, the ice cream man, and three different Mexican dancing songs flowing out the windows of nearby homes, I wonder how we can stay in this driveway much longer. We've been given a new lease on life, and today's peek into a world far beyond the Hood makes me yearn for a step up, even a little one.

## February 20, 1992

My new job is glorious! I am teaching myself to type from a *Teach Yourself to Type* manual, while I smile and greet members as they enter the Country Club, and answer occasional phone calls. All told, my duties could fill a short half-hour workday. I think my job title should be Front Desk Ornament. The most staggering aspect of all is that I get insurance and a steady paycheck. Whoever thought life could be so strange and exotic?

## February 25, 1992

The past week-end made me actually appreciate living in the Hood, far away from pretenders.

Last week Joe phoned Brent Fox, an old roommate from his pre-UCLA days in Newport Beach, to catch up on things. When Joe first moved away from Colorado to go to college in California, he spent a year waiting tables and surfing in order to get residency for in-state tuition. He shared a beach apartment on the Newport Beach peninsula, south of here, with two guys he barely ever saw. They had real jobs. One of them, Brent, had kept in touch with him sporadically over the years, and the other day (since we are slightly low on friends) Joe looked him up. We were invited to come visit him and his wife, Page, in Marina Del Rey, a coastal city north of Torrance.

I knew from their appearance when we first met them that we might not have much in common. They were both tan-addicts as indicated by their dark, leathery complexions, had identical twin hair colors—an unnatural platinum yellow, and had tried overzealously to make their trendy outfits look relaxed and unaffected. I admit that I prejudged, but in this case I just had a bad feeling.

At first, they were cordial, seemed down-to-earth and genuine, and showed an interest in our goings-on, but gradually their true personalities began to show through. We all went down to the beach—an unusual pastime in February prompted by unseasonably warm weather—where Page set up a portable tanning salon of sorts, complete with strategically placed lawn chairs, side tables for several brands of tanning lotion, special eye goggles, and the like. While she and Brent oiled themselves and positioned their chairs with nuclear precision, Joe and I lathered on 30 SPF sunscreen. We borrowed their unused beach umbrellas to hide from the sun, and I slipped on a hat and sunglasses. Page wore a tiny bikini. I wore a 50s style one-piece with a little skirt. Thus began our descent into hostile territory.

Joe spent most of the day beachcombing, his favorite hobby, while I was subject to a barrage of rudeness aimed at my apparently stupid desire to remain pale.

"Why don't you want to get tan?" Page asked with a grimace, not trying in the least to conceal her horror that I would voluntarily use sunscreen.

Before I could answer, Brent piped in sarcastically, "She doesn't want her skin to age."

"Well, that's part of it," I said, confused at why I would have to defend the blatantly obvious reasons to avoid sun exposure. "It also causes skin cancer, and I personally got too much sun as a teenager, so now I break out in hives after five minutes of sun, and I also like having pale skin." I could have really emphasized that last point, but I could tell by their expressions that they found my reasons ridiculous. They didn't push the issue verbally but their stares indicated total distaste. I changed the subject safely to weather, hoping that tanning philosophy would never be heard from again, but found it difficult to keep myself from feeling self-conscious and angry the rest of the day.

Weatherworn and hungry, we returned to their condo around 3:30 to clean up for an evening on the town. Let me preface this entire evening by noting that both Joe and I are hell to be around when we are hungry. We are irritable, impatient, negative and, if conditions persist, volatile. We warned Brent and Page of this fact several times, hinting that we should probably have a snack before venturing out. But their refrigerator was empty, and  we were told by Page, "Chill out. We'll get to the restaurant soon enough." She said it in a teasing, supposedly cute way, but it came across as sadistic.

While they dressed, we meticulously scanned their condo, as we do everyone's homes, for artistic inspiration. Our paintings, inspired from people's homes, make every visit to new interior spaces a busman's holiday for us. One's environment speaks volumes about its inhabitants, and we tried to fight back our hunger to listen carefully to what this typical Southern California residence had to tell us about Brent and Page. There were few furnishings in the living room: a black leather sofa, a glass coffee table with four remote controls encircling a half-dead spider plant, an entertainment center larger than Lucy's bedroom. No art adorned the walls, an unforgivable crime in our rulebook. The room was shouting the California credo: "There is no time or money leftover after purchasing a fancy car, buying trendy expensive clothes, and eating out all the time to do anything with the house except to watch movies on the VCR, which help keep one posted on the hottest movie stars with whom to wish an acquaintance."

They finally emerged from their bedroom as starvation began to nudge us into snapping at each other. Page was scantily dressed and heavily made up; Brent had fastidiously tousled hair.

"What kind of place do you want to eat at?" Brent asked.

"How about some place quiet and inexpensive," Joe replied, having given the awful details of our financial wreckage earlier that day.

"Oh! I know! What about Rock 'n Roll Sushi?" Page exclaimed, "They might not be too busy yet." I bit my tongue, holding back my disgust with sushi, reasoning that I could always order chicken teriyaki.

"Yeah, you'll love the food. And it's not expensive at all," claimed Brent. Being out-of-town guests, we naively assumed they knew what they were talking about.

We piled into their BMW and drove to a restaurant designed to look like an old boat dock. From the large, festive outdoor patio overflowed Hawaiian-shirted drunks bouncing up-and-down to thundering pop music. I gripped Joe's hand in the back seat—hard. We were too hungry to protest. I knew if I opened my mouth at this stage of starvation, I'd likely spill untold profanities and end up stranded at that godforsaken place. We went in, wincing our ears shut. I whispered to Joe, "Try to remain positive, try to remain positive."

When a skinny hostess with huge boobs popping out of her tight t-shirt quoted us a one and a half hour wait, I nearly screamed bloody murder. Joe's eyes shot wide open and my heart pounded in terror. Brent immediately put his hand on the gal's shoulder and said the horrific word, "Fine," then leaned over to Joe and confided, "We'll get drunk and have appetizers while we wait", avoiding contact with our eyes and quickly heading out to the patio. It was clear he had no intention of eating anywhere else.

My blood rises as I write about this episode; even though my hunger is gone now, I have the urge to hatchet those idiots into edible tidbits.

We very reluctantly followed, looking at each other like forlorn concentration camp victims trying to mash our way through the throngs of obnoxious, shouting humanity. By the time we caught up with Brent and Page, they held fishbowl size margaritas and asked us, shouting, if we wanted some, too.

"No thanks," we protested, "we're on a budget."

After some physical struggling with alcohol-crazed patrons, Joe managed to round up two waters for us. To our dismay there were no available tables, so we were forced to stand for half an hour, without appetizers, being bumped and stepped on. It got worse when Brent ran into an over-muscled, tight-shirted acquaintance from his workout club named Jeff, and jumped into a name-dropping contest designed to impress everyone within a twenty-foot radius, a feat that would challenge the most uproarious opera singer.

"Yeah, he ran into Arnold there last week, said he's a great guy. Said Michael Keaton also goes there, and Cher."

"Cool. Say, I got tickets to Jay Leno at the Strand. My buddy knows one of his assistants. Got me good seats."

"I saw Howie Mandel there two months ago. Sat behind Dennis Quaid and Meg Ryan. Nice people. Real Salt of the Earth."

Joe and I pinched each other's legs alternately, wishing we had a tape recorder. Sometimes, I actually revel in surreal situations such as these, knowing Joe and I can live off the laughs for months to come. But claustrophobic insanity threatened to topple me, and instead of laughing, I excused myself, went into the ladies neon bathroom, locked myself into a stall, plopped down on the toilet, and bawled. I begged God to get me through the night without flying into a rage in front of Joe's friends, promising to never come to Marina Del Rey again.

After I gathered myself together and wiped away all running mascara traces, I emerged a calmer individual.

Bathroom breakdowns are a familiar and necessary survival tool to most women in the hectic restaurant business, and can be used in social situations as well. To my ecstatic relief, the hostess had found a table on the patio for us, for appetizer sushi only. I would still have to wait for my chicken, but this was a huge breakthrough nevertheless. Unfortunately, our tiny table was in the middle of the swarming multitude, and we were to be nudged by surrounding California rock-hard butts for another half-hour.

Brent and Page, now joined by the supposedly well-connected muscle man, Jeff, finished their third margarita before appetizers appeared, adding inebriation to their long list of faults. We allowed them to order the food for us, responding unwillingly to their claims of sushi connoisseurship, and while we waited for food, Brent and Jeff insisted on standing up, forgoing the precious chairs we had accosted for them. At first I couldn't figure out why they had to stand, but gradually caught on as I watched their constantly roving eyes, puffed out chests, and their even louder than before name-dropping. They were showing off. Meanwhile Joe and I were trying to make polite conversation with Page, who was half drunk by this time and slurring her words. Just as our coveted food came, a waitress announced, "Your table's ready!" I nearly shit my pants.

The whole glorious moment, when I thought I could finally make it through the night, was dashed by Brent's quick reply, "We'll just stay here and have appetizers."

Joe's usually calm demeanor rapidly changed. "No we won't!" he shouted.

Brent ignored the objection and replied, "We three want to stay here."

I backed Joe up by stating quite frankly, "We'll go in and eat then."

This brought the loser to his senses. He realized we meant business and succumbed begrudgingly to our outrageous idea of eating real food. Waitresses carted our food and drink indoors, followed by Joe and Dori Chop-lickers and the now sullen threesome. They had finally achieved the most sought-after position in the restaurant to pose and scope, only to be hauled away to the confines of the indoors, where lurked the boring prospect of talking with us pale flabby folk without movie star connections.

By the end of the meal, Joe and I had consumed seventeen glasses of water apiece, and half orders of the cheapest thing on the menu, which was fine with us. The devil trio had taken in countless margaritas, sushi, shots of Johnnie Walker, the most expensive entrees available, desserts, and coffee drinks, which was fine with them, especially when the bill came. I don't know if they were drunk or mad at us for ruining their swinging evening, but when the bill was brought to the table, it was automatically assumed to be split between all of us, meaning $60 for us instead of $12. I sat in a daze of disbelief, too bewildered to be angry or fight back. I just wanted to go home. Joe told me later that he was in shock, as well, just hoping our long, loud nightmare would be over soon. Sadly it was not over soon enough.

Jeff insisted we hang out for just a few more drinks on the patio, and since we had been driven here in their car, we were at their mercy. We found a choice spot right next to the pulsating speaker blasting Midnight Oil, where we strained to hear Jeff's thigh-neck, loudmouth, boring weight lifting stories, sprinkled with boasts of celebrity-sightings and hot babes that wanted him. Page was plastered by this time, hanging on Brent for support, and smiling. Finally, the evening ended after too many obvious yawn-and-stretch hints on our part. We were never so happy to say goodbye, and we meant positively forever.

I'm a little embarrassed that I've written more about this one bad evening than I have about any other one event. Maybe my frustrations and feelings of inadequacy about our life are easier taken out on someone I don't know very well and will never see again. Whatever the case, I feel better. And those tacky, pretender, lowlife, imbeciles deserve every rotten word I can write about them anyway.

**February 27, 1992**
Tonight is the first time since moving to the Hood that I wish we could sleep inside with Elga and Hilda. I'm not only scared for myself; I've lost that unreasonable security that women sometimes experience when they have a man with them. For some crazy reason, when I'm camping in the woods with nothing to protect me from being mauled by a grizzly but a skimpy tent and an unarmed male companion, I feel safe. At this moment I do not feel safe, even with Joe snoring next to me and a herd of cop cars driving slowly up and down our

street, their search lights occasionally sweeping a blinding flash in Lucy's little back window.

We watched *Studs* with Elga in the garage after the sun went down, seated on matching 1960s kitchen chairs with fuzzy stuffing oozing out of the upholstered seats and our feet propped up on an old metal milk crate; happy to relax and numb our minds after a tedious workday. We sported the usual reactions to the mildly amusing gutter humor: Elga would raise his eyebrows and make a little circle with his mouth while we responded in unison with a long, drawn-out, disgusted "OH." Any other evening we would have lingered to see which ludicrous Made-for-TV movie was waiting to bore us, but tonight we thought it best to return to the camper to start some new paintings—a pastime nearly forgotten since the last art show, due to the bankruptcy and all.

The old garage screen door slammed shut behind us. As we walked the thirty-or-so feet down the driveway to Lucy's resting spot, we noticed the dark silhouette of a human figure in the neighbor's yard hiding behind the tiny stucco house and breathing heavily. His back was pressed against the outside wall. Having seen too many suspicious characters every day and all day in our neighborhood, it did not register in my absent mind that anything was amiss.

"Hello," I said cheerfully.

"Hi," said the stranger, in a tense, raised whisper.

"Nice, night out, isn't it?" I asked.

"Uh, yeah."

I could only tell through the shadows that he was Mexican, in his 20s, with a medium build. I kept walking, still oblivious to any danger or unusual goings-on, until suddenly I was blinded by the swinging searchlights of several police cars on our street. It immediately registered in my foggy skull what the cops were looking for, at which time I swirled around to see Joe loitering back at the malefactor's hideout, chatting. I supposed Joe to be ignorant of the search party, so I began, from behind the shield of Lucy's white hull, to signal him to get away from there. I jumped up and down, flailing my arms wildly, whispering as loud as I could manage, "Joe! Get over here! Quick!"

Joe seemed as relaxed as ever, amiably nodding at the bad guy and ignoring me. My heart raced as I tried to think of a ploy to save him from the clutches of a potential madman, my mind picturing my husband being held hostage in a SWAT shoot-out. Joe then calmly said goodnight to the guy, strolled over to me and said, "What's you're problem?" As we darted into the motor home, I relayed in my most dramatic tone the scenario out on the street and its dreadful implications, only to be told, "I know."

"Then why the hell are you standing around chitchatting with a fugitive criminal?"

"I didn't want to piss him off! He was saying all these crazy things to me, and I thought I better remain calm so he didn't go nuts on me."

"You sure were calm. What did he say?"

"Well, he started out OK with 'Hi, How're you doing?' Then he started going on about how he's not a bad person or something. He said I'm not a bad person. It's not like they think. I'm a good person'."

"What did you say?" I asked.

"I said 'OK, I believe you'. But he kept going on, saying the same thing over and over. I thought I'd never get out of there. He ran off after that."

"Didn't you see me waving at you?"

"Who couldn't? You were just making things worse, you know."

"I thought you didn't know! I thought you were being a dunce."

We sat in silence for a few seconds until Joe said, "Should we go tell the police where he is?"

"Don't go out there again!" I shouted, panicking all over again.

We left it at that.

No art was made this evening. We sat and stared, listening for yells or gunshots outside the camper, which we never heard. I said I didn't want to live here anymore and Joe said me neither. We went to bed, and Joe fell asleep in less than a minute. I'm still pumped with adrenaline and will probably not sleep at all.

## February 28, 1992

Hilda showed us the morning paper with a small mention that the motorcycle Christmas murderer has been caught. He was a Mexican in his 20s, of medium build, and lives a few doors down from us.

I asked Joe if last night was his first conversation with a murderer: he said yes.

Mab has been telling us at work of this great apartment complex about a mile from here, still in Torrance, but right on the edge of Redondo Beach. She says it's cheap—if you call $500 a month for a tiny efficiency cheap—and obviously a lot safer than here. We are ready. We can afford it, barely, and we can't live in a driveway forever. This last incident has convinced us to get the Dodge out of hell, as Joe says too often.

**March 2, 1992**

Everything happened so fast. We called the apartment complex that Mab recommended (its claims of "mature landscaping" spurred us to jump on the deal), and set up an appointment to go look at it. We met with the managers and after being told that our credit history would be checked, gave the sob story about astronomical medical bills. We got accepted easily, and moved in. Moving in required literally no effort on our part. We started Lucy, drove a mile, and parked. We did have to carry our paltry belongings inside, a job that took all of 15 minutes. For once I am reveling in the freedom of owning next to nothing.

The Duke of Kent is the name of our new happy residence. Its name has inspired plenty of snickers on our part, because it implies some semblance of English architecture or stateliness, if not a Californiafied version thereof. Yet it looks identical to a 1950s beach motel, with every one-room apartment facing a central courtyard with a shining aqua swimming pool and giant palm trees.

We moved Lucy's foam bed—our only piece of furniture—into our little room, then laid upon it to appreciate the dreamy, fantastic way the ceiling was out of our reach. (We only have to jump slightly to reach it from a standing position, but it feels like Madison Square Garden compared to Lucy's six-foot ceiling.)

Now maybe we can get on with the business of becoming rich and famous artists.

**March 4, 1992**

It didn't take long for us to decipher the reason this place charges rock-bottom prices and allows recently bankrupt boneheads like us to move in. I don't want to use the politically incorrect term "cheap white trash" so I won't. Let's just say we won't be fraternizing with any of our neighbors.

## March 8, 1992

Now that we have a real life with jobs, an apartment, a car, and our bills paid, I can't seem to find a thing to write about.

## March 10, 1992

DORI AND JOE'S LIFE—A REPORT

1) Car: Betty's running beautifully; we've grown very attached to her. We were quoted prices at Earl Schibe for a pink paint job to spruce her up, but decided we're not that attached to her.

2) Home: Aside from our pathetic neighbors, we love our new place. I will never in my life take for granted the enormous luxury of long, hot showers.

3) Work: Both Joe and I have received substantial raises and are deluged with constant praise at the Country Club. We've never been so dedicated to jobs before, probably because they're the only things we have going in our life.

4) Art: We've only eked out a few paintings since we moved in, as our creative energies are nowhere to be found. This is the first time since I started studying art in college at age twenty that I've been so unable to paint prolifically.

5) Spousal Relationship: Love is still in the air, and fighting is limited to "No, you may not fart under the sheets! Go in the bathroom!" One doesn't have to be a genius to know who issued those words.

6) Lucy: She sits peacefully out on the street in front of the "Puke of Kent," empty and safe from car thieves due to her unique appearance. No one would get far stealing a vehicle that looks like a white version of the Oscar Meyer Weiner-mobile.

7) Weekends: Fun has been limited as we adjust to our new life as ordinary people. We've planned some real extravaganzas, though. We'd like to take trips to both Death Valley and Sequoia National Park sometime this spring.

## March 14, 1992

Today I learned at the Country Club not to use the term Latino for the Mexicans there. They are from Mexico and they are Mexicans.

**March 16, 1992**

There is an old folks home right across the skinny alley from the Duke of Kent. In fact, our windows—all two of them—face directly into the windows of two elderly people. Now, rather than gunshots, the ice cream man, and/or Mexican music, we hear the moanings of a sad, old woman. She sings funny songs out-of-tune and stops halfway through, in mid-sentence, as if she has forgotten the words, but fails to start crooning again. Now, instead of the ice cream song, we find ourselves filling in the tunes of her unfinished songs and humming the tunes the rest of the day. The songs were hits in her heyday, like "Stage Door Canteen" and "Sentimental Journey." She sometimes cries out, calling for someone. "Help me! Somebody please help me!" Her voice sounds desperate and panicked, like someone is trying to kill her. The woman's calls grow louder and more hysterical until, after some time has passed, a nurse invariably shows up. Then the old woman cries, "What are you doing here? Get away from me!" The nurse leaves, apologizing (and probably cursing after she gets out of earshot), and the old woman settles down again. This happens at least once a day and has begun to fade into background noise like gunshots in the Hood. Sometimes the woman just moans softly for hours.

**March 31, 1992**

This weekend we finally went up to L.A. to explore the numerous galleries. We were expecting to be depressed by their superstar artists and high prices and sold stickers and snooty gallery owners. We investigated the Santa Monica area, where we had been told the highest concentration of "high art" galleries are located. To our relief, we have returned to our dinky apartment with several of our long held preconceptions about big galleries blown to bits.

"I can't believe how nice all the gallery owners were! I kept expecting them to turn around and ignore us the minute they found out we were artists, like Denver dealers do," I said after plopping onto our foam pad. "They don't have to act like pretender-snooty-assholes here. They have good art, nice gallery spaces, the art sells—they don't have to pretend they're big shots because they sort of are."

"That's where I want to be someday."

"Where?"

"Exhibiting in one of those galleries.   And on the cover of Time magazine. And I want to shake hands with the President."

"Which President?"

"Any one will do."

"What if you don't like his politics?"

"Or her politics. I don't like any of their politics. I just want to see the White House and be able to tell my grandchildren I shook hands with a President. Besides, just because I don't like their politics doesn't mean they might not be a nice person."

"You've got a point there. What did you think of the art we saw today?" Joe asked wearily, simultaneously rubbing his tired feet and stroking my hair.

"It was all big."

"Yeah. And expensive," Joe sighed, switching feet. "Who was your favorite?"

"That Brian O'Connor guy who did the dark figurative ones."

"I liked the one who painted the freeway overpasses."

"Yeah. He was good too. Do you think our paintings would be appropriate in any of those galleries?" I asked with some hesitance, not wanting to hear an honest answer.

"Nope. Not really. Our work's too tame."

"You're right," I admitted.

"That sucks."

"Yeah, it does."

## April 1, 1992

Occasionally, I play what Joe calls "Lucy schemes," named after the most famous perpetrator of unsuccessful mischievous ploys, Lucille Ball. I began my career as a bumbling trickster in childhood with my slightly younger sister, Debi, in an attempt to pester our even younger siblings, Derick and Dana. (My maiden name is Duckels—my Mom lived life speaking a perpetual tongue twister). Our only successful feat of tomfoolery was when we blasted Dana with raw eggs and bologna from the roof of our house, undetected. But in every other case our efforts to annoy were thwarted and usually backfired. We tried to dig deep holes and cover them with grass (traps for the kids to fall in), but our victims would always walk up to our deadly snare and exclaim, "What's all this dead grass here for?" We'd tape-record scary messages and put them under Derick and Dana's bunk bed at night. As we listened with our ears pressed to the door we heard, "Hey! Look what

Dori and Debi left in our room! Let's make a tape!" They were
completely oblivious to our recorded chants about the ghost
with the golden arm. When we short-sheeted Derick's bed and
poured sand in it, we were punished by my Dad with the
atrocious task of cleaning out the storage room nicknamed
"The Dungeon" and making it into a cozy new bedroom for
Derick. It took us a week of hard labor and discouraged jokes
of any sort for a long time.

Even though my pranks have yet to fool Joe, I can't resist
keeping up the tradition. The prospect that they will never have
the proper effect actually makes me love to do them all the
more, because I always get to laugh at myself and my stupid
idea and Joe's head-shaking reaction to them.

Today, after we'd finished breakfast (toast, not carrots!) Joe
came out of the bathroom to find me sprawled across the
carpet in a dead person's position with jelly/blood oozing out
of my mouth. "Dori, why is there jelly smeared around your
mouth?" he asked, with a grin. He knew I wouldn't be able to
answer for 15 minutes, my obligatory laughter session that
follows every Lucy scheme played out, with me shaking
violently and silently while holding my stomach until I am
forced to breathe at intervals. I am fully aware that my game is
not funny in the least and that is why I laugh so. "You really
outdid yourself this time, Lucy. Very clever."

After I gained control of my wits, I told him he should be
grateful he isn't married to some boring old gal with a normal
sense of humor and an aversion to rubbing jelly on her face.

"You're right", he said. "I'm very grateful."

## April 28, 1992

Just when we think our life will finally be relatively secure
and mindless for a while, when I find myself writing about
pranks instead of primal fears, we get slammed with another
reason to believe in crisis as a way of life. The riots. We don't
have a phone or a TV, so we learned of the emergency by
overhearing our loud, drunk, loser neighbor yelling at his
television, "I can't fucking believe it!" We stepped outside our
room and noticed several ratty apartment dwellers milling
about on the other side of the swimming pool, all smoking and
loudly discussing something about South Central L.A. We
hurried over and asked a young but weathered, crackly-voiced,
bleached-blonde woman with gray teeth what was going on.

She excitedly explained about the not guilty verdicts of the
Rodney King trial and the ensuing pandemonium. We assumed
she was drunk when she relayed the stories of looting and
burning, but we believed the episode was worthy of further
investigation. Joe ran to a nearby pay phone to ask Hilda and
Elga if we could come over and watch their television, while I
stayed back at the apartment to put on lipstick, the essential
accoutrement to all important events.

The streets of Torrance were uncommonly sparse this
evening and there was an air of impending disaster. As we
drove into our old neighborhood, we wondered if it too was
experiencing the aftermath of the injustice and proceeded
cautiously as though we'd be set ablaze by a flying Molotov
cocktail at the next turn. Nothing out of the ordinary was
occurring in our old stomping grounds, except for the absence
of Mexican music. We suspected all eyes and ears were on the
television at the moment.

We hurried into Hilda's TV parlor where she and Elga filled
us in on the action we'd missed. This was one night we'd all be
watching together.

The television footage was spotty and mostly taken from
the sky due to the obvious dangers, but it was clear that a great
number of buildings were on fire. The announcers talked of
looting and death, of brutal attacks on white people, of chaos
from Los Angeles to Long Beach. There weren't many images of
it yet—mostly just burning buildings from the sky—but the
magnitude of the situation was apparent, making it difficult to
grasp the fact that it was all taking place a few miles from
where we sat reclining in La-Z-Boys. We watched in frustration
as jerky cameras filmed a black night with nameless buildings
in flames and wished we could see more. It sounds morbid that
we would be yearning for scenes of all the gory details instead
of just reports, but we were. This is history.

We're going to sleep now, in our (hopefully) safe bed on
the floor at the Duke, after the long, philosophical discussion
that these kinds of events will always warrant. Tomorrow we'll
see the aftermath of the destruction on the big TVs that loom
over the dining room at the Club House and until then sleeping
will just have to suffice for entertainment.

### April 29, 1992

On our way to work, we saw lines gathering at gas stations
as some people prepared to exit the city. We hadn't heard any

news since the night before and assumed that it was all over, until we arrived at work to find the RHCC staff and members alike crowded below the television in silence.

"What's going on?" Joe asked the gathering.

"It's gotten worse," Mr. Culp told us. "They're burning or looting every business in their neighborhoods. It's spreading all over the city, too. They're not far from here, now. Look out the window."

It was a beautiful, clear morning. Below us the fresh greens of the golf course were scattered with golfers in pink or green Izod shirts and plaid shorts, relaxed and oblivious to the scene behind them. As usual, the backdrop of an endless city loomed in the distance, but now there were billowing smoke clouds rising from hundreds of small points in the great expanse, and even flames could be spotted without much effort. Many of the fires had to be colossal to be seen from such a distance. Mr. Culp was right. It was apparent the chaos had spread to neighborhoods not far from Torrance, including Compton (a dangerous place under any conditions) where many of the Country Club staff reside.

Today, all eyes were hypnotized by the television, even at the insistence by the managers that we actually work, but of course, the members didn't mind or even notice the slow service. The escapades of the thousands of looters pillaging the city seemed more like sad comedy than the shocking tragedy that it actually was. Television interviewers stopped thieves as they exited demolished stores with armloads of goodies, and asked them how they felt about looting (a fine question). "Great!" was the answer. Folks took the time to comfortably sit down on stools and try on shoes before running off with them, and hold outfits up to their small children to make sure they fit before stuffing them into garbage bags and flying away; all in front of national television cameras. We found ourselves laughing, but shocked at ourselves for it, as a most surreal day unfolded before us.

It was announced at regular intervals that all citizens of Los Angeles and its surrounding cities should absolutely not be venturing outside their homes today. Almost all businesses were closed or being ordered closed by the governor. Wives of the golfers were calling the clubhouse incessantly, telling us to beg their husbands to come home immediately, a request that never came to pass, as the men would no sooner leave the golf

course on a sunny day than loot a department store. Through
the frantic women callers we were informed that the spreading
mania had reached Torrance, and that looters were annihilating
Del Amo Mall, the massive galleria near us. Later we found this
to be sheer lies, but it fueled a panicked response from
members and staff alike, as we imagined the danger so close to
home. We were not allowed to go home early, like the millions
of other lucky workers throughout L.A., probably owing to the
management's feeling of the Country Club being "above it all,"
both literally and figuratively. When we left at 5:00 p.m., a strict
after-dark curfew imposed on all L.A. area residents gave us a
ride home like none other. We drove down the normally
busiest thoroughfares to see not a single car in sight.

We drove slowly along Crenshaw Boulevard with our
windows open, listening to the quiet. The windows of
businesses and their accompanying signs were dark, and a
weird smoke that smelled like burnt beach balls hung in the air.
"We'll never see anything like this again," Joe softly and
reverently stated.

**April 30, 1992**

It's hard to believe the insanity is still going on. The
National Guard was called in today, but basically did nothing
about the situation except to stand around in full riot gear and
look tough. I guess the situation is touchy, what with the riots
being set off by bad cops and all. No one wants to start it up
again. The multicultural diversity of the Rolling Hills Country
Club has given me and Joe an up close view of the opinions of
various ethnic groups about the riots, an upsetting education.

The Mexicans voice disgust with the destruction, calling the
rioters filthy names, and stating that if they were in charge,
they'd call for bombs to blow them away. Gina, an African -
American herself, is saddened by the riots, but furious about
the injustice of the Rodney King verdict. I've gathered she
believes that the riots are a necessary evil to call attention to
the grave crisis in our justice system. The Country Club
members, for the most part, have all lived through a few wars.
The sampling of opinions that Joe and I heard from their ranks
probably isn't universal, but all of the members we listened to
were outraged at the violence. Although they all sympathized
with the anger of the masses about the trial, they believed
strong and swift force on the part of the National Guard was
the only answer to stop the pandemonium.

The only opinion I care to voice is the ever-pressing riddle of our little household—how to get that poor old, old woman across the alley to quiet down at night or at least close her window. I've been humming... *summertime and the living is easy*...over and over for three days. That's all the words I know. Since it isn't summer and living isn't easy right now, I really wish she'd start me on something more appropriate, like "When the Lights Go on Again."

## May 1, 1992

Tired of writing about riots. Two new annoying sounds to contend with at the Duke:
1) loud, howling, raspy-voiced cat wandering around swimming pool at night.
2) drunk next-door neighbor now on fifth day of TV and Jack Daniels binge. Yells obscenities at television and armchair.

## May 2, 1992

The National Guard is still standing post throughout the city in case of a flare-up. Joe is dying to take a leisurely drive to go look at building carnage, but I told him it isn't going anywhere soon. I'd rather wait to be sure we don't get our heads bashed in with bricks, like other unfortunate white people.

## May 3, 1992

TODAY'S LIST
1) I'm ugly.
2) I'm fat.
3) I'm really fat.
4) I write like a sixth grader.
5) I'm a terrible artist and we'll be poor forever.
6) I hate everybody.
7) Everybody hates me.

I read my list to Joe and he said, "It's that time of the month." I guess he is right.

## May 4, 1992

That darn cat is still howling and whining all the time. Joe has declared war, vowing to clobber the cat if he can catch it. Our loser alcoholic neighbor is quiet, though. I think his weeklong bender has left him nearly comatose. The old lady

across the alley must have been uplifted by the riots; her
wailing has been reduced to a mere hum.

**May 5, 1992   Death Valley, CA**

A spontaneous idea seized Joe in the middle of last night,
resulting in our present location, Death Valley.

"Wake up!" he nudged me, "We've got to get out of here!"

"What is it?" I sleepily whispered.

"We've got to get out of town. Go somewhere and get away
from this crazy place." Joe was much too excited for 2:30 a.m.

"Right now?" I slurred into my pillow.

"No, but this weekend. We've been wanting to go to one of
the National Parks, how about that?"

"I thought you meant leaving forever," I said, a little more
coherent.

"That would be nice, but no, just for a little bit."

"O.K.," I agreed as I rolled over, "But do you think Lucy's
up for it?"

"Yeah, sure. We've got our Ultra Van manual. We can do
it," he stated unsurely, but still ready for adventure.

"O.K. But don't we have to get up early?"

"How about I set our alarm for six?"

"Are you out of your fucking mind?" I cussed
uncharacteristically.

"Definitely," he laughed.

After dead silence and a few coercive kisses on my neck I
moaned, "OK, but you're in charge."

I immediately fell back to sleep, and dreamt that Henry
Fonda was trying to sell us a used boat. Abruptly, my weekend
started a few hours later.

"This better be good," I warned Joe.

"It's going to change our life," he said, smiling. "Oh yeah."

So here we are, at the Death Valley campground (officially
and literally the hottest place on Earth) surrounded by other
RVs. I am practically dead from the heat. We couldn't sleep on
Lucy's rear bed, which is overheated from the engine again, so
we are lying together on the two front seats,   stark-naked, and
madly vigilant about keeping our skin from touching each
other. The curtains are closed, but a scorching wind
occasionally blows through, revealing full, frontal nudity to any
passers-by. We don't care. It's exhibitionism or death.

We arrived here safely, but not without trouble. Lucy's
temperature gauge began escalating past the medium range just

as we began our descent into Death Valley. We used the trusty but miserable remedy: driving slow and keeping the heater on high power until we stopped. We were able to experience this hostile land much the way its first discoverers did, with unreliable transportation, no air conditioning, and a lust for adventure. Hopefully we won't end up like they did, as rotting carcasses covered with maggots. I can think of better ways to spend my vacation.

Tomorrow we'll discover some of the weird attractions to be found here, all named after the Devil.

## May 6, 1992

We awoke this morning, shivering and snuggling together for warmth, only to be sopped with sweat two hours later as we drove around to the various geological features of the park.

Our favorite attraction was Devil's Golf Course, a flat stretch of land covered completely with otherworldly mineral formations that seemed to grow out of the ground. This gray expanse of clumpy, craggy, brittle desert extended as far as the eye could see, and was our main source of Kodak moments: Joe jumping at Devil's Golf Course ... Dori sleeping among the lumps at Devil's Golf Course ... Dori and Joe holding hands among the lumps ... Lumps alone ... Lucy parked among the lumps ... Joe looking out into the great expanse ... The great expanse alone.

Other favorite stops included Devil's Cornfield, Devil's Sand Box, and Devil's restrooms. One attraction should have been called Devil's Penis, but this is a National Park, after all. We departed late this afternoon, hoping to find a place to sleep with temperatures that actually register on a thermometer. On the way out of the park, Joe noticed the gas gauge dropping rapidly and said as we drove down the road, "Go back to the engine compartment and see if you see anything unusual." I ran back and opened up the volcanic blast furnace and squinted down into its depths, fearing my hair to be singed completely off.

"Anything unusual?" Joe yelled.

"Is it unusual to have gas pouring out all over the road?" I hollered.

Joe came to an immediate stop by the roadside, the very same vast desert road side used in countless movies where motorists end up stranded and eventually crawl with cracked lips, crimson faces, and tattered clothes to their death, just after seeing a mirage of ladies in bikinis and palm trees. I looked around in terror at the parched, cracked, endless vista while Joe calmly got out the Ultra Manual and looked up our problem. To make the time go faster, after pulling myself together, I took pictures of Joe's feet sticking out from under Lucy. He mumbled something about jerry-rigging a fuel filter as he fumbled through the manual and pulled things out of his toolbox, while I looked on, positive that his efforts would be fruitless.

They were not fruitless. Within 20 minutes, my genius husband had fashioned a makeshift fix-it filter that solved our problem and had us back on the road, although we still had to drive 20 mph with the heater on. I dreamily gazed at my perfect man, my knight in shining armor, as we drove out of the land of the Devil to cooler weather here in Lone Pine.

Lone Pine is a desert town against the towering spires of the eastern slope of the Sierras, where numerous Hollywood movies, especially Westerns, have been filmed since the silent era because of its large, bulbous rock formations that jut out just below the mountains' faces. We immediately recognized it as the location where our favorite movie, *Tremors* (with Kevin Bacon and Reba) was filmed. We're lying here relaxing and listening to the quiet while a happy, cool breeze emphasizes our distance from LA.

"Do you like LA?" I asked Joe earlier.

"I hate living there as a poor person."

"Why haven't you said this before?" I asked.

"We went through a lot of trouble to get here. We had a lot of big plans. I didn't want to give up so soon."

"Wouldn't it be nice to live in Lucy and travel around the whole country and sleep in places like this every night?"

"Don't say that," Joe sadly replied.

"Why?"

"You have to have money to do that."

"That's my dream, then. This is heaven."

"Yes. It's heaven."

We allowed ourselves to pretend we could fix Lucy up to perfection and took ourselves on imaginary journeys around the United States as we lay staring at the snow-capped Sierras just outside our window. Someday.

**May 8, 1992**

Back at the Duke now. Work's boring, except for the fact that the managers are on a witch hunt, trying to find the culprits who stole over half of the new $50,000 English cutlery set.

I've gained ten pounds since starting my ass- mushing secretary job. Everybody says I look much better with some flesh on my bones and they're probably right, but I'm not used to it and feel fat sometimes. I've had to buy new clothes that fit at Ross Dress for Less. We've been trying to save money now that we're out of debt, and it's going rather well so far, so I hate spending money on clothes that I wouldn't need if my size hadn't changed.

Joe finally got his revenge on the yowling cat. At least he thinks he did. I came around the corner of the ugly Duke building to the parking lot, where I caught Joe stooping under our car, engaged in some high-concentration activity.

"What are you doing?" I asked.

"Throwing carrots at that darn cat", he replied with a predatorial growl. (We now keep carrots in the fridge, to remind us of where we came from).

"Why carrots?"

"They were all I could find."

"That's not very nice," I scolded.

"It's the food chain," he replied.

**May 16, 1992**

We're leaving. Last night we saw the movie Leaving Normal with Christine Lahti and Meg Tilly—now the single most influential movie night of my life. The movie is about two directionless women who decide to follow their hearts for the first time in their lives and set out in a (what else) motor home to discover their destiny. I cried six times, laughed dozens, and was hit over the head with the message that I was destined to get sooner or later: it's time to leave L.A. I left the theater not wanting Joe to know how I was feeling, for fear he wouldn't agree with me, or that my instinct was wrong.

"I want to get out of here," I eventually said. "I honestly hate it. The riots really made me see I don't want to be here."

"Let's do it, then. I think you're right. It's time," he decidedly stated.

It all happened so quickly. After a late night of discussion we've decided that in one month we're leaving LA in our motor home to be homeless vagabonds, stopping to work when the money runs out, just like adventurers have done for centuries.

## May 18, 1992

We gave the Country Club our notice three weeks ahead of time, just to be nice and fair. I'm going to miss that place a lot. Best job I ever had. Joe, too, he says.

## May 21, 1992

Before we leave town, we'll take one more excursion—to Sequoia National Park. We're actually planning ahead this time, so hopefully, I'll get some sleep the night before.

Last night the old lady across the alley was out of control. She wailed and moaned so long and loud that the nurses stopped coming to her rescue. I was feeling particularly naughty and was so fed up with her shrieks that I stuck my head out of our window just eight feet from where she sat and began howling loudly like a coyote. I made sure my head was hidden by our ratty curtain, to avoid being arrested by the authorities. Joe was just inside the window, telling me to shut up, but I could tell he was trying not to laugh. Miraculously, the woman stopped her hours-long ruckus and listened to my howls as if in a trance. Then she was silent. We didn't hear a sound from her the rest of the night. Maybe all she needed was a little healthy competition.

## May 24, 1992

Too busy to write. Working a lot to make money for the road. Sequoia trip this weekend.

## May 27, 1992

WEEKEND REPORT, IN 17 EASY STEPS

1) Left L.A. at 7:00 a.m. Saturday, after night of little sleep due to yowling cat—made worse by Joe's carrots, I presume.
2) Drove Lucy as far as Bakersfield, stopped for gas and noticed transmission fluid pouring all over pavement.
3) Looked up Ultra Van owners who might be able to help us and found Melvin and Millie  Dineson of Bakersfield, CA. Called and was told Dineson home was in sight distance from gas station.

4) Drove Lucy one block to Dineson home and arrived just as last drops of transmission fluid spilled from Lucy.

5) Dori listened to Millie explain how kids watch too much TV while watching *Marilyn Monroe: The Mystery of her Death* on ABC. Joe poked around the Ultra Van with Mel (very nice man) with no luck fixing transmission.

6) The Dineson's neighbor, a transmission mechanic, came home from work at 5:00 p.m. and fixed our problem in 15 minutes.

7) Spent night in Dineson's driveway, sweating, but relieved that our car trouble was so miraculously taken care of.

8) Left Bakersfield early Sunday morning, drove through orange groves and sunshine, then steep, winding roads to Sequoia National Park. Lucy did not like the steep hills; never went faster than 25 mph.

9) Read all required park literature about bear safety, i.e. "Don't do anything at all or a bear will eat you alive."

10) Went for hike, saw really big trees. Too worried about bears to notice. Yelled "Sergeant Pepper's Lonely Hearts Club Band" as loud as possible to ward off bear attack.

11) No bear attacks to speak of.

12) Slept well Sunday night as long as no sounds whatsoever met our ears. Every time a camper rolled over in nearby tents, I woke and shook Joe awake to fend off impending bear attack. Still no bear attacks.

13) Hiked next morning to some Look Out Vista View Mountain Thing. Saw millions of acres of land covered with blue smog sent from San Francisco and LA. Happy to leave California.

14) Saw more really big trees. Walked through really big tree forest, took pictures of really big tree trunks, stood on really big tree stumps, read literature about really big trees. Want to become a conservationist and kill people who hurt really big trees.

15) Departed late afternoon. Lucy's brakes almost insufficient to manage steep winding downhill roads. Brakes barely working after that. Drove to the Pacific coast on minor roads, headed south on Pacific Coast Highway as sun set.

16) Joe turned on lights , smoke began billowing from dash. Turned off lights, smoke stopped. Drove 25 miles in the dark on major Los Angeles freeways during rush hour with no lights and barely responding breaks.

17) Happy to be alive. Hate Lucy's guts.

## May 31, 1992

This past week at work was not as boring as usual. The fact that we're moving on makes the end much easier. The Mexicans, the members, the management, and even the American employees have been expressing their sadness at our impending departure, and we too will miss this strangely endearing place.

Friends and acquaintances have been presenting us with various going-away tokens, the first time in either of our lives we have been showered with such appreciation. Perhaps our short tenure here hasn't garnered enough negative relationship situations to warrant a good-riddance kick out of town. It makes the prospect of being roving ramblers all the more presentable. After all, a rolling stone...

We received an adorable goodbye card signed by all the Country Club employees, the only multi-signature card I've ever been given. Maybe I should get laid-up in the hospital once in a while. Mr. Waterman gave us a $50 bill. That was appreciated, I can tell you. The RHCC Lady's Bridge Club pooled together a 50-spot as well. Elga and Hilda gave us a five-inch, portable, color television to carry around in Lucy. It doesn't make sense, but these people that we've only known for nine months seem like lifetime friends. I guess it feels like we've lived a mini-lifetime here, having gone from financial ruin to having a small savings, from a dream of instant fame and fortune to a dream of being homeless wanderers, from living friendless and in fear of starvation to having cards and $50 bills being thrown at us by our friends. Yes, we feel very different than when we first arrived here.

## June 1, 1992

We are back in the Hood with Elga and Hilda. Joe and Elga have been working on last minute repairs, which consist primarily of chants and prayers to the Mechanic Gods. Other tries at fortifying our road queen include installing a new water tank for the sink, getting the front headlights to work, buying a new foam pad for a bed, and attempting to fix the breaks. Every small attention paid to Lucy adds to our comfort and security down the road, so Elga's help in these matters is appreciated more than he'll ever know. How do you thank someone enough for uncountable acts of unselfishness? We have nothing material to give, and a thank you note or a hug hardly seems enough. I told Hilda today that we could never thank her and Elga properly, to which she replied, "Just do something nice for someone else down the road, and tell them to do the same. It will come back to all of us."

## June 2, 1992

The last day at work was a smiling, tearful goodbye party with a few small tasks thrown in to pass as labor. Each of the managers, even the head honcho upstairs, Mr. Bahman (called Meester Mama by some of the Mexicans who pretend they can't pronounce Bahman) made a point to shake our hands and expound on what an asset we've been to the Country Club and how we'll be missed. We collected addresses from everyone including old Jesus, the dishwasher, who can't speak a word of English.

An hour before we left, we explained to Manager Greg that we hadn't yet sold Betty.

"How does she run?" he asked.

"As well as when we first bought her. One of the most reliable vehicles we've ever owned," Joe answered honestly.

"Can I take her for a test drive?"

"Sure. Are you thinking of buying her?" Joe asked greedily.

"I don't know. How much are you asking?"

"We'd like to get $500, but we're leaving in a few days so we may not be able to get that."

"How much did you pay for it?"

"$200, but it's definitely worth more than that."

"I'll try her out."

Greg came back rather impressed with Betty's smooth ride and well-preserved interior, but unwilling to lay down cash. We were more than a little worried about being stuck with an automobile, so Greg helped us circulate throughout the restaurant, asking, "Do you want to buy a car?" Betty's famous engine was of interest to some of the hatred lovers, so interest was perked immediately, but money was, of course, a problem.

Marco came up with the raffle idea.

We were skeptical, but within 15 minutes (literally), Marco and Greg had rounded up $30 apiece from ten eager gamblers (including themselves), waiting for their chance at a new old car. I, always completely mystified at the attraction of gambling, was stunned beyond measure. Thirty dollars is food money for their children, I thought, but kept quiet for selfish reasons. No one needed my Holy Roller lecture anyway.

Names were assembled on little paper bits in a baseball cap, and I was chosen to pull the winner. As I nervously reached in, nine sets of big, brown, hungry eyes bore into me, making me wish I had never agreed to this thing. I was even more aghast when the winner turned out to be Greg. Greg, who probably makes $60,000 a year and has a wife who will have Betty hauled to the junkyard the minute Greg isn't looking. I will never forget the looks on the faces of the losers. The Americans had won again. Joe and I got their money and Greg got their car. My stance on gambling still holds.

## June 6, 1992

Lucy is packed, and as mechanically sound as can be expected. Will we ever drive down the road without wondering whether she'll fall apart within the next mile?

We spent our last evening with our surrogate grandparents, discussing our plans of a gypsy lifestyle, which the Greens heartily approve of due to their usual six months a year on the road in a motor home.

"Where will you go first?" Hilda asked.

"Well," Joe started, "We'll go back to Colorado for the summer, to be where it's cool and make some more money painting houses. Then, who knows? Probably go South somewhere for the winter."

"You can always come back here anytime, you know," Elga offered.

"We'll be back soon, I'm sure," I assured them.

"What about your art?" Hilda asked. "Are you going to keep painting?"

"Oh yeah," Joe replied. "We've got a portable studio in the camper so we can set up anywhere, anytime. We plan on traveling to places all over the country, so we can look into galleries everywhere we go."

"Are you going to miss living here?" Elga asked.

"Only for the people," I said.

We're leaving early in the morning to try to get through the desert before it gets too hot, so we gave our kisses and hugs before retiring to the driveway.

"You've gained weight," Hilda said as she squeezed me. "You look better and you're much nicer to hug."

"Thanks," I said," I feel better."

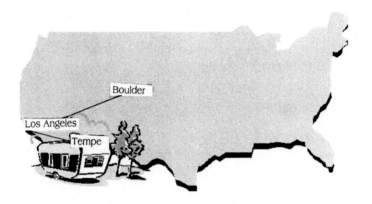

# PART 2

Finding the Road

**June 7, 1992   Rest stop, middle of nowhere, Utah**

We're parked next to one of those 48-foot RVs that look like a Greyhound Bus. Earlier this evening, the inhabitants of this big rig spent one and a half hours graciously giving us a crash course in full-time life on the road, one of the more valuable lessons we have ever been taught. I doubt schools will be catching on to "Gypsy Lifestyle 101" anytime soon.

Some of the useful tips included how to have your mail forwarded to you on the road through a motor coach association, free places to stay around the United States, how to avoid having your throat slit at roadside rest stops after dark, and how to empty a holding tank without covering yourself with human feces. We were also informed of the open invitation for an overnight stay at all Wal-Marts and McDonalds parking lots and shown the proper usage of our courtesy light, just outside Lucy's door. (One turns it on at RV parks to light the way for other campers at night.)

The retired couple gave us a tour of their enormous motor home, which made us feel like Spartans, in comparison. They had a wet bar, a shower and a full bath, a bed you could walk around, three TVs, a microwave, and the crowning touch: a washer and dryer. They explained that they'd sold their lifelong home in California to buy this rig after they retired and had been "full-timing-it" ever since. They were very convincing when they assured us that the Gypsy lifestyle is the best thing anyone could hope for. We gave them some homemade

muffins for their help (made in Lucy's dinky oven) and said
goodbye for the rest of our lives.

I've forgotten their names already.

### June 10, 1992   Cedar City, Utah

I'd like to report on the majestic beauty that is Cedar Breaks
National Monument, but I have no idea what it looks like.
Tonight we're parked behind a parts shop in Cedar City, having
never made it inside the park because Lucy's brakes have failed
us again. This time our stopping power is almost non-existent.
The parts shop guy says it'll take three weeks to have a new
master cylinder sent in because this particular part is from the
Chevy Corvair. We have no intention of waiting three weeks
here, so we will test our adventure stamina and try to drive all
the way to Denver from here, braking as little as possible. The
mechanic-on-duty says we're nuts and he is correct.

"Can't we just go into the park for one day? We're right here
and who knows when we'll be passing through here again?" I
whined earlier.

"You know we can't, honey. The road up to the Breaks is
as steep and windy as the one to Sequoia. We have no choice.
We'll come back here someday."

"I guess so. This sucks really bad."

### June 15, 1992   Boulder, Colorado

I haven't had time to write for a few days, what with our
arrival into Boulder, finding an apartment in one day, and
having Lucy sent to the repair shop. The journey here was
treacherous but successful; we managed to use the brakes only
three times between Salt Lake City and Boulder. For future
crazies attempting this feat, here is the procedure:

1) To drive as far as possible without stopping:
   a)   Take turns peeing in the camper toilet while the other
        person is driving. (Turning over the wheel is difficult).
   b)   Eat pre-made food from the refrigerator while driving.
2) How to stop when absolutely necessary:
   a)   Make sure you begin slowing down long before
        freeway exit ramp. With the right timing, you will
        come to an almost complete stop once off the ramp.
   b)   Wildly pump the breaks until your legs feel like putty.
   c)   Pray.

The first night in Boulder we stayed with Dan and Patty Tomlin, who live not far from the Stank Shack. They said we looked a little frazzled from the trip. Over dinner we talked about our unintentional, hair-raising travels. They talked about their purposefully frightening vacations such as mountain biking to the top of 14,000-foot peaks, safaris in Africa, and hundreds of miles of hut-to-hut skiing in the high country. I much prefer our experiences because they are cheap, unexpected, and take little physical exertion.

The next day we pored over the newspapers to find a place to stay temporarily and ended up finding our present home, a small apartment shared with three college-aged roommates named Nelson, Julian and Kate. Before we met our new roommates, we agonized over the decision to spend at least a month with college students—potentially party-crazed, horny, loud, immature humans—but so far they have proven to be quite civilized, as much as we've seen them. I have my eye on them, though.

Lucy was carefully driven to the shop today, so we are on bicycles until further notice. We extracted the bikes from our storage space in Arvada before moving into our new home. We are going to paint houses again, subcontracting for our dear friend, Mark Ackermann, who got us painting jobs regularly when we lived here before. I actually look forward to working outside instead of sitting on my butt eight hours a day. And Boulder is beautiful.

**June 20, 1992**

Yesterday, our first day back to work as house painters, Joe fell off a ladder and broke his arm. After four years of painting on high, slippery rooftops, or standing on the top rung of unstable 28-foot ladders in the wind, he decides to maim himself by tripping off one of the lower steps of a six-foot stepladder.

**June 22, 1992**

We painted today. A house, not a painting. Joe is working left-handed, which he says is awkward, inconvenient, and slow, but we have to make a living. What we thought was a substantial savings (and it was, for us) has proven to be an insignificant speck after driving from California, paying for Lucy's new brakes, eating out for a few days, and getting Joe's arm taken care of. But life is different now, and even work feels like a vacation.

"Boulder is so different when you're not settled here. I feel like I'm a tourist," Joe said dreamily as we lay in the shady grass, eating homemade tabouli on our lunch break and staring up at the sunlit Flatirons.

"Why do you think it's different than when we lived here before?" I asked.

"Well, we have no home here, really. And we know we'll be leaving."

"Yeah, I actually enjoy painting houses, knowing we won't be doing it forever."

"I wonder what we'll be doing this fall."

"Me too."

"Yeah, ain't it great?"

## June 25, 1992

I met two adorable kids today at the house we're painting. In all of the madness of the past few years, we've had very little time to think about children. The truth is we want children, and have been going without birth control ever since the ovarian cyst operation, with no luck so far. The implications of getting pregnant at this time in my life are hard to imagine. We would have to get off the road and make a whole new set of plans. But because we didn't get pregnant right away or even after trying for a while, we fear we may never be able to have kids. If there is any chance that we can get pregnant, at any time, we're ready to take it.

Most of the time I don't sit around and think about my desire to have a baby, and Joe and I don't discuss it much. I do want one, but it only comes up when I see a cute kid.

## June 27, 1992

NEW BUSINESS
1) We're going to be in a group art show at Hassel Haeseler Gallery in Denver, Colorado. It opens in a few weeks. Great space, good opportunity. We'll exhibit paintings we did in our Post-College Pop phase.
2) New roommates are stellar. They are responsible but fun, and let us watch their big TV at will. Kate is an Olympic skier, so she is always training and never here.

3)  Haven't touched Lucy. She's parked out in the lot while we ride bikes to our jobs. Mark Ackermann transports our supplies to houses each time we change jobs. Great guy.

4)  Joe's arm doing well, healing quickly. He still climbs tallest ladders with abandon while I shout safety lectures to him from below.

## June 30, 1992

I love the bicycle ride to and from our latest painting job. We ride along the shady streets by historic Victorian homes intermixed with unconventionally painted houses owned by ex-hippies, and every sort of Eastern Religion Institute the world has to offer. Invariably we pass one of the resident transients who has been skulking the streets since our college days. TRANSIENTS:

1)  Kick Man: the painfully skinny guy who wears jeans cut off at the knee with a zigzag, muttering to himself and kicking himself in the leg every few steps.

2)  Sad Man: a tall, dark, and handsome man who seems clean-cut until you get close enough to smell him. He ambles along with his head bent perpendicular to the ground at all times, staring at the sidewalk as if his head was stuck that way. The only thing that will cause him to raise his head is a pretty girl walking by.

3)  Monk Man: an Asian gentleman with a shaved head, who dresses in flowing orange robes and walks with huge steps and at high speeds all over town and out into the country, while banging a giant drum. He might not be an official hobo, but a lone practitioner of some obscure Eastern religious ritual.

4)  Skirt Man: (the most obtrusive character). His plaid skirt is nothing like a kilt, which would give him the Scottish excuse, but rather a J.C. Penney's-type women's skirt from the 1970s. He smells atrocious and accosts unassuming tourists on the Pearl Street Mall and often yells obscenities at small children.

Our bike ride takes us briefly through the Pearl Street Mall, the favored place for tourists, transients and hippies, sidewalk performers, people watchers, weirdos, college students, and business people. We'd lived here ten years before we left Boulder and saw the number of unusual, exotic, eccentric people gradually drop as the prices of everything rose and Boulder became a sough-after place for yuppies and millionaires. The unique, independently-owned stores along the Mall which sold trinkets and products only non-conformist Boulderites would appreciate have been kicked out in favor of the big chain stores found in every city in the country. And the ratty hippies who lounged in the park, begged for money, danced expressionistically to no music at all, and sported smelly dreadlocks have been replaced by rich teenage pretenders who lounge in the park, beg for money, dance expressionistically to expensive boom boxes, and wear recently purchased $150 dreadlocks. Unoriginality grows like a disease.

The ride home is infinitely less interesting. Hunger, sore arms, and sun or windburn propel us quickly and blindly back to our apartment. We eat sandwiches and fruit and watch the Olympics with Nelson and Julian.

## July 6, 1992

We drove our paintings to Denver this afternoon for the show next weekend. We peeked at some of the other art that will be in the show; ours are the only paintings. The other work is photography, silk-screens of photography, or mixed media. At least paintings will stand out, I guess.

## July 13, 1992

We arrived at the art opening early, as many of the artists did, while the sun was still above the horizon and few art patrons had yet ventured out. Our bold, colorful paintings contrasted with most of the computer-age sterility of the other art (and I mean that in the kindest way) even though we chose the least warm-fuzzy pieces we had. I felt proud of our paintings, because of their visual and postural differentness and the obviously greater amount of time spent on them than the other art. I fully realize in today's art world these attributes are far from admired by the "experts," critics, and tag-along wannabes of those same experts and critics, but Joe and I are somewhat old-fashioned in our artistic views. Maybe that makes us mavericks.

We enjoyed one woman's small photographs of machinery silk-screened on canvas, encircled by sketchily drawn schematics of the same machines in colored pencil. We also liked some of Larson Reddick's mad dog portraits. But Sale Chisbut's giant penises topped with poorly transferred faces of political figures were tiresome and just plain dumb. How many more insecure males have to plaster their phallus all over kingdom come, all under the guise of being political or passionate, before the rest of us cry, LOB OFF THOSE WEINIES, I SAY!

Joe and I mingled casually with old art acquaintances, catching each other up on our careers (or lack thereof) and complaining about penis art.

A little later our families showed up. Debi, Derick, Dana, and Mom had driven down from Steamboat after work (a four hour drive) and planned to drive back that night. Joe's family live in Denver, and his parents and siblings Mike, Tony, David and Julie came with their families. We walked down to Larimer Square and pretended to look in the fancy shops around the historical district for an hour, commenting on the building renovations and Denver's plans for Coors Stadium until our bladders suggested we head back to the gallery. Our conversations may not have amounted to more than chitchat, but somehow I felt we were communicating on the deepest level of human contact. We were together. After the past few years of struggles, Joe and I are much more able to appreciate the important things we have.

### July 15, 1992

We're in the newspaper! We're in the newspaper! It's a miracle we even found it. At a picnic table in the backyard of the Shamsuddin's, who are having their house painted Igloo White, we were eating lunch and thumbing through the latest issue of Westword (the arty and sometimes rather whiny Denver weekly) when we were suddenly jolted by the sight of a large, color reproduction of one of our paintings from Hassel Haeseler. A full-page article, titled "Pop of the Heap" told all about the show and featured paragraphs of several of the artists, but ours was the only photograph included. The review of our work was complimentary and said we ..."stroke a clever compromise between large and small"...because our works..."resemble miniature James Rosenquist paintings". We've been in newspapers before, but never so unexpectedly. What if we hadn't grabbed that Westword at the supermarket yesterday?

This is a perfect time to document the path of our artistic career thus far, a short but possibly interesting report.

THE ART OF DORI AND JOSEPH, A WRITTEN
RETROSPECTIVE

Dori studied art in college and painted large, expressionistic
interiors. After graduation, Dori started an experimental phase,
intended to convey her ultimate artistic goal: to make art that
appealed to both the high art world and to regular people. This
included snapshots of cows in flea market frames and a series
of minimalist-appearing pieces with "I am the greatest, most
respected, rich, and famous artist ever" written thousands of
times on each of them.

Joe studied writing/literature/other stuff in college.

After marrying, Dori taught Joe how to paint. Dori and Joe
commenced an artistic collaboration, still hoping to achieve the
idealistic art goal of making art everybody likes. They began
with a colossal all-white installation of displays of everyday
items, semi-ironically conveying conservative values. The mini-
James Rosenquist Pop stuff followed this. Joe and Dori decided
experimental art was fun but not anywhere close to achieving
their art goal, so they gave up on concept art and returned to
Dori's original love—paint and interiors.

END OF RETROSPECTIVE

We'd better love paint and interiors; we could be doing
them both on a much larger scale for a long time.

**July 17, 1992**

Yesterday I called the Schleichers, good friends here in
Boulder. We met Don, Edith, Sebastian and Lucas and Stony,
the dog, last summer while painting their house. Edith was
happy to hear from us but a little disappointed that we hadn't
called sooner. They are leaving the first of August for Germany
for one month. She did, however, offer a housesitting job for
their spectacular, newly beautified home to us while they
travel, an offer over which I nearly fainted. We get to have our
own nice home for a while!

After I gave the full report of the phone call, Joe and I
locked our arms and swung around like square dancers,
shouting, "Yeee-haw!" until we were dizzy.

**July 25, 1992**

We've discovered a new calling in life. It's called making a
living from our art. We attended a party last night to celebrate
Julian's 24th birthday, which was held at the home of a very

amicable artist couple, who introduced us to the idea of selling
our art at outdoor art festivals. They don't sell their work this
way, or any other way for that matter, but they have heard
from friends that it can be quite lucrative. I, having attended the
University of Colorado and receiving a Bachelor of Fine Arts
from this illustrious institution, was trained in the Sacred High
Art Fancy Pants Tradition that looked down on such lowly
endeavors as outdoor festivals, commercial art of any kind, and
the production of art that would sell to anyone except New
Yorkers in black turtlenecks. The mere mention of peddling my
superior artistic wares at a tasteless, middle class, vulgar
outdoor festival would have been unthinkable a year ago. What
a difference a year of eating carrots and living in the Hood can
make. Now the idea of living solely off our paintings sounds so
delicious, I don't care if we sell them at Elmer's Used Furniture
Emporium. When we asked Julie, the artist woman, how we
could find out more about the festivals, she knew absolutely
nothing, but was highly encouraging when she learned we had
a motor home. She said many festival artists did what is called a
circuit—traveling with the good weather from show to show in
a van or RV. It may just be our jillionth attempt at some lame
new art scheme, but we're going to look into this.

**August 1, 1992**

We moved into our enchanting new home for the month,
complete with our own dog, Stony. We were a bit somber at
having to leave our friendly roommates, but promised to have
them over to our swank new pad for cocktails and casual
munchies one evening soon. The Schleicher's house, thanks in
part to the gorgeous paint job, is a fresh, airy, roomy place,
right out of the pages of *Metropolitan Home*. They have a big
tree with a swing hanging from its branches, a great deck for
entertaining, and a huge yard, at the back of which runs a
brook. Brooks are good.

**August 3, 1992**

I spent the whole day calling Chambers of Commerce, art
associations, and even museums all over the United States of
America to see if I could drag up some information on these
outdoor shows. I got nothing. We'll see what I can come up
with tomorrow. But I did find The Motor Coach Association of
America, who, for $25 a year, will be our mailing address and

will forward our mail to Post Office General Delivery in whatever location we call them from each week. Our mailing address will be in Cincinnati, Ohio! I've never been there but from the derogatory manner in which Ohio cities are depicted on television and movies, it sounds like the worst place in the world. What if people think we are from there? I guess it's no worse than the truth, being from nowhere.

### August 9, 1992

I found it! I found *The Harris Rhodes List* of outdoor art festivals! I am a genius! After days of expensive telephone calls to nearly everybody on Earth, I finally found a woman who had a friend who had heard of someone who used to do the festivals who used some sort of list as their guide to the best shows. After several more frustrating dead ends I finally located Larry Harris, the author of this legendary list, who promised to send me one immediately. He even offered—if I send $45 dollars for the list—to look at slides of our paintings to determine which shows would be best suited for our work. Apparently, some festivals are geared toward a very conservative, country craft crowd, one that we would be wise to avoid. Two weeks ago I would have laughed in the face of someone who attempted to squeeze $45 out of us for a piece of paper, but now I feel as though I'm getting the bargain of a lifetime. After finding out how impossible it is to obtain nationwide information over the phone on this subject, I've never felt better spending my money.

### August 14, 1992

The list arrived today. Larry Harris, I salute you! Joe and I tugged on either side of the precious document, fighting for a look at our traveling future. After settling in with our heads resting together, we quickly became so overwhelmed at the 200 shows in every state in the country that we decided to give it a rest until tomorrow. It's hard to believe that after so many years of artistic failure we could possibly become so enthralled about yet another attempt to make it work. We have no idea whether this undertaking will succeed, and we're ready, once again, to plan our whole life around it. We must be wacky.

## August 15, 1992

SAMPLE OF INTELLIGENT ARGUMENT BETWEEN TWO ARTISTS:

Joe: What are you doing? The color of that room is too dull!

Dori: Well, you're being mean to me!

Joe: I haven't said a word until just now.

Dori: And it was mean!

Joe: I wasn't mean before.

Dori: Well, you were just waiting to be.

Joe: Alright dear, maybe we should discuss that color before you continue.

Dori: This color's fine.

Joe: I think it should be brighter. That orange window stands out too much.

Dori: I've done too much work on this already to just erase it. You can make it brighter on the second coat.

Joe: Sounds good to me.

Dori: And you better watch how you criticize my paintings! I could pulverize you with one comment when you least expect it.

Joe: I'm sure you could.

Dori: OK then.


Conversations such as this only happen when we are hungry.

We have been painting paintings during our every spare hour, which aren't many. To keep from accidentally besmearing anything inside the Schleicher's fair villa, we have set up painting camp on lawn chairs in the yard. We are certain that Monet's Giverny could never have been so inspirational as our resplendent view of the babbling creek, cobalt blue skies, and Stony's doghouse.

For the first time, the totally empty interiors of our paintings are beginning to call for objects. A chair in a corner, a table with a vase, a cord plugged into a socket; our rooms are showing some signs of humanity. When we started painting empty interiors, we had just unwittingly emptied our life of just about everything, including hope. Now these things are seeping their way back into our life. I think that until now we actually feared humanity, especially our own. And now, somehow, it is not so scary.

**August 16, 1992**

With the help of our trusty *Harris Rhodes List*, we have finally created an exciting itinerary for this fall and winter. If these festivals aren't fruitful, however, we are doomed to a life of misery and suffering.

The first festival on our course takes place in San Diego in November, followed by a humongous 600-artist show in Tempe, Arizona in December. If these supposedly profitable endeavors fail, Lee Green (Elga and Hilda's son) has offered us a job painting his house in West Hollywood. The next festival on our circuit will be in (gasp) Tampa, Florida, in early March, which will relocate us in the highest concentration of winter art festivals in the country. This schedule is dependent on one small supposition—that their juries accept us. Thousands of artists send slides to be judged by jury panels at each of these exhibitions; only a select few are admitted, usually between 100-300. Some festivals have more artists, some less, but all can be difficult to get in to.

We are looking into purchasing a booth in which to exhibit our paintings. They are not inexpensive. It seems as though my hatred of gambling is being put to a test. We are being forced to risk what paltry dollars we have on a chancy enterprise, and I absolutely abhor the whole situation.

We were making art today, finally a weekend, out near the creek on lawn chairs in the shade. We came inside for lunch to medicate another absurd argument that would never have happened if we had the discipline to tear ourselves away from our work long enough to eat. We need an assistant to stand over us with a cattle prod, and poke us when lunchtime is nigh. (Got that *nigh* word from "Away in a Manger").

We returned to our creative perch to find that little creatures had invaded us. Our eyes followed tiny tracks of various colors trailing all over our wet paintings, up the lawn chairs, through our palettes, into the grass and up a nearby tree. Squirrels, apparently. Although hours of work would need to be repainted, the sight was so cute we just shrugged our shoulders and took photographs of the scene for our scrapbook. This is the kind of occupational hazard we can handle.

### November 1, 1992   MONTHS LATER!

I have failed to write for nearly three months because the boredom of painting houses and painting paintings finally caught up with me. Here is a recap of the highlights:

HIGHLIGHTS, FALL OF 1992

1) The day after we finished painting one house an ugly taupe, a sports car flew headfirst into the side of the garage, completely destroying the wall and the new car parked inside. We were not to blame.

2) The Schleichers returned and benevolently invited us to remain at their home until we leave for California, provided we help with a few chores and paint a few bedrooms. We tried to stay out of their hair as much as possible, but may have corrupted Lucas and Sebastian slightly. They now yell, "SHUT UP!" in several different languages.

3) During a short trip to Steamboat we stayed with Debi. Her boyfriend, Bob, accidentally set 35 acres of their land afire by improperly burning their trash. Debi was shown on the front page of the *Steamboat Pilot* in her boxer shorts, helping firefighters put out the blaze.

4) We acquired at no small expense an EZ-Up canopy for our outdoor art festival booth display!

5) We were accepted into the San Diego, CA and Tempe, AZ art festivals!

6) We again became fed up with work-a-day life and are absolutely rabid with hunger to make a living from art.

The most important event of the fall has been excluded from the list, as it deserves its own paragraph.

We got a dog.

She's eight weeks old; her name is Ruby; some farm folks gave her away for free; she was the smartest girl in a litter of eight. In Steamboat, her breed is referred to as Dingo, but technically she is an Australian Cattle Dog of the Blue Heeler variety. We have been training her to come, stay, sit, and not poop in people's homes.

### November 3, 1992

We are departing tomorrow for San Diego. My excitement exceeds that of our last exodus from Colorado tenfold. There is

actually a possibility that we will be artists! It doesn't get any
better than this.

**November 4, 1992  Somewhere in Utah**

Edith might very easily have been overjoyed at the sight of
Lucy pulling out of her position in the Schleicher's driveway
this morning, but she didn't let on. Joe and I showered the
family with thank yous as we drove away, with Lucas and
Sebastian chasing Lucy for a few hundred yards on their
bicycles waving and screaming, "*Calle La Boca*, Man!"

We drove all day. The freeways between Denver and Los
Angeles are becoming familiar to us.

**November 6, 1992  Joshua Tree, California**

Another long day of driving yesterday deposited us last
night in Saint George, Utah. Wal-Mart hosted us there for the
night. We were awakened by the maniacal Parking Lot Cleaner
Man, in his loud bristle-laden truck, swooshing around light
poles and cart depositories on two wheels. He must have been
trying to make a statement because he circled the Ultra Van so
frequently and so closely one would have thought we'd
dumped a camper full of garbage and sludge around our
perimeter. Since we were up, we ventured out early to our
destination in Joshua Tree. We've been informed, via the Ultra
Van newsletter, of the High Desert Mini-Rally in Joshua Tree,
hosted by Jim and Marlene Craig. It's the Ultra Van fanatics
ultimate must-do. We plan to stay there for a few nights before
our show in San Diego.

The secondary road that leads through the 29 Palms and
eventually Joshua Tree was very, well, secondary. A thin two-
laner with no shoulder and no services for long stretches, it was
pot-holed and cracked from the extreme desert temperatures
and no maintenance. Part of it wasn't even paved. But along its
embankment on either side were written the names of decades
of previous travelers, formed with little rocks in letters four feet
high. The names continued for miles and miles, on both sides
of the road: John Sue Adrian Bob Mary Lexy Anna Jenny Joe
Carl Betty Jeff. They continued until we grew tired of reading
them. Names flashed by, mingling with the miniature cacti and
yucca plants that grew among them, like an unending electric
sign board of the Old West. An urge to join our names into the
Desert Hall of Fame was squelched at the idea of trying to find
a yet unturned stone or the space to fit it.

The Craig's modest ranch in Joshua Tree had already welcomed several Ultra Vans to the rally by the time we arrived. A large gate in the high chain-link fence was opened for us by a leathery, good-looking middle-aged man who introduced himself warmly as Jim. He pointed to a slot in the row of six or seven Ultras where we were to park.

"Welcome. We're sure glad to have you. After you park and get all settled, we'll all get together in the house for some home movies. And don't forget to take a look at all the Ultras. You'll get some good ideas on how to make modifications on your own coach."

"Thanks!" we said as we excitedly pulled into the compound.

Marlene came to welcome us as well and introduced us to a gathering crowd of Ultra members from places like San Francisco, Canada, Arizona, and even Australia, most of whom couldn't have been younger than 65. Before the evening gathering, Joe and I set out to explore the desert outside the chain-link fence, which, we've been told protects the Craig's cats from becoming a coyote's dinner.

"Your shoes stink," I told Joe as we wandered through the cactus, Joshua trees and sand. "I can smell them from here. They're ruining my fresh air walk."

"Don't give me any guff," he replied, and that was the end of our hiking conversation.

We would have loved to wander for hours, but our walk was cut short by a hungry coyote looping circles around our perimeter, eyeing Ruby. We carried her home.

After dinner we were treated to two hours of scratchy, silent Super 8 movies of the Craig family dune-buggying in the 1970s when their kids were little. I was very near the projector, hence the present rattling in my ears, back at the camper. Dune Buggies. I don't get it.

## November 7, 1992

Spent the day receiving "tech-tips" from every coach owner here. (There are now ten Ultra Vans here, not counting the four owned by the Craigs). Our rear suspension should be the focus of our utmost attention, we are told, if we plan to travel far. The work to be done is costly if done by a mechanic shop, and only someone well-versed in Ultra Van problems should attempt the task. Few Ultra owners are eligible for this procedure; Jim Craig is one of them. He offered to attempt a temporary fix, at a very reasonable price, if we return at a later date. For now we're content with getting a new windshield wiper flicker installed.

We laid all of our paintings out on our green turf carpet (our instant yard) for all the folks to see, at the request of Christy Barden who drove in today. He'd just come from a nudist colony in Somewhere Else, California, and would have been in superior spirits had it not been for the catastrophic mechanical problems of his own Ultra Van. He showed us photos of his travels, all in which he was working on the underside of his coach, or grimacing and pointing to a new Ultra problem. He was fully clothed in all shots.

Our paintings were well received by Christy, Jim and Marlene, and one other person, but we could tell that our brightly colored rooms with a spattering of sad furniture didn't appeal to most of the other senior citizens. Everyone was very polite, however, and congratulated us on all our hard work. For dinner tonight, we all piled into the Craig's Chevy Step Van and headed to the Joshua Tree Senior Center for a meal of boiled chicken, overcooked brussel sprouts with Velveeta sauce, cold, white dinner roll with rock-hard butter pat, and the quintessential senior staple—green jello. It was strange comfort food, bringing back memories of school lunch and Furr's Cafeteria.

Joe says our life is surreal.

## November 9, 1992   San Diego, California

We arrived late at my brother Derick's apartment after driving through the desert where the main points of interest were:
1)   Jillions of windmills twirling at once.
2)   The Stonehenge of Date Palm Tree formations: Clusters of these palm trees were planted to form geometric shapes along the roadside. Too hurried to stop.
3)   Joshua Tree National Monument: There were lots of Joshua trees.

Derick goes home to Steamboat during the summer to work for Dad, but winters find him being schooled at a college in San Diego (forgot which), not far from this one bedroom apartment he shares with his girlfriend, Christine. Joe and I are sharing our Ultra bed—the foam thing—on the living room floor of this clean, sparse apartment that has, among other things, a giant entertainment center, four remotes, and a spider plant. Now that we have begun adding objects and furniture to our paintings, we are even more observant about the interiors of people's homes. One's living space and belongings say so much about them! And the more a place says about the person who lives there, the more it inspires us to want to paint it. I don't think we would have any interest in painting a designer home, which generally has little personal connection with the person that lives there. We took over a roll of pictures for our paintings.

## November ?, 1992   Thanksgiving Day

Christine prepared the turkey and opted to stay home while Joe, Derick, and I did the Turkey Day sports thing. Instead of watching Thanksgiving Day football, which Derick the sportsaholic so bigheartedly gave up this year, we went to the beach and played nerf football until Ruby shredded the ball into little Styrofoam bits. Then we went to a nearby basketball court to shoot hoops. Joe, who admits he is the world's worst basketball player, just sat on the sidelines and watched Derick kick my ass.

I cooked the remainder of Thanksgiving dinner when we returned to the apartment, which we wolfed down. Then we watched *Silence of the Lambs*.

## November 27, 1992

The first day of our first art fair is over and I wish I were never born. We didn't sell a single painting.

We woke at 5:00 a.m. to be sure we had plenty of time to set up our booth. We arrived at the festival grounds, a roped-off section of streets in a quaint historic district, where our Artist Parking Pass was recognized by a semi-happy gentleman who admitted us into the arena by swinging back a few long sawhorses. He stared wide-eyed at the Ultra Van and, when he thought we could no longer see him, burst out laughing.

We meandered down the van-filled streets, around white cargo vans, mini-vans, three-quarter ton vans, and even moving trucks, occasionally asking one of the 40-something bohemes with armloads of art where we could find space number 78. It looked and felt very much like a circus setting up for the day. Tents were being raised, dozens of people were unloading and setting up their allotted paraphernalia as if they'd been doing it for years on cue, and there was a sense of concentration in the air that suggested a deadline; a performance to come.

Our booth space was marked on the street in chalk, and by the time we arrived, the two booths on either side of us had already been erected with little regard for our chalk marks, leaving us exactly four inches on either side of our booth to set up. We had practiced "popping-up" our booth in the Schleicher's backyard this summer but hadn't anticipated this obstacle. Joe the genius surveyed the scene intently and solemnly while I stood by waiting and watching his every move, our ritual now when things go wrong. Within five minutes we managed to raise the booth under Joe's careful directions without scraping or otherwise bothering the neighbors' booths.

Then our self-invented system of hanging the paintings didn't go quite as planned. Most artists have several very handy, attractive standing panels, perhaps seven feet high and four feet across, which their work is placed on. As these panels are both cumbersome and expensive, they were not an option when we purchased our booth set-up. We were forced to jerry-rig an arrangement by which our paintings hang from little white pieces of string that are attached to one of the canopy's aluminum crossbars at the top of the booth. The paintings are somehow supposed to hang (and stay) against the white canvas sides of the booth, the theoretical end result being a stark, gallery-like simplicity, with the little strings relatively invisible against the white walls.

One word. *Wind.*

It all seemed like a great idea until about 9:00 a.m. when the festival opened to the public, and sudden gusts of warm sea air began lifting our paintings away from the walls. They sounded like wooden wind chimes as they bonked together (not good on our painted frames), and the spectators had an impossible time seeing them. We embarrassingly tried to hold them down with our outstretched arms, which made viewing even more difficult for people. We finally gave up by 9:15, figuring we'd touch up the nicked spots that evening and allow the crowd to tackle the flying paintings manually to see them. No one seemed to mind having to catch a painting to look at it; in fact, it added a little sport to the process, and most people left our booth with a smile. I can't honestly say they were smiling at the art itself.

As each art patron scanned our booth politely, we strained to hear their comments. For the first time in our art lives we have had the opportunity to hear verbal feedback from someone other than a snooty art professor.

The variety of comments amazed us. I had expected a day of condescending looks from everyone, the modus operandi of the gallery and art school world. But I came to realize quite quickly that we are very far from the art world. These are real people. Comments ranged from "nice work," "great colors," and "I love the angles" to "weird," "these are twisted," and "you guys have sick minds." I loved all the commentary and interpretations.

Just as our rookie nervousness began to subside, our money fears began to escalate.

"What if we don't make any money?" Joe mumbled in my ear.

"We will."

"Yeah, but what if? Do we sell our canopy and panhandle our way around the country?"

"We said we'd try this. We still have the Tempe show in two weeks. Don't come to any conclusions yet. Why don't you walk around the festival and pump some of the artists for information. That'll keep your mind off money."

So Joe set out to scout the other artist's work, their booths, their vans, the way they dressed, their prices, their sales techniques, and their propensity to bring a puppy to the fair. (We left Ruby in Derick's care for today).

Joe's findings were helpful.
1) Our paintings are inexpensive, in comparison. For the price of two "Country Expressions" painted sweatshirts (that's the booth across from us), one can purchase a DeCamillis original.
2) Our Ultra Van is more original than our paintings. E very artist that had seen us drive in earlier asked Joe "What kind of motor home is that? It's great! Where'd you get it? What year was it made?" And so on.
3) The wearing apparel of a circuit artist is not something we'd like to imitate. Two modes of dress were typical—one was a watered-down version of the 1968 Haight-Ashbury look and the other was jeans and an art festival t-shirt. Hoping to look presentable to art buyers, we dressed up for the

occasion; I wore a cotton dress and Joe wore khakis and a nice shirt. Already we're rebels.

4) No one brought a puppy to the fair and we were told it was prohibited. Ruby will be hidden contraband at future festivals.

5) Most of the other artists are far more professional than we are. They take credit cards, some with portable phones for verification, they hand out color postcards and brochures, and their booths cost in the thousands of dollars. There are a few riffraff booths like ours, but no one else has art swinging from strings.

6) Our most important concern is art quality. Happily, we feel confident about our work. We could easily rank our art among the most original and forward thinking of the San Diego Art Festival. In galleries, we had exhibited with artists that focused more on their ideas than their talent as crafts people; here the opposite was glaringly apparent. Expert painters, photographers and sculptors displayed their gifts by illuminating the  most trite and overused subjects and styles in the art language. Crisp photos of baby seals with big brown eyes. Stroky Parisian street scenes. Wooden figurines of howling coyotes. And the worst—sparkly painted sweatshirts. We thought that the fairs' opportunity for making money would render us less judgmental of these artistic atrocities. But no. Money or no money, we were embarrassed.

And now that it's 3:00 in the morning, I can be assured a miserable day of overtired grouchiness at the festival tomorrow. I have no idea how these circuit artists sleep at night. After the crowds, their questions, the nine hours of sunshine, the physical labor, the rejection, the previous travel, and the bad art, I feel like a fly carcass after a spider has sucked the life out of it. Except that I can't sleep.

### November 28, 1992
Day two—San Diego Festival—it's over. We sold one small painting called *Cherry Bomb*  for one hundred dollars. We are the biggest losers. I don't know why we ever decided to be artists.

"Don't give up," Derick said as I sat on his leather couch with my head in my hands.

"This is only your first show. Wait and see how the next one goes."

"This is not our first show, Derick," I grumbled. "I've been showing for five years. I should have been an insurance salesman. Anything is better than this."

"But you really haven't given these festivals a chance. You've got that Tempe show coming up. You guys are good artists. It'll happen for you someday."

This statement got my tears flowing. "Oh, yeah! I've been saying that same thing since my sophomore year in college. 'It's going to happen for me soon, I can feel it', I mimicked sarcastically. "Here my little brother has to pat me on the back because my life is going nowhere."

"She just needs to cry it out," Joe offered from the black leather chair with ottoman across the room. "I feel the same way, honey, but several other artists told us it was a bad show for them, too."

I apologized for my childish attitude and excused myself for some extra childish blubbering on Derick's bathroom floor.

Tomorrow Derick and Christine are taking us to see the San Diego sights, which may or may not bring my spirits up to a respectable level.

### November 29, 1992

I feel much better. The elaborate Hotel Del Coronado and Rubio's Fish Tacos took my mind way from Loser Land, if temporarily. Usually my success-obsessed mind wouldn't be kept down for more than a few hours, so waking this morning with no foreseeable positive thoughts was a bit of a shock. Even now, 24 hours later, I must focus solely on the present moment to avoid a downward spiral of negativity and fatalism. But I am much better than yesterday.

We leave tomorrow morning for Los Angeles to visit Elga and Hilda before the Tempe show.

### November 30, 1992

We arrived at the Green's near lunchtime and were welcomed enthusiastically with a lunch of pot roast, potatoes, and asparagus. It was so nice to spend time with our dear ones. I turned vaguely sullen when Hilda asked if we plan to have kids one day. We told her our story—that we want to have them but aren't sure if we can. Keep trying, she told us. You'd be surprised how many people have kids even when doctors say it's impossible.

I hope so.

### December 8, 1992   Still at Green's

It's a good thing Lee and Bruce in West Hollywood have offered us a job painting their house after the Tempe show. That San Diego fiasco has raised some serious doubts about this festival business. Lee will pay well and we can stay with them while we work. I don't know where we'll go from there. We entered that outdoor festival in Tampa, Florida (a gazillion miles from here) but we don't know if we've been accepted and if Lucy will make it or if we even want to go that far, especially if Tempe is a bust.

### December 9, 1992   Tempe, Arizona

I'm writing at night in Lucy, at our little table, with Ruby passed out at my feet, both of us exhausted. We left Los Angeles around 10:00 this morning for the Tempe Art Festival, with naive and positive thoughts of a big success fueling us forward. We sang every Sons of the Pioneers song we could think of as we drove, as well as numerous Johnny Cash hits, and the theme song of our life, Side by Side. It is 100 percent true for us because:

1)   we ain't got a barrel of money
2)   we're ragged and funny
3)   we don't know what's coming tomorrow (maybe it's trouble and sorrow)
4)   we're travelin' along, singing a song, side by side.

See?

Troubles were nil until we tried to stop a few rest areas before Phoenix, where to our horror, our brakes failed to work again.

"PUMP 'EM HARDER," I screamed at Joe as his right leg bounced up and down wildly on the brake pedal with no response from Lucy.

"I'm trying!"

"I'm going to jump out and run ahead to warn all those people," I decided, seeing the crowd of unsuspecting tourists milling around the rest area ahead of us.

"You can't! We're still going 30 miles per hour!"

"PUMP 'EM HARDER!"

My crazy plan to save the innocent bystanders never materialized, thanks to Joe's muscular leg, which miraculously slowed the Ultra to a snail's pace by the time we pulled into our "RVs Only" spot. We slammed into the curb with enough force to significantly disturb Ruby, who had been shivering in the corner, already alarmed by our screaming. She peed on the floor, jumped up, and stood with ears pressed back, eyes wide, shaking by Lucy's door, ready to fly out and find new owners immediately.

We waited until our composure was regained to exit the coach as all watching eyes were fixed on our motor home, not because of our sudden stop, but because Lucy always attracts such attention. We felt in one way like movie stars who must always wear a dignified face for the constant scrutiny of the public. Joe and I managed to regally step down to the pavement with no visible signs of a near-death experience, but Ruby bolted out the door and headed for the doggie area, where she cowered under a tree. A few tourists with cameras approached, asking the typical Lucy questions while we politely tried to gather up our dog and our wits. How old is that thing, where'd you find it, what kind of engine does it have? After doing what folks do at rest areas, we gathered for a conference in the "safety" (yeah, right) of our own home to decide how to get to Tempe without brakes.

"We did it on the way to Boulder; we can do it again," I offered.

"But we don't know our way around Phoenix. We could cause an accident. And we still have to get back to Los Angeles."

"Joe, think. We have less than $30 left. We can't afford to get the brakes fixed or get back to L.A. unless we do this show and make some money. We have no choice."

"Yeah, well you better stop panicking and contain yourself. It doesn't help to have you screaming and carrying on every time something goes wrong. The next time you lose your cool, you're driving."

"I'm sorry. I'll be better. I promise."

And here we are. The no-brakes technique was indeed more stressful in an unfamiliar place, and (God forgive us) we had to run more than one red light to arrive safely. If anyone knew the peril under which we put ourselves and other drivers, we would be arrested for a crime that is significantly more dangerous than drunk driving—driving under the influence of Lucy.

We arrived and set up our unprofessional booth in its designated spot. We're located in a far corner of the festival down a skinny alley, presumably where they put all the low-life cheap booths. With 600 other booths at the show, I can hardly see how anyone will find us back here.

It is beginning to rain hard. I'm going to bed.

## December 10, 1992

After a breakfast of uncooked toast (which is technically bread slices) and jelly, we stepped out the Ultra Van this morning into a pouring rainstorm and an ankle-deep puddle. The times I've been to Phoenix in the past it has been bone-dry, blistering hot, and cloudless for days. I think the average annual rainfall just fell last night. We trudged soggily to our booth in the boonies, wondering how many art fans would be venturing out into the first deluge of weather in a year, and how many of those few would have the stamina to seek out our hidden art den.

We sat in our $15 Kmart director chairs.

And we sat.

And the rain poured harder and harder.

A few umbrella-covered spectators in knee-high rubber boots and ponchos glanced our way as they ran down the alley carrying bags of other artists' art that they had purchased over on the main street of the festival where all the choice artists were located. Around lunchtime, the rain gained such momentum that a few artists on our row started packing up to leave. Within five minutes we had a knee-deep river running swiftly through the center of our booth, but, having no place to go, we stood forlorn and soaked, gripping our director chairs to prevent them from being whisked away. Our art-on-strings hung unaffected, as oil paintings are virtually waterproof.

This crap continued for nearly a half hour until, suddenly, the rain stopped, the sun came out, and the clouds disappeared. The artists that had been packing to go claimed they were still leaving because the rain had ruined some of their humidity sensitive mattes. Joe and I had a moment of gratitude for the robustness of oil-on- masonite canvases and hand-painted flea market frames.

We sat some more.

And then it was 6:00 p.m. and time to pack up.

No one bought a thing.

We still had the artist's dinner to look forward to. They're charging $4.25 a person, which is more than we ever spend on a meal. We were waiting hungrily in line with 600 other hungry artists when a forty-something, ex-hippie-type who looked as dejected as we did leaned over and asked, "Why do you think they have to charge $4.25 for a dinner when they already charged us $400 for a booth space? There are 600 artists here. Where does all that money go?"

"It's a racket," I replied eagerly, excited to have a conversation with someone other than Ruby or Joe.

"I've never been to a festival like this before," he complained. "Usually they charge under $250.00 and provide free food, at least."

"Maybe they're serving filet mignon," Joe offered.

"For $400 they should serve filet mignon AND lobster for free," he laughed.

"How long have you been doing festivals?" I asked.

"Twenty years."

We gasped.

"Things were different back in the early days," he added. "People sold everything. Macramé. Painted figurines. There's a lot more competition now, so you see more fine art. But the best time for the shows was in the 80s. We all made bucket loads of money then. It's a lot less lucrative now."

"Pardon my asking," I said, "But what do you consider 'less lucrative'?"

"I average about $3,000 a show. I won't do a show again if I make less than $2,000."

Joe and I stared at him a moment, then stared at each other, then stared at him again.

"But the rain might ruin this show for everybody. You never can tell."

$2,000! Joe and I couldn't speak until we arrived at the food table. They were serving Mexican food with no meat.

"You're right," our artist friend decided. "It's a racket."

## December 11, 1992 Home of Warren and Nobia Suckow, Phoenix, Arizona

It's a long story, how we ended up here at the Suckow's. A hint: they're Ultra Van owners. But first, a recap of the last day of the Tempe festival:

It didn't rain.

Fifteen people entered our booth all day.

Someone stole our $9.99 calculator—one of our most valuable possessions. We argued over whose fault it was to watch the calculator.

At 5:00 p.m. on the last day, a woman entered our booth and looked long and intently at *Rich Chocolate and Squash*, a neutral-colored painting of a living room with a fireplace and a strange light glowing from behind a couch, priced at $185. I sensed she was interested in it and asked her friendly questions about her day at the festival and chatted about the weather. Joe was off somewhere milking other artists for festival tips.

"Do you like that painting?" I nervously asked.

"I love it," she replied, "But I'm Christmas shopping for other people and I can't afford to spend money on myself."

"Well if you really like it I might be able to give you a deal on it. A really good deal."

I couldn't believe the words had left my mouth or where they came from. I hate sales and salesmen and anyone that looks like a salesman. But I knew that if we didn't sell a painting we would be looking for jobs in Phoenix, Arizona the next morning. I felt like a street panhandler.

"Well," she countered, "How good?"

I couldn't believe she was considering it! "Why don't you decide what you can afford and make an offer. Honestly, we need the money to get back to Los Angeles, so I'm willing to go really low." I knew a good salesman would be kicking my butt for that self-effacing comment, but I was, in fact, begging and had no pride whatsoever.

"Oh, I know this will sound like an insult to you," she winced, "but would you take $100?"

I tried to act as if I was considering the offer, but lost my composure at the intoxicating thrill of a sale. "That's exactly what I had in mind!" I happily lied, having expected to get $20 if I was lucky. I nearly dropped the painting while wrapping it for her.

"MERRY CHRISTMAS!" I shouted loudly in her ear as she walked away with a glow of satisfaction. This was the first time I had even acknowledged the holiday season, or had even known it was coming.

So here we are at the Suckow's. We called them from a pay phone after the festival, their address acquired from the now coveted Ultra Van Motor Coach Association Directory, told them of the trouble with our brakes, gave them our references (Jim Craig, The Greens, Christy Barden), and accepted their kind offer to come to their home so Warren could look at our mechanical troubles. We were very rude, we thought, to give them such short notice, but our grotesquely stressful life makes us rude, we think.

We very slowly drove to the Suckow's modest one-story home in a middle-class neighborhood where we were greeted at the door by the cutest, shortest, smiliest old couple we'd met so far. We were ushered in and offered hot showers, food, and a soft couch to sit on.

We didn't converse for more than 20 minutes before going to bed. It's late and we're all tired. We'll talk tomorrow.

## December 13, 1992

Nobia Suckow. (Nobi, I am allowed to call her now). I spent the last two days indoors, sipping water and conversing with her on every subject from dealing with the death of family members (only she has been through that one), to Warren's religious fervor, to Ultra Van Club gossip, to her escalating property taxes and my art career. We had an instant rapport, one that I only have with women that are both good listeners and good storytellers. I had plenty of time to soak up their home décor—perfect for one of our paintings. I photographed many scenes, but the best was their bright aqua couch with raised paisley design under a huge painting of a roadrunner sniffing a cactus, in matching aqua.

Joe and Warren spend their days in the driveway examining Lucy. The brakes should be fine now; that's what Warren told me. And then he told me that I would go to Hell if I didn't go to his church.

"I don't like it when he says that," Nobi confided back inside the house while we prepared dinner of roasted chicken and green bean salad. "He's excited about his religion, but I don't think he should push it on others. I don't say anything, though, because it's so important to him."

"That's nice of you," I said. "Do you think he really believes it? That I'm going to Hell?"

"Oh, I don't know. He's really very accepting of people. He just thinks it's his duty to help save people. I hope you're not too upset about it."

"No, just a little mystified."

"I think it's fine for people to believe whatever they want," she said, standing taller.

I didn't hear any more sermons during dinner, but after we womenfolk finished with the dishes and joined the men, our living room conversation was forced up a volume to compete with the All Christian Channel booming from the television.

"So you met Christy Barden," Warren asked with a smile.

"Yeah, he's a character," Joe replied, laughing. "One night, at the Mini-Rally, we were sitting around in the Craig's living room—about ten of us—when Christy started going on about the nudist colony he'd just visited and the weird lady who rents his house in Boulder and who spent $17,000 trying to get enlightenment at the local Buddhist center, and about his latest macrobiotic diet. You know how he is, with his eyes open wide, slowly telling the craziest details of a story. The lady sitting next to him is new to the Ultra Club—she's from Australia—and after each one of his stories, she would inch her way a little further away from him until she was practically leaning off the other end of the couch."

Warren and Nobi laughed.

"But he's the nicest guy," Joe continued. "And underneath his eccentricities he's as sensible and intelligent as they come."

"That's so true," I said. "He has really gone out of his way to make us feel welcome in the Club, and he's very generous with his time and knowledge."

"Well, there's someone else with an Ultra who's a lot like Christy," Warren told us. "He's one-of-a-kind."

"Who's that?" Joe asked.

"His name's Walt Davison. He and his wife Marilyn live in Miami, Florida. If you ever visit there, they will be the most hospitable and generous people you ever meet in the Club. They let you stay in their home and they treat you like family. Walt's just an original, that's all. He really knows how to make life fun."

"How's that?" I asked.

"Well, this story will just about sum up Walt Davison," Warren began. "Before he retired, he flew planes for Eastern Airlines. One night, he was flying a big plane full of passengers over the Canadian Rockies under a clear sky and a full moon. He said the snow was sparkling and it was bright as day. It was the most beautiful thing he'd ever seen. The passengers were crammed at the windows staring out in total silence. He couldn't stand it. So he got out his loud speaker and told the passengers, 'I probably shouldn't do this, folks, but we're never in our lives going to see anything this beautiful again.' And he turned the plane around and flew back dozens of miles in the direction they'd just come from, and flew over it again. He really got in trouble for that one. I think he almost got fired. He wasted expensive fuel and got the planes off schedule. But to this day, thirty years later, he gets letters from people that were on that flight, thanking him for one of their best memories."

"Wow. What a story. I hope we meet him someday," said Joe.

We leave tomorrow morning for Los Angeles. Joe helped Warren sand one of his Ultra Vans for a future paint job. Nobi and I talked all day. We'll miss the Suckows.

## December 15, 1992   Home of Lee Green, Bruce, and Jinny

Lee and Bruce came out to welcome us as we pulled up in Lucy. Handsome guys. After the craziness of the past few weeks, seeing familiar faces and knowing our stay here would be longer than a weekend felt like falling into a warm sea. After scrutinizing their home for future painting material and then photographing every inch of it, we sat in their living room drinking pop with our feet propped up on the coffee table. Jinny came home from work at the American Heart Association and joined us, and we continued our easy conversation into the night.

Tomorrow we are going to look for a Christmas tree with Lee and Bruce. We'll start painting after that.

## December 20, 1992

We got a tree.  A perfect tree.  The most perfect tree known to exist on planet Earth—of that much I am certain. Here's how we found it: first we went to the Christmas tree lot across from the Hollywood Bowl and looked at every tree there, front and back, from a distance and close up, with and without sunglasses. This was Lee and Bruce's idea; Joe and I just milled around and people-watched. No movie star sightings to speak of. The perfect tree was not to be found at this location.

So we piled into their compact car and drove to a downtown lot where trains were arriving with boxcars full of Christmas trees freshly shipped from Canada. We looked at every tree that had already been unloaded into adjacent lots; by

the time Lee and Bruce were through, every needle had been
scoured for imperfections. No trees were good enough. Joe and
I were getting hungry, so we wandered off to find the nearest
hot dog stand.

We returned to find Lee and Bruce in a crowd of bidders
circling an open boxcar. One worker would toss a tree from
the depths of the boxcar to another worker in the center of the
multitude. The tree-holder would prop the tree up, spin it
around a few times, and call out a price starting at $25. This
price was considerably cheaper than any trees we'd looked at
so far, and each tree thrown in the ring looked positively
flawless from our point of view. The price rarely escalated over
$30, but Lee let tree after tree go by; for what reason, I have no
idea. Lee stood with his hand at his chin and would shake his
head in disapproval as each tree passed.

Occasionally an exceptional tree would perk the interest of
Bruce (they all looked exactly the same, I swear), who would
glance to his left at Lee for approval. Lee would shake his head
slowly, rejecting some flaw that only he could see. We would
have teased them at this point, but they were so serious in their
quest I am quite sure they would have been insulted. We were
enjoying the Monty Python-ness of it all, anyway.

Finally the monumental moment came. Without warning,
Lee, in an uncharacteristically thunderous voice, shouted,
"Twenty-Five Dollars!" Joe and I jumped a foot in the air. I
nearly wept with gratitude that no other bidders countered his
price, and as we walked up to claim our prize, I strutted
proudly, knowing that the other spectators must have been
jealous as sin that we won The Most Perfect Tree on Earth.

The Perfect Tree was erected upon our arrival back at the
house, with Lee in charge of the lights. His Mom, Hilda, is
famous for having over a thousand lights on her tree, and Lee
is always responsible for the task of faultlessly placing each of
them, so he has garnered a shining (pun intended) reputation
in tree-decorating circles.

The blemished side of The Perfect Tree was made to face
the wall, and Joe spent 15 minutes trying to find the "flaw" that
Lee had discovered, all without letting Lee know what he was
doing. Nothing out of the ordinary, Joe claims.

Later this evening, while Bruce and Jinny sipped vodka and
Joe and I sipped Coke, Lee put the final touches on the
glorious Perfect Tree. The rest of us lazily admired his hard
work and expertise, worn out from watching his performance.

The grand finale came when Lee demonstrated that he had wired the Tree up to "The Clapper," as seen on TV, which turns the lights on or off when one claps twice. Hysterical laughter resulted for the remainder of the evening as we clapped the Tree on and off probably a hundred times and ultimately found the exact pitch to yap twice that would voice-activate the thing. Lee finally kicked back and enjoyed the fruits of his festive labor with a Diet Coke and Melba toast.

## December 21, 1992

Lee took Joe to the store today to buy the paint for the house, while I stayed here and started scraping. We got a good start on the house today. At 1:30, a neighbor passing by on the sidewalk yelled to Joe, "You missed a spot!" and I heard Joe mutter "asshole" under his breath.

## December 22, 1992

Painted Lee and Bruce's house until dark. After dinner (tuna sandwiches) Joe started a new painting of a lonesome little table in a brightly lit white room. I began a super-bright picture of Lee's breakfast nook. With Lee's insistence, we set up our studio in the middle of their living room, the only place we could comfortably spread out our tarps, paints, mediums, thinners, palettes, brushes, rags, Masonite sheets and ourselves. We had intended to paint in the camper on Lucy's pop-up kitchen table, but our hosts wouldn't have it. It's cold outside, they maintained, and besides, we want to see what you're doing.

We lay on our stomachs on our protective drop cloths, forcing anyone wanting to get through our mess to step over our legs. No one complained. In fact, we reveled in the abundance of unsolicited compliments and admiration. A better studio has not been found in our travels yet.

Jinny, a Sunday painter herself, was interested in how we work together. Before she saw us paint, she couldn't imagine how we could collaborate so closely. But after watching us for a while she said it seemed second nature for us to paint on the same canvas at the same time. Occasionally I'd ask Joe where he was going with this color or that shadow, or Joe would ask me to scoot over so my brush wouldn't leave a shadow on his work area. Since we get asked about our collaboration frequently, it's nice to have someone see it in action without having to explain.

**December 23, 1992**

Painted all day: house in sunlight, paintings by TV light. Christmas dinner will be at Hilda and Elga's in Torrance. What will we do for Christmas Eve?

**December 25, 1992**

It's Christmas morning. Instead of opening stacks of presents, I will write about our Christmas Eve celebration. We returned home too late last night to report. The sun is shining through Lucy's front window onto my page and a fresh breeze (in L.A.!) comes through the side window. It's not very Christmas-y, but nice anyhow.

Yesterday we painted until dark again, and after our nightly showers inside the house we were offered a fancy and expensive dinner out as a Christmas present from the three of them. We gratefully accepted their offer, especially when they told us we'd be going to a chic and exclusive underground gay hustler bar/restaurant.

"What exactly goes on at a gay hustler bar?" I asked.

"Well," Lee offered, "Young, handsome gay men, usually boys barely over eighteen, cruise the bar and offer their services to older gentlemen, for money. Pretty good money at a nice place like this. Regular street hustlers are usually poor or not as good-looking and make a quarter of what these guys do. You can watch all the deals made while you eat, for no extra charge. And the food is excellent."

"All right!" I exclaimed, eager for an extra-cultural Cultural Encounter and a nice meal out with good friends.

"Are we going to be out of place?" Joe asked.

"Not at all," Bruce jumped in. "Straight people go there, too. It's a beautiful restaurant and very classy."

"I love it!" exclaimed Jinny, a woman in her 70s.

We arrived at the restaurant late, what I call late—for dinner anyway—at 8:00 p.m. I was raised in the small-town American tradition of eating at 5:00, 6:00 at the latest, and I am still usually insane with hunger by 7:00. I have trained Joe into this same schedule, however unfashionable, so our friends that plan to dine with us are forced to feed us or put up with our meanness. It must have been our classy clothes—borrowed from our hosts—that kept our attitudes civil while famished; we enjoyed drinks at the bar while our table was prepared without a hint of foaming at the mouth.

The place was, as Lee had promised, underground—a veritable cave entered by a descending spiral staircase. The walls were covered with floor-to-ceiling mirrors to enhance the small amount of available light and space. The maitre d' went far out of his way to be gracious, apologized for the wait, asked us where we were from, and put his hand on Joe's shoulder.

We were eventually seated in a large booth facing the bar—a good seat, according to Lee, with its unencumbered view of the bar area where all the scoping and pouncing goes on. I seriously doubted at that point whether we would really be able to witness actual pick-ups and not just a few discreet notes passed or sideways glances among the patrons. I couldn't ask Joe what he was thinking, but he told me later he was so goddamn hungry he couldn't think straight.

Lee was right. There was plenty of visible action amongst the suave gentlemen at the bar, and we gawked unfettered in our front row seats at their routine.

A desirable young man would approach the bar. He'd either sit next to or put his hand on the shoulder of an older gentleman—also attractive and tastefully attired—and the two would converse for a few minutes.

Then they'd leave.

Then they'd come back.

We saw this scene perhaps fifteen times throughout the evening, but it might have happened significantly more; we also had our food and company to amuse us. After a time it became less of a wonder, once we realized that it really happens and that's the way it is.

After dinner I scooted to the end of the booth to exit for the ladies' room. Lee smiled and stated, "You had better get the key from the maitre d'."

"What do you mean?"

"The ladies' room is locked."

"Why?"

He leaned over and whispered, still smiling, "Not many women come here so the patrons will use the ladies' room to turn their tricks unless it is locked."

I stared at him. "OK."

I gracefully requested the key from the obliging maitre d', but he insisted on escorting me. We climbed the long spiral staircase to the restrooms near the front door, and he unlocked the women's room for me, informing me discretely and courteously to alert him again when I returned downstairs. I couldn't help but imagine while I peed all sorts of acts that might be going on in that very stall, if, well...anyway.

Thus ended our curious Christmas Eve. We were ushered out with the same splendor that had greeted us, the maitre d' again paying special attention to Joe.

It's Christmas Day. We're going to Hilda and Elga's today for an old-fashioned family Christmas dinner. Somebody pinch me.

## December 25, 1992  Late at Night

Being in the Hood again on Christmas Day brought back the unreal memory of the bloody murder in front of the Green's house. The bloodstain's gone but we will always have the special Christmas memory.

Janice, Hilda's daughter who lives in Pacific Palisades, and her family were present along with the five of us West Hollywood people. We sat most of the day in Hilda's grandmotherly living room talking about this and that.

Joe and I photographed every inch of the Green's house. Now that our paintings are gathering more details and objects of the people who live in these interiors, we are obsessive about noticing everything in the homes we visit. We barely say hello before our eyes sweep the room to gather a feeling of the place, to survey the furniture and items, their placement and lighting. Our first question is, "Can we look around?" So far everyone has welcomed us to scout around, especially if they've seen our work. With no hesitance we dart into every room, including bedrooms, bathrooms, and closets. Most people apologize for the mess or say they are planning to get this or that thing fixed, but we assure them it is perfect just the way it is. To photograph we often turn on every lamp in the house. The way lamps illuminate the articles beneath them or lay their beam over the arm of a sofa is what makes our paintings sing. We hate overhead light when we are hanging out, but sometimes for a painting we include them, especially if they lend a glaring, interrogation-room look. Most people have been surprised at how quickly we photograph and how seamlessly we work as a team. We pass the camera (a cheap automatic) back and forth, pointing out a particular angle, commenting on a great scene, or telling the other to move out of the way. The whole process takes no more than fifteen minutes.

The Green's house was especially inspiring because of the memories it holds for us. I just wish we could portray in paint the smell of that Christmas dinner.

HIGHLIGHTS OF CHRISTMAS 1992
1) Bruce dressed up as Santa and handed out presents.
2) Hilda was thrilled when she received a crotchless, fire-engine red, Frederick's of Hollywood teddy, from Santa. (That's lingerie, not a stuffed animal).
3) Lee, for his part in the meal preparations, had, over a course of three days, made a 14-layer Jello mold. It glowed every color of the rainbow, plus each of those same rainbow colors in its pastel version. He explained that he had to wait hours until each 1/8 inch layer jelled in the refrigerator before pouring the next layer on top. The pastel layers were mixed with sour cream. It was as delicious as it was beautiful, and was the main topic of conversation and Kodak moments before and after we ate.
4) I did a bit of frowning in the corner because I was embarrassed that I cut my bangs too short this afternoon.
MERRY CHRISTMAS.

**December 28, 1992**
Today at the supermarket on Santa Monica Boulevard, we were standing in a typical California long checkout line, waiting our turn and staring into space like everyone else when two non-English speaking, older Russian ladies trudged straight to the head of the line with their groceries. The rest of us—not necessarily all English-speaking or legal citizens, but respectful of the *No-Line-Butting-Law-of–the-Universe*—watched in disbelief as the gray, grim-faced women shoved the front-of-the-line people out of the way and nestled into their new spots. The shocked and irritated complaints of the people in line fell on deaf ears as the perpetrators pretended not to understand English. Joe, the enforcer, wasn't having any of this. His death stare, the one that frightens me no matter who it's directed at, bore a hole into the back of the women's gray heads as he stomped around everyone in line to get at them.

He tapped on their shoulders and said, "Don't mess with me," in a voice exactly like Clint Eastwood's. "I don't care if you speak English or not. Go to the back of the line like everyone else." His big arm pointed to the place.

They began protesting in Russia n and turned to ignore him, but he stood with his big arm steady and continued staring at them. Within ten seconds, they began shouting foreign, surely unpleasant things and gesturing wildly, all the while dragging their things to the back of the line. I was red in the face, and the others watching pretended nothing happened. And Joe's usually such a quiet guy.

### December 30, 1992

I was waiting in line at the post office to pick up my general delivery mail from the Motor Coach Association of America in Cincinnati, Ohio while Joe waited outside with Ruby. When I came outside, Joe had a story.

Our status as vagabonds must be apparent to everyone, he told me. He was sitting on the pavement outside the post office, leaning against the building, with Ruby lying next to him, her head on his leg. He was wearing his ripped jeans and one of his only t-shirts that wasn't ripped or stained with paint. A Russian woman walking by stopped and held out her fist with something for Joe to take.

Joe took it.

It was a quarter.

"Oh, no!" he objected, "Here! I don't need this!" She had no idea what he was saying, but waved at him to please take the money.

"Here, take it," he insisted as she tried to get away, embarrassed.

She got away, and Joe got a quarter.

I told him he should have just said thank you, and let her feel like she'd done a good deed for a poor hobo man.

"Yeah, you're right," he said, "But it shocked me. I didn't want to take her money." Then after a moment of silence, "What do you want to do with our new quarter?"

I opened our mail upon returning "home", as Joe was setting up the ladder for painting. In the mail pile was hidden an envelope from the  Gasparilla Festival of the Arts. Had we found it earlier back at the P.O., I would have violently torn it open on the spot.

Dear Artist,
Congratulations! You have been accepted to exhibit in the...

I stared at it abstractly, not sure whether to jump for joy yet. The letter went on to say that thousands of people had applied for the show and only 300 artists were selected to exhibit and compete for over $60,000 in prizes. That sounded fine.

But Tampa, Florida is a long way from Los Angeles.

"Joe, look at this," I said, as he hauled paint cans outside. He saw by my demeanor that the envelope I held must be thought provoking and eagerly came to grab it.

"Hmmm," he said, after a minute.

"What do we do?"

"I don't know. What do you think?"

"Do you think Lucy would make it?"

"Maybe. We'd have to stop at Jim Craig's for that rear suspension work."

"If this show is a flop like the others, we're stuck without money in a place where we don't know anyone. In fact, I don't think we know anyone east of the Mississippi!"

"But what else are we going to do? We're making all these paintings, and for what? We've got to try something."

"Let's do it," I said, still unsure.

"Yeah, we have to."

We painted quietly today, both mulling doubts and hopes around in our brains, occasionally looking at each other for support with pensive, distant smiles.

This could be it. Our big chance.

Oh God. How many times have we said that?

## January 1, 1993

Last night's New Year's celebration is certainly not to be compared to New Year's Eve last year at the Rolling Hills Country Club. We went to bed early after a long day of painting. Then today we examined the Porn Superstore on Santa Monica Boulevard. We bought a postcard of some tattooed, naked midgets.

## January 3, 1993

Bruce came home tired and worn from his manager job at a nearby bank today. "The bank was robbed again today," he mumbled while pouring his drink after work. "This is the fourth one this month."

"Why didn't you tell us about it before?" I said.

"Oh, it happens all the time; I forget to tell you," he said as he plopped back on the sofa.

"What did you do? Were you scared?" I couldn't wait for details. Joe and I were sprawled out on the floor with our paints, drinking Cokes.

"Yeah, I guess," he replied blandly. "We just do what the robber tells us to. Today there were three guys in black masks. Usually there's more. They took $14,000 today. The last bunch, the idiots, only got $2,000."

"You only had that much available?"

"Right, the rest is back in the safe, which even I can't open."

"Since you're the manager, do they come to you?"

"Yeah. They make everyone lie down, like in the movies, and then ask me to gather up the money from the tellers. Usually."

"At gunpoint?"

"Yep."

"And you're not afraid?"

"Well, I just do what they tell me to, so I don't get hurt."

"Is that the policy for everyone in the bank?"

"Yeah. All the tellers are instructed to do exactly as the robber tells them."

"Why does it happen so often? Don't you have a security guard?"

"Uh-huh. The thugs just work around his schedule. We just got a plainclothes guy, after the robbery last week, but he didn't fool anyone. He was dressed like anybody else, reading a paper on a chair, and regular bank customers would ask the tellers, 'When did you get the new security guard?' The last robbery should never have happened, you know. The cops told us afterwards that a witness had seen a Toyota full of men in black masks driving circles around the bank before it happened. I don't know why someone can't do anything about it."

"Does your bank get hit harder than other banks in California?"

"Maybe a little more. They all get it pretty bad. Not usually four a month, though. I think the Christmas season contributed to that."

"Yeah," Joe finally spoke up, "Criminals have to give presents, too."

## January 5, 1993

We're finally working on the finishing touches of the house. We'd like to leave by the fifteenth so we can fix Lucy and have plenty of time to get to Florida; six weeks should cover it, we hope.

## January 9, 1993   Home of Jim and Marlene Craig

We left West Hollywood with heartbreaking goodbyes to Lee, Bruce, and Jinny. I'll miss The Clapper and evenings on the floor, painting, and Lee's Norman Rockwell collector plates, Jinny's good cooking, and decadent West Hollywood in general.

On the way here, we stopped at the big Dinosaurs in the desert, where, in his Big Adventure, Pee Wee Herman told about his dream where a snake in a vest was rolling a donut...you had to see the movie.

We arrived late morning to a hero's welcome at the Craig's ranch. No ticker tape but a mighty good lunch.

Jim did what he could, with the short amount of time and limited resources available, to service our rear suspension so our bearings don't burn up. And he charged us next to nothing. Our suspension "should" make it to Florida without trouble, he says. Jim, like Elga, is calm and diligent when working on an Ultra Van (and probably any other mechanical entity), much like Joe and I are when we paint. I can now see why some men become motorheads; machines become their art, their escape, their therapy, their accomplishment, their love, hopefully among other loves. Joe says the only reason he's becoming a fix-it guy is because poverty and necessity force him to, although one can easily see his wonder and pride at repairing any of Lucy's ailments. I think this Ultra work is empowering him.

It feels like life on the road is officially beginning for us now. We will be certified itinerant wanderers, going to places we've never been before.

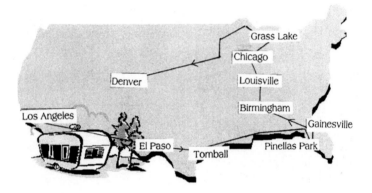

# PART 3

The Road

**January 12, 1993  Algodones Imperial Dunes, California**

It's 2:15 a.m. Joe and I are wide-awake listening to the roar of the 20 dune buggies flying around the mountainous sand dunes that were earlier thought to be our peaceful backdrop for the night. We pulled into our free camp spot at 4:00 this afternoon, situating ourselves on an open plain of hard-packed sand, aiming our side picture window for a full, spectacular view of the quiet, mountainous dunes in all their barren splendor. Their dense covering of motor vehicle tracks somehow escaped us in all our excitement to stretch our legs and feed ourselves before the sun went down, and only hindsight has demonstrated to us that the motorheads must have been taking a few hours off around the dinner hour to gain strength for the frenzied orgy of dune terrorism we are experiencing now.

After relaxing over a dinner of sandwiches, salad, and ice cream bars (a rare delicacy around here), we treated Ruby to a long and taxing game of fetch—a game she is slowly mastering. While we tossed the slobbery tennis ball again and again, we talked with excitement of our adventurous life ahead. This feels like our first day of actually living on the road, a wonderful, freeing, frightening feeling—intoxicating and sobering at the same time. I've never felt so in charge before—of my life or my fate. If I stop to ponder it too long, I realize my life has probably never before been so out of my hands.

As we walked toward Lucy to retire for the night, an extra-stretch limousine pulled up on the sand field near Lucy. A uniformed chauffeur got out, walked around the car, and opened the door at the tail end of the super long car. A bride and groom stepped out, laughing, both holding champagne glasses. Algodone Dunes are as close to the middle of nowhere as any place in the United States, essentially hundreds of miles from mentionable civilization in the lower California Mojave Desert, very near the border of Mexico.

"This is right out of a Fellini movie," I whispered to Joe.

"I think it's a mirage," he said.

The drunk, blond-haired, blue-eyed newlyweds shouted, "Hey! Ya want some champagne?"

"No, thanks," we said in unison, smiling, but too mystified to say much more. Now I'm wondering why the hell we said no. I can't imagine the next time free alcohol is going to fall from crystal glasses into our laps.

"We just got married," the groom slurred.

"Congratulations," we offered, again together.

Before we could stop her, Ruby greeted the chauffeur by attacking his shiny shoes, growling and biting while shaking her head as if to wrench his feet off. The man was obviously not a dog lover, and began to dance a jig of sorts, while swearing and yelling at us. We called her off, while the bridal couple laughed enthusiastically, spilling champagne on the groom's tux, then laughing even harder. Before we could find out where they came from or where they were going, the chauffeur whisked the couple back in the car, and ran around to his own door while eyeing Ruby distrustfully, and sped off in a cloud of dust.

"Weird," I said.

"Yep," said Joe. "Let's go to bed."

Ten minutes after lying down, prepared for a night of dead silence under the stars, the screaming dune buggies revved up their muffler-free machines and have not ceased since. Peckerheads.

### January 13, 1993   Quartzite, Arizona

I have, over a span of 10 minutes, completely changed my outlook on dune buggies. This morning we woke early to the silent sands of Algodone; the demented and inconsiderate dune buggyists had crawled into their hi-tech tents as the sky began to lighten in the east. We managed to get a few hours of sleep somehow, and in our excitement about our new lifestyle we were happy to get up. We're free!

Before heading east toward Arizona today, we took a long, exploratory walk into the dunes, mostly to see how far we could launch Ruby over the edge of sand cliffs. Joe would heave her over the edge while I stood camera-ready, attempting to capture her in mid-flight, as she sailed, legs outstretched and ears perked, at least 30 feet down through the air to a cushiony spray of sand at the bottom. She never tired of this amusement, and was impatient and perturbed when an approaching dune buggy interrupted her festivities.

"Hey!" the dune man called out. "Do you want a ride?"

Without hesitation, without remembering our hellish tirade condemning anything to do with the sport of dune-buggying the night before, forgetting our condescending giggles in bed the night after Jim Craig projected his Super 8 dune movies in Joshua Tree, we instantly yelled, "Sure!"

We almost fought over who got to go first.

I, with my cutest smile, persuaded Joe to let me go first. Dune Man introduced himself as Gary and with a crisscrossing mess of safety straps, secured me to the front of the vehicle. The buggy's construction had me a little worried. Its body consisted only of monster tires, a few roll bars, and an exposed engine—nothing at all between me and the elements.

Gary took off. We swirled around the inside of sand bowls, flew over the top of mountainous dunes, and sped through the desert like a slalom racer. As far as the eye could see, there was sand, and we were the only beings out there—racing, turning, skidding, jumping. I involuntarily shouted with joy a few times and was sure that Gary, sitting behind me, must be feeling extra manly about his ability to make a woman scream so early in the morning. I understood the deeper meaning of dune buggyism and was one with the sand and sky.

My turn was plenty long enough, but when we pulled up to Joe so I could get off, I regretted that it had to end so soon. I eyed Joe with a knowing smile as I was unstrapped from my seat.

"What?" he said.

"You'll see," I said wisely.

While I sat in the sand patting Ruby, I actually allowed myself to dream of one day owning a dune buggy (I dream of owning pretty much everything I see anyway). When Joe returned from his sandy roller coaster of fun, he said, "We need to get one of those things." We thanked Gary exuberantly and left.

Thanks, Gary, wherever you are. We will never see you again, as long as we live, probably.

I now admit that dune buggies are OK, but I still want to make it clear that no matter how fun it is to buggy at night, I would never race around in the dark when tired, innocent campers are nearby. I'm nice that way.

Then we drove to Quartzite. We've heard about this weird place from several Ultra Owners, only because it is a free place to camp for up to two weeks. This alone makes it a desirable attraction to many motor home types.

Quartzite is a barren flat spot in the central Arizona desert, dotted with sage and a few short cacti, just east of the California border, and home to an immense permanent flea market. Not much town to speak of, just rows of tents, plywood shacks, and spaces for wayward junk collectors to set out their shabby wares. Quartzite is most famous for its Annual Rock and Gem Show, held in the spring, when tens of thousands of "stone heads" converge on this Mecca of rock collector trading. Today the place is scattered with an occasional single motor home like ours, all spaced so far apart we can barely see each other.

During our afternoon investigation of the area, we came upon a tiny, pot-bellied pig owned by a fat man in a Harley Davidson t-shirt. The pig was tied up to a retired school bus with hand-painted words— *Spirit* and *E Pluribus Unum* and *Buy American* and *North American Meteorite Recovery Team*—emblazoned across it.

The market was for the most part deserted of humanity except for a few ratty, weathered, old people who obviously live here and run the booths. A rickety building named The Camel Stop sells nothing but goofy lawn ornaments: green smiling frogs in tuxedos, knee-high pigs dressed up like sheriffs, Indians pulling arrows out of their pouches, and the Virgin Mary. A life-size camel stands in the center of the multitude with a real estate ad sandwiched over his back.

The camel reference, we soon learned, has to do with the legend of Hi Jolly the camel trainer, who was brought to the American desert from Syria in the nineteenth century to help train camels and be a scout in the Arizona Desert. The U.S.

Government had a plan to use camels for some brilliant military strategy—now long forgotten—but as usual, the scheme failed and the camels were left for Hi Jolly to take care of. Hi Jolly's grave sits behind the flea market in a strange little graveyard, his tombstone an eight-foot pyramid constructed mostly of petrified wood. On top sits a metal camel silhouette. His epitaph reads: *The Last Camp of Hi Jolly. Camel Trainer, Packer, Scout. Over 30 years a faithful aid to the U.S. Government.*

## January ?, 1993 A rest stop near Dragoon, Arizona

We arose the morning after our exploration of Quartzite to crisp blue skies and a man peering into our front picture window. We hadn't closed our gingham curtains the night before, thinking we were far enough away from all the other campers not to need that kind of privacy. The man smiled and waved. If there is such a thing as a normal-looking guy, this fellow was it. Ward Cleaver (only plumper) wore a blue down parka, jeans and tennis shoes. Joe stepped out and greeted him, expecting to answer two-dozen Ultra Van questions—which he did—while I hurriedly got dressed in Lucy's tiny hall space. I didn't want to miss a valuable and coveted second of interaction with other humans. By the time I stepped from Lucy's door, the conversation had turned from Lucy admiration to Ruby compliments. What an interesting looking dog, boy she's smart. Randy, a "full-timer" himself, was enthused that we, too, were inhabitants of the open road.

"Nine-to-five people have no idea what they're missing," he assured us. "And there's not a way in hell you can explain it to them. I have no bills, no schedule, no one to answer to. When I run out of money, I just get me a job for a few months, and then I'm free again for a while. And when you only work a job for that short of time, you don't get sick of the work or the people."

"How long have you been full-timing it?" I asked.

"About a year and a half," he replied. "I had a great job as a writer for a newspaper, but I was always under pressure, with deadlines and long hours. I just gave my two weeks one day, and haven't regretted it. I bought a motor home with my savings and took off with no plans of where to go and started figuring things out as I went along. And you know what?"

"What?"

"I love it. Did you realize that living in a motor home has the least impact on the environment of any way of living? Think about it. You don't use much water, because you don't want to fill your holding tank up too fast, right?"

We agreed, thinking about our infrequent showers and our obsessive attention to minimal water use while washing dishes.

"And you certainly don't use much electricity. You're either on battery power, which you have to conserve like crazy so you don't run them down, or you're hooked up at a RV park, which we full-timers rarely do, to save money. And propane. Think about how little propane you use. One tank lasts a month and that's if you're really using your heater in the winter."

"Yeah, but what about gas?" Joe had to be the Devil's Advocate.

"We do use gas. But most RVs rack up less miles a year than cars even if they're full-timers because there isn't this back and forth commuting thing. Usually we drive a long distance, stop and park, and then explore a place on foot or bicycle (that's me, I have a bicycle)."

"You've really thought this out, haven't you?" I asked.

"I am so grateful to have the opportunity to see this country like very few people ever do, so yeah, I do think about it a lot. Walt Whitman wrote a wonderful poem that I think says it best about our life on the road. Would you like to hear it?"

"Absolutely!" I said, interested that such an ordinary looking man would be so contemplative and literate. I expected his poetry recital to be something Joe and I would joke about and mimic for months to come. Poetry, especially something as nineteenth century as Whitman, can come across as intensely sappy and melodramatic with the wrong interpretation. But this plain man, standing in the desert with his hands in his parka pockets, captivated us with his earnest, down-to-earth, rendition of Song of the Open Road. It was like a forward in the book of our brand new life.

Afoot and light-hearted I take to the open road,

Healthy, free, the world before me,

The long brown path before me leading wherever I choose.

Henceforth I ask not good-fortune, I myself am good-fortune,

Henceforth I whimper no more, postpone no more, need nothing,

Done with indoor complaints, libraries, querulous criticisms,
Strong and content I travel the open road.


The Earth, that is sufficient,
I do not want the constellations any nearer,
I know they are very well where they are,
I know they suffice for those who belong to them,


(Still here I carry my old delicious burdens,
I carry them, men and women, I carry them with me wherever I go,
I swear it is impossible for me to get rid of them
I am filled with them, and I will fill them in return).


So then we drove through the cactus and sand vista and got here. Here being a rest stop where we are sandwiched between two rumbling, ground-shaking semis. They keep some motorized part of their rigs running at night, for refrigeration. We are trapped in a canyon of anti-slumber. Tonight I hate truckers. Peckerheads.

### January ?, 1993  Las Cruces, New Mexico to El Paso, Texas

Everywhere we stop—every gas station, grocery store (still too poor to ever eat out, even at Taco Bell or Burger King), every rest stop or scenic pullout—we are approached by curious Ultra Van admirers voicing one or more of these questions or comments:

What the hell is that? It looks like a big floating marshmallow. What year is it? It's the greatest motor home I've ever seen. Did you make it? Is it in production? Where can I get one? It looks like a converted VW van. I thought it was older than 1970. Thumbs Up. It looks like the Oscar Meyer Wiener mobile. Have you ever seen that Lucy and Desi movie "The Long Long Trailer"? I've been around RVs my whole life and I've never seen anything like it. You should paint it yellow and it would look like a big banana. You've really done a nice job with it. Where'd you find it? Boy you'd better hang on to that. It looks like Buckminster Fuller's Dimaxion. It must have lots of power with a Chevy V-8 307. It's so roomy and airy, it has more room than our 38-footer. It looks like a giant loaf of bread. I'll bet you don't have any problems with it, huh?

We can never go anywhere without people noticing us.

Yesterday we drove all the way from Dragoon, Arizona, to White Sands National Monument, New Mexico. This drive would be an insignificant, lazy jaunt for regular vehicle owners, but Lucy should not be driven over 50 miles per hour, so we felt like Almighty Road Masters to have made such distance in a day. White Sands was our first exploit that involved going out of our way, 60 miles in and 60 miles out.

We arrived at the White Sands National Monument Visitor's Center by early afternoon and perused the maps and flora/fauna information, Indian dioramas, and clean restrooms. We got charged half-price because the whole place is under water from flooding!

It looked like snow. Snow everywhere. The temperature was a moderate 70 degrees. The skies were swept with high cirrus clouds, so it didn't feel like winter, but the sugar dunes of sand reminded me of the powder-covered fields and mountains of my girlhood home in winter.

We drove down a white road with white sand banks, and scanned a vista of white hills, occasionally dotted with a brown-leafed tree, still hanging onto its last crumbly leaves from a recent Fall. We didn't notice the flooding at first; we stayed on some higher dunes to play before venturing into the flood plain. Our probe of the area was much like at Algodones, with Ruby-tossing, kamikaze dune jumping, Ruby-burials up to the head, and a sexy photo shoot. (Which will produce one photo of me standing in my gray sweats, baggy green shirt with paint stains, greasy hair and no make-up in front of a dune lump).

We were tired then, so we drove Lucy to the flood zone. A sign just before the slight descent into the picnic grounds eerily read, SLOW, CONGESTED AREA–a lone sign on a desolate landscape that suggested a multitude of people that were no longer. We continued over the small promontory that overlooked the restrooms and picnic area to see a white lake speckled with half submerged picnic tables and trashcan foursomes. Even the large, modern restrooms were mostly underwater. The picnic tables had an unusual umbrella-type covering, resembling the wind-filled sail of a boat. The short, identical reflections beneath each of these futuristic, machine-like objects on the milky lake, with a bleached-white shore was a bizarre sight—like UFOs hovering in nowhere.

Five o'clock was fast approaching; we pulled some leftover spaghetti with Ragu out of the fridge and ate it cold. Too lazy to turn on a burner. We left quickly and drove to Las Cruces. We're in a Wal-Mart parking lot, ready to be woken early by Parking Lot Cleaner Man.

## January ?, 1993  Las Cruces, New Mexico to El Paso, Texas

Got up. Drive. Drive. Drive. Still light when we entered El Paso.

"This is the ugliest place I've ever seen in my life," Joe stated as we rode I-10 into the city. The Rio Grande paralleled the highway, and across it was a dirt-covered hillside brimming with leaning shanties, broken-down rusty cars, and refrigerator boxes—all homes for the extremely poor. Tattered clothes hung out on twine clotheslines; trash was scattered about; everything was brown.

"That must be Mexico," I said, staring at the map. "It says that's Ciudad Juarez over there. How strange that people live like that, just over the river, where they can see right into America. I'd swim the river in a second if I were one of them." We gazed, speechless at the sad sight, in awe of the squalor. I looked down at my red-painted toes. The last thing on their mind is toenail polish, I thought, then wondered why I thought it.

The freeway turned away from the river, heading east. It was still ugly even though the view into Mexico was gone. There were no trees, no color (except for brown), no beautified median, no landscaping of any kind. Just dirt, utilitarian businesses, factories, intersecting telephone poles and lines, and smoke stacks all crammed together. It was as if no one had ever thought about making anything look good here. A city whose only function is to function, in a land with nothing but land.

We found the local AAA office just off Highway 180/62, the road to our next tourist destination, Carlsbad Caverns. The AAA lady strongly suggested we pay $8 each to take a trolley into Juarez, Mexico for a day of shopping and sightseeing. We thanked her, claiming we surely would take her advice, grabbed a pile of maps to direct us to Florida, and walked out the door.

"Sure," I laughed sarcastically when we climbed back into Lucy. "No problem. We can just drop $16 any time someone has a nifty idea. I'd love to go into Juarez. That Bitch."

"Honey, you've been cussing a lot lately. You never used to cuss."

"Why don't you mind your own goddamn business, you big wiener."

"I think your period is coming."

"What would you know," I mumbled inaudibly, admitting only to myself that he was right.

So here we are, on the outskirts of El Paso, in a small RV space at the Desert Oasis Trailer Park. (They got the Desert part right, but this is hardly an Oasis. Like the rest of the area, this camping place is void of all flora, with only a windowless cinderblock office, a few RV hook-ups, and a surrounding chain-link fence.) The only other campers here are a converted 70s station wagon, a dirty old Winnebago, and a dying pick-up with a pop-up on the back.

We took a hike into the desert after dinner to let Ruby stretch her legs. Ruby was delighted to run free through the sage and beer cans, but we were aghast at the crazy amount of litter. We marched through a gauntlet of discarded La-Z-Boys, doll arms, flannel shirts, couches, liquor bottles, and Cheetos sacks. A half of a mile down the trail, fully disgusted, we saw no end to the Trail of Trash.

We turned around to flee from the barbarous inhumanity, when Ruby began growling and tugging on a couple of decrepit mattresses nearby. Our minds moved from dejection to childish abandon in less than a second. We ran over, at Joe's suggestion, and joined Ruby on the mattresses for a trampoline fiesta, rivaled in fun only by the dune buggy excursion of days ago. Our road weariness was quickly bounced out of us as we hollered and sprang as high as we could, rusty springs creaking and desert dust flying. Ruby tried joining the fun by nipping at our heels, but frequently got her nose bounced on, and eventually just stood back barking. We only gave up our sunset fun when the darkening evening threatened to leave us lost in a desert garbage heap. We sprinted back to camp, laughing and howling, not caring whether the other campers heard us.

I think about our friends and family, back in Colorado, probably watching TV or out to dinner at a restaurant—doing things most people do in the evening, in America. And then there's us.

### Late January, 1993   Carlsbad Caverns, New Mexico

Huge news: Lucy has driven one-third of our journey without any huge breakdowns or catastrophes.

Tonight we are parked in front of an abandoned gift store/gas station on the side of a highway just outside the Carlsbad Caverns area. We drove into the area just after dark, with no intention of paying money to park for the night. We were turned away from every available parking space along the roads or in parking lots by signs that read NO RV PARKING EVER. We circled the area four or five times and then headed out of town, tired and grouchy. We reluctantly chose this spot—an unlit, unfriendly, deserted building, with broken windows, trash strewn around, and no other establishments in sight. I've been laying here for three hours and haven't slept yet due to fears of:

1) Indian Ghosts
2) An escaped convict with a hatchet
3) Police who could arrest us for trespassing and throw us into a stinky cell with a drunk and some prostitutes

### Late January, 1993   New Mexico rest stop (near nowhere)

The caves ended up being a colossal surprise. I didn't expect anything so massive or amazing or unearthly. After paying our money in a carpeted, hi-tech visitors' center, we chose the guided tour that led us on foot down a labyrinth of paths toward the main cave, or BIG ROOM. The tour took an hour. Looking back, we've decided that it would have been better to take the elevator straight down to the Big Room.

Our tour guide was a true nerd. A skinny, bespeckled woman in a Ranger Rick uniform, she gave a long, rehearsed intellectual-sounding speech every 20 feet or so. This, in and of itself, would have been bearable, had it not been for her attempts to excite her listeners with the word "mystery": "The mystery of the cave; that's why so much mystery surrounds this cave; bats are very mysterious creatures; the mysteries of spelunking." Ironically, she was explaining every detailed, scientific aspect of caves one could think of, taking every ounce of mystery out of the cave. She gave us something to roll our eyes about in the back row.

Disney could never dream of making an attraction as spectacular as Carlsbad Caverns. Our tour down the path was marked occasionally with interesting stalagmites and stalactites

of all sizes and colors and textures, but the Big Room, larger
than the biggest football stadium, was filled with them, from
teeny-weeny ones to skyscraper-sized ones. We meandered
along a concrete path through a maze of grotesque formations,
colored pools, dark holes that led into the center of the Earth,
dripping stalactites whose milky liquid dropped faithfully onto
its stalagmite mate below, towering monoliths and groupings of
wet, minuscule stone outcroppings, green with moss. Joe liked
the boob-shaped stalagmite, (automobile-size, complete with
nipple). I liked The Kiss, a stalagmite and stalactite combination
that are millimeters away from touching each other, and will
someday join the ceiling and the floor of the cave. As we
learned from our mysterious tour guide, these formations grow
at a rate of less than an inch every hundred years, so visitors
are encouraged to appreciate the time it took Nature to create
this wonder. We sure did.

I think all Americans should be required by law to visit
Carlsbad Caverns. Or at least get a tax deduction for doing so.

The temperature inside the cave always remains at 56
degrees, year-round. When we emerged at 2:00 p.m., we were
surprised to see the temperature outside had dropped at least
20 degrees and snow was falling. Ruby was beside herself with
excitement when she heard us approach the camper; she
barked and wagged and licked the windows until we let her
out to tear circles around the parking lot and bite falling
snowflakes.

We then drove slowly to here, the world's most primitive
rest stop. Its existence on the map puzzles us, as it is void of
any facilities whatsoever. It's basically a dirt pullout, which
means I will have another night of worrying about murderers,
rapists and ghosts. I think the fact that we survived last night's
stop has given me a little confidence, though.

## January 31, 1993   Good Samaritan Church, Dallas, Texas

I have much to write about. We left New Mexico four days
ago and we just arrived in Dallas. Reason it took so long: *Texas
is big!* Texas seems to be half of the United States, and not
necessarily the most scenic half, either. Cotton. Peanuts. Dirt.
Lots of sky. Small towns that haven't changed since the 1940s.
Pickups. Cowboy hats. Silos. Barbecue restaurants. I guess this
is how I imagined Texas would be, and I am not disappointed.
It's wonderful in a big, quiet sort of way. I just didn't imagine it
would take so long to drive through.

At a roadside stop somewhere between Abilene and Fort Worth, while eating our dinner of peanut butter and jelly sandwiches, canned green beans, and Progresso soup, I started crying.

"Joe, I'm really scared."

"Why?"

"We're leaving the West. Only once have I been east of Brush, Colorado. And here we are, practically moving out East, for all we know. I have this weird feeling, as if there's no turning back once we cross the Mississippi. What's that all about?"

"That's funny. I feel the same way. It's like there's some imaginary line down the middle of the country that we have to cross. But what's the difference between the East and the West, I wonder?"

"The West is home, that's what's different. And the East is far away from it. My instincts are telling me to turn around and head back."

"Is that what you want to do?"

"Hell no! I'm just scared, that's all."

"Me, too. It's weird, isn't it?"

Well, we made it over the imaginary line, and we still have a strange sensation that there's no turning back. But we're going ahead anyway.

This morning we drove into Fort Worth with the intention of exploring its finer attractions. I had no idea it had so many BIG fine attractions. I guess everything about Texas is big. First, we drove downtown to visit the art museums and galleries. The '80s were good to Texas and allowed them to build kingly museums—far more impressive than what we expected. The Amon Carter Museum dealt mostly in Western/Cowboy/American art, and although we ho-hummed through the Remingtons and Russells (seen too many reproductions), we thrilled at Thomas Eakin's *The Swimmers* and Grant Wood's *George Washington Cuts Down the Cherry Tree* (or whatever that one is called). The contemporary museum had Picasso and Hodgkin and Tansey and George Segal and Red Grooms. I still get horror flashbacks from writing college essays about contemporary art, so I will only say that it was all "very nice."

Poverty forced us to skip the Kimball Museum, where were asked to part with $16 for the *Vast Empire of Sultan Rajhadad*

*Traveling Exhibition* (or something like that). I don't care if they have Elvis Presley's last fart in a jar, we can't afford $8 a person.

We checked out a few galleries in Fort Worth. They were much like the ones in Denver—a little less important than they thought they were. We doubted our paintings would be suitable for the galleries we saw, anyway.

The drive here to Dallas was the easiest ever; there were no cars on the road. We wondered what was wrong with this place. The freeways of a major city were virtually empty! Then we got lost, incredibly lost, thanks to the illogical, completely wrong signs we followed. We had no idea where we were. We drove back and forth, arguing and searching the map, then yelling at each other and tearing the map, until we finally saw a shining beacon of a sign. *The Good Samaritan Church.* We assumed there could be no other place on Earth where we would be more welcome to park for the night than here. We'll see what the priest says in the morning. Although it seems safe, trespassing on private property seems like something I'll never get used to. The priest could be a hypocrite and call the cops on us. Lucy could catch fire and we'd get sued in the morning. Angry church ladies might surround us with picket signs that say, *Yankees Go Home, Sayeth the Lord.* You never know.

We finally deciphered the reason for the emptiness of Dallas/Fort Worth. Today is the Super Bowl. Joe figured this out when, from all over the city, just minutes ago, arose the sounds of honking horns, rebel yells, and cries of "We're number one!" We will probably hear these noises far into the night, and I am glad because I was beginning to seriously worry that we were the only people left in the world.

### February 1, 1993

A friendly priest/pastor/minister guy knocked on our camper door this morning while we were eating stale bagels.

"Good Morning!" he said.

"Hey, Father," Joe greeted the man, not sure how to address a non-Catholic man of the cloth. "We hope it was all right to park here for the night. We got kind of lost after dark last night."

"You're welcome here. I'm just surprised you found this place. It is surely off the beaten path of a camper."

"Like I said, we were lost. We were pretty relieved when we saw your Good Samaritan sign, though. It was late and we were tired."

"Well, feel free to stay another night if you like. We don't often get overnight guests here."

"Thanks, a lot," I replied gratefully, a little guilty that I had, just last night, secretly fantasized that this nice man would look like Quasimodo and carry a tire iron.

A DAY IN DALLAS, TEXAS

1) Joe threw Ruby in a nearby lake so she would learn to swim. It worked, barely, but Ruby hated him for four hours.

2) Discovered in our Texas Tour Book the story of the Hogg family—very wealthy patrons of the area. Mr. Hogg named his three daughters Ima Hogg, Ura Hogg, and Bea Hogg, then stipulated in his will that any name changing would disinherit them.

3) Went downtown and gazed at the skyscrapers. Ate at McDonalds (BIG TREAT).

4) Experienced the pinnacle of American tourist adventures: we saw the infamous Grassy Knoll, the spot from which JFK's mythical second assassin allegedly fired his rifle. It was a most anti-climactic experience, although our expectations shouldn't have been very high. After all, the thing is called a grassy knoll, and that is exactly what we saw.

5) Saw the book depository from the outside. It was closed to visitors. Also nothing to shout about. Our life will be forever altered, however. Every time we see the television footage of JFK's head being blown off, we'll be able to picture precisely where it happened.

6) Returned to Good Samaritan Church. Will have a peaceful night, knowing we are allowed to be here.

## February 2, 1993   Home of Dick and Mary Herrman, Tomball, Texas (North of Houston)

I am now writing from a charming bedroom of mauve and green, with flowered wallpaper, pillow shams, bed skirts, and matching bedroom furniture. I have just eaten a huge, fantastically delicious dinner of fried chicken, fried okra, mashed potatoes, and apple pie; all cooked and served by the nicest people imaginable. And I took a long, hot shower. The humble way we came upon this bonanza entailed what would be considered unthinkable to most respectable people.

We drove south from Dallas toward Houston on I-45, and only made it to the outskirts of Houston by nightfall. I couldn't bear the thought of another night worrying about our safety. We also hadn't had a hot shower since El Paso, Texas. So I looked in our Ultra Van directory for anyone in the area that we might be able to stay with for the night. Notice would be too short for whomever we hooked up with, but it was worth a try.

We stopped at a Giant Truck Stop, which was giant, and I called from a pay phone, nervous and stuttering.

"Hello?" answered a friendly woman with a southern accent.

"Hi, my name is Dori DeCamillis and we own an Ultra Van. We found your name in the Ultra Van directory and wondered if you might know of a good, really cheap place to stay for the night around here. We're just north of Houston."

"Oh! You own an Ultra Van," she laughed. "Well, we sold our Ultra Van after only using it a couple of times. I'm surprised we're still in the directory. I'm not sure about places around here because we don't own an RV, but let me think for a minute..."

"We've traveled all the way from Los Angeles in the past few days and we're exhausted. So we're not picky."

"Well, you're welcome to stay with us for the night if you want." (The words I had been waiting for and impudently hinting at).

"Really? Oh, that's so sweet of you. Are you sure?"

"Absolutely," she said sincerely. "Let me give you directions."

This isn't our first foray into the world of imposing on total strangers, but it seems distinct from the other times because these people don't own an Ultra, they are east of the imaginary line down the United States, and we could give no references that they were familiar with. We can officially be considered brash.

When we pulled into their country, English Tudor-style home, Mary and Dick came out to their large driveway to greet us with hugs and a "How was your trip?" as if we were family members. They loved Ruby and introduced her to their two beagles, Chelsea and Bubba, who inhabit the swimming pool and gazebo area of the back yard. They are in their late 40s, I am guessing; Mary is a schoolteacher and Dick is an engineer of some sort. We were graciously treated to dinner, showers and an indoor bedroom, without any indication whatsoever that they were uncomfortable with our presence. It's as if we've known each other for years.

The Herrman's home is ideal material for our paintings! In the living room, Mary displays her very elaborate and detailed ceramic Christmas Village, which she made herself from a kit. She said she hasn't had the time since Christmas to take it down. Dick showed us his books on guns and was proud of his stuffed bobcat, which stands regally on the hearth. We took lots of photos, and Mary kept saying, "Are you sure you want to take a picture of that?"

We sat and chatted through the evening after the dishes were put away. One of the  Herrman's dreams is to own an Excalibur—one of those super fancy 1930s-remake cars. They talked about the economy, their rapidly developing neighborhood, and the problems with public schools. Their secure, normal life makes me feel like a weirdo.

I think as long as we are alive we should send at least a Christmas card to the Herrmans. Our whole lives we are trained to be wary of strangers, and the evening news would have us believe that all of humanity is out to destroy each other. Why does it appear to be the total opposite, now that we're actually testing this theory?

### February 6, 1993   Crystal Beach, Texas

Joe, who was a positive, friendly, good-spirited man most of the day, eventually cracked under the weight of too many new experiences. His end of the day quote: "If I see another historical log cabin, I'm going to grind it up and stuff teddies with it. I'd rather slide across the Astrodome turf on my naked butt in front of a sell-out crowd with my penis dressed up in Barbie clothes than see one more damned tourist sight." (This comment came after seeing the zoo and the contemporary art museum in Houston).

We drove hurriedly to Galveston, where we did nothing but stop to find out where the ferry departed. I have now seen Galveston. It has knee-high curbs, in case of hurricanes.

Lucy took her first ferry ride across Galveston Bay, and we ended up here, parked right on a deserted beach by ourselves with no signs to tell us where we are. The map says we might be on Crystal Beach. It's a nice name, so we'll settle with that.

**February 7, 1993**

Beach life is divine, but two things about this beach will send us to our next destination tomorrow morning. One, Ruby keeps finding decomposed animal carcasses and bringing them to the door of the camper for us. The first putrid toad skeleton with white meat hanging off its bones was tolerable, because Ruby was so proud of herself. But, after a large decaying fish and an indecipherable species of rodent were left for us, we became annoyed. Ruby's mouth smelled exactly like the new friends she was bringing home, which meant we had to run for our lives when she'd try to lick us, which was frequently.

The other dreadful aspect of this beach occurred last night in our sleep. Somehow, even though our coach is supposedly airtight, some clever killer mosquitoes found their way in. Flying bugs have never accessed Lucy's interior before, so we had to give credit to these resourceful mosquitoes for their superior intelligence, but we wanted them dead nevertheless. Joe and I threw a fit trying to bat them away from our ears and slap them on our skin, but they kept coming in droves. We finally surrendered when it was made apparent that the buzzing, swirling maelstrom around our heads was only going to get worse. We pulled out a flexible mosquito screen (a Vaughn Gizmo saved in case of an emergency) and laid it directly over our bodies, like corpses in the jungle. Then we put pillows over our ears and, voila, no mosquitoes on Joe and Dori! We could still hear Ruby scratching herself through our pillow earmuffs, which served her right for smelling like a carcass all day. The next morning Joe had a swatting jamboree and left black splats all over the walls, ceiling, and counters for me to clean up. He says I should be happy that I didn't have to do the squishing but, honestly, who wouldn't rather be the squisher than the squish cleaner?

**February 9, 1993   Home of Byron and Eleanor Elliot, Lafayette, Louisiana**

Rather than giving our usual short notice, we just showed up at the Elliot's. Byron answered the door, at first with a confused look, then a big smile of recognition.

We met the Elliots at the Rolling Hills Country Club. They were among our favorite members, and showed gracious interest in our art career and our lives. They even invited us over to dinner one evening at their beautiful home on the Palos Verdes Peninsula. We vowed to keep in touch with them, not knowing at the time that we would be frolicking around the United States and that they would be moving to Louisiana. Our correspondence since then gave us their address.

I felt highly awkward entering the Elliot's lavish, well-appointed home in my sweatshirt, cutoffs and dirty sneakers, but Byron made us feel right at home. Eleanor is out of town, he told us, visiting their children in Texas. He offered us a bedroom for the night. We settled in by showering, changing, and examining and photographing the entire three-story condo and all of its expensive antiques. Then, over a dinner of crusty French bread and homemade spaghetti from fresh basil and vine-ripened tomatoes, Byron entertained us with his stories of his businesses overseas, his dealings with various nationalities of people, his goings on at his new country club, and his politics. Joe and I listened, mesmerized, without much to say in return. Our stories of pouncing on putrefied mattresses in the desert, spending the night at the Venice Beach car impound lot, or bathing with a garden hose in the Hood, didn't sound too impressive.

So here we are, in our gorgeous mahogany king-sized bed with fresh, all-cotton sheets, staring at art on the walls that cost more than everything we own.

### February 12, 1993   New Orleans, Louisiana

Since Lucy can't go very fast on the freeways, we took the back roads through Louisiana with the impression that we'd make it to New Orleans in the same amount of time. Big Mistake. Highway 90 through Cajun Country was like a 300-mile long cattle guard. Potholes riddled every mile, and no shoulder at all existed. Lucy's ancient suspension makes potholes feel like teeth-shattering explosions (no exaggeration) and, if we were ever forced to pull off a road with no shoulder, we would be dead (small exaggeration). Either Lucy's weight would sink us into sand for good, or we would be bumped to death, or we would tip over. Ruby sensed our white-knuckled tension and lay on the floor with her ears back and her sad eyes peering woefully at us. Some would-be scenic encounters were passed without a look, as taking our eyes of the road could have been fatal. Even the passenger had to be on guard for malicious potholes ahead that might be missed by the driver.

Somehow, with all the obstacles to contend with, we managed to see Louisiana. Romantic, lush, haunting, liquid, primitive, erotic, and musty. We saw eerie primeval swamps and marshes, black bayous, knobby live oaks with overhanging moss, and lingering shacks on stilts above water, one-room shanties with abandoned cars poking out from waist-high grass. And garbage. Lots of garbage along the road, in people's yards, and pretty much everywhere.

Just before entering New Orleans, we played Typical Tourist again by spending a few hours at the Jean Lafitte National Historic Swamp (or something like that). We must have taken six rolls of film of various swamp ecosystems. Being from Colorado, I had never seen a swamp before this trip, and Joe had certainly seen nothing as vast as this. We walked miles and miles on boardwalks that hovered six inches above the water, overlooking endless forests of partly submerged bald cypress and other trees draped with Spanish moss. I will never forget the trip because, after hiking two miles out on a boardwalk trail, I suddenly needed to use the restroom, and I don't mean number one. There were no shortcuts, no switchbacks, no way to abridge my trip back to the public john, unless I wanted to wade with the water moccasins and gators. And I certainly wasn't going to hang my rear end over the rails. Joe teased me the entire way, but admitted he did feel sorry for me. Fortunately I made it just in time. This is one problem you don't anticipate when swamp exploring. Any other outdoor environment would have posed no problem in this sort of emergency. Something to remember.

We drove away playing "Bad Moon Rising" by Credence Clearwater Revival on our rickety boom box. We had to strain a little to hear it over Lucy's loud motor, but the spirit was there anyway.

INTERESTING ATTRACTIONS OF LOUISIANA
1) Town of Rayne: Frog capital of the United States. Murals of high, artistic merit painted on many of the town's buildings, all depicting frogs. Frog crossing signs everywhere. We saw not one live frog.
2) Evangeline Tree: Supposedly the live oak tree that inspired Longfellow's famous poem. Joe's summation of poem: "Some Cajun princess from Nova Scotia or somewhere like

that came down to Louisiana and lost her lover or
something, and turned into an oak tree, I don't know."
Thanks, Joe.

3) Mardi Gras Museum in a tiny town: a musty place
containing costumes of past Mardi Gras in that community.
Most special exhibit is a decorative costume reenactment of
the spider wedding held in the 1800s in that very town.
Joe's summation of spider story: "Some rich guy wanted a
fancy wedding for his daughter so he imported spiders from
Africa or South America or somewhere and let them go in
the trees above the wedding area to make their webs and
then lit gas lights to make them shine." (This is not correct.
The spiders were from China, and the guy let them lose in
the night so their webs would make an elaborate canopy
covered with dew for a morning wedding). Thanks,
anyway, Joe.

We got to New Orleans this evening, with only enough
time to find a place to park for the night, behind a large office
building out in the suburbs.

### February 13, 1993   Mardi Gras

Thank goodness we drove down to the French Quarter at
9:00 a.m. this morning, or we would never have found a place
to park. At that hour, the streets were empty except for a few
straggling drunks leftover from last night. We took advantage of
the morning quiet and toured the Quarter with Ruby: Marie
LaVeaux's House of Voodoo, Jackson Square, the French
antique shops on Royal, and the bars on Bourbon Street, curio
shops with vampire paraphernalia, and a few praline stores.
(We are not allowed to buy pralines but we enjoyed smelling
them). We even squeezed in a graveyard before lunch. Much
pain and gnashing of teeth occurred when we had to eat
peanut butter and jelly sandwiches in Lucy for lunch instead of
sampling even one morsel of New Orleans' cuisine.

The first of the Mardi Gras festivities began at 2:00 p.m. -
with a parade. From a pamphlet someone stuffed in my hand
while the crowd assembled, I learned that organizations, or
krews, each have a float in the parade, and that there are
parades all twelve days of Mardi Gras. We left Ruby in the
camper for this part of the day, to prevent her from being
trampled.

Joe and I acquired a prime spot across from the Pearl Street Oyster Bar. The theme of the parade must have had something to do with Hollywood horror movies. One float was a giant fly with a human head; another was a two-story Freddie Kruger. There was an immense green Frankenstein, a super-size Jason from the Friday the 13th series, and a gruesome Night of the Living Dead float, with severed limbs and all. There were many high school bands mixed in with the floats, all playing patriotic-sounding versions of horror movie themes. The floats were overflowing with drunk krew members whose sole purpose was to throw plastic Mardi Gras necklaces, drinking cups, and fake coins at the crowd. We street observers gradually stirred into a frenzy of competition for Mardi Gras souvenirs, and halfway through the festivities most people were waving, screaming (and I mean bloody murder), and snatching flying goodies from the air. The iron filigree balconies above us joined the competition and would occasionally drip Bloody Marys on heads below them, I think purposefully sometimes.

To prove how rowdy I was, my neck was covered with so many fought-for necklaces, that float-throwers would look at me and yell, "You have too many already!" And I wasn't even drunk.

The parade was long. As the end approached, we screamers had sore throats, and the marching bands looked like zombies. I leaned over the plastic fence that kept us crazies out of the street and asked one of the sweaty, haggard clarinet players how far they'd come. She replied, half-dead, that they'd marched all the way from City Park, five miles from where we were watching the parade! And they planned to go all the way back! I thought I had it bad, eating PB & Js in the camper.

The nighttime Mardi Gras celebration was nowhere near as fun as the parade. Perhaps when I was just discovering alcohol in college and didn't get hangovers so easily I would have enjoyed the scene. Everybody was sloshed. The epicenter of the party, on Bourbon Street, was jammed with loud drunks, all pushing and yelling and being gross. Gatherings of frat-boy type males would yell, "Show us your tits!" up to the balconies, where inebriated women would then oblige. Joe and I tired quickly (although I'm sure Joe could have held out for more of the boob-flashing,) and we trudged over to Jackson Square where he rubbed my sore feet while we rested on a park bench. A homeless man saw what Joe was doing and said,

"Now that's love". Then a tourist guy said, "Can I be next in line?"

We left New Orleans shortly thereafter, to put the city behind us before tomorrow morning's traffic. We are in the parking lot of a trashy grocery store only because we were too tired to look for a proper place. I am too tired to be paranoid about robbers and psychopaths in the night.

### February 16, 1993  Pensacola, Florida

Oh my God, the beaches here are absolutely unbelievable! California beaches look like a sewer in comparison! After landing in Pensacola, we played for hours today in sand as white as snow and crystal clear aqua blue water. In oil paints the color would be a mixture of cerulean blue and manganese blue. Never mind that the wind-chill factor was below zero. We buried Ruby up to her head in sand, watched her chase the sandpipers, and generally frolicked about until I thought I had frostbite. I never imagined it could feel so cold in Florida.

After we warmed up again by the propane wall heater in Lucy, we had to set up our paintings to photograph for slides. We need slides of our work to send in with show applications, and of course can't afford a photographer, so we've developed our own primitive system. Our methods must have looked mysterious to passers-by on the highway. Right off the road, we hung long pieces of black velvet over Lucy's side, sat the paintings in front of this backdrop on a chair covered with black velvet, and dug our tripod into the sand to shoot. We received some questioning stares from drivers, which made me feel like a typical, romantic, weirdo artist, something I have aspired to be for a long time.

We're now illegally parked on a pullout just over the sea grass mound from Santa Rosa Beach, huddled together under the covers for the night. Joe is telling me that writing is a lame thing to be doing right now.

### February 18, 1993  Carrabelle, Florida

Well, it has finally happened. Lucy broke down. I will start from the beginning.

We traveled along the Gulf Coast at a leisurely pace, stopping occasionally to admire the beach. Night fell, and we still kept driving, trying to make it to Perry for the night. On a narrow stretch of road right along the gulf waters, we were gazing at the moon over the sea and relaxing, when suddenly we heard a horrid sound from the back of the camper, like a jackhammer drilling into our right side. I hollered and panicked while Joe pulled over onto the sand shoulder—always a dangerous prospect for Lucy. We only sunk slightly into the sand. We rushed out with anticipation and dread to see nothing out of the ordinary. Our noses got the full story, though, and Joe explained to me that our rear bearings must have disintegrated or burned up. Jim Craig had warned us back in Joshua Tree that this might happen, and he did all he could to prevent it.

The night was lit only by the half-moon, which gave us enough light to see that civilization was nowhere nearby. Our thoughts remained surprisingly clear, and immediately we agreed that we better start hiking to find a phone. We left Ruby in the coach to protect it. We slid down a short embankment to the beach—the only place to walk except for the middle of the two-lane highway. We continued in the direction that Lucy had been going, listening to the gentle surf, and hiking through white sand lit by the dim moon. Not far ahead, we encountered the rusty and splintered remains of what appeared to be a demolished house and a few cars partly submerged in sand and beach water. Under different circumstances, the ghostly remnants would have been fun to explore, but this night it gave us the creeps. Less than 100 feet farther down the beach we came upon another pile of gnarled, nearly indistinguishable fragments of someone's ex-beach house. Shredded tires, a crumbled fireplace, the rusty twisted hull of an automobile, a corroded cement slab, splintered and mildewy wood beams. We tramped under the moonlight through five of these ominous ruined homes, all spaced with equidistance along the shore, and we became more disquieted as we passed each.

Eventually a light appeared in the distance, across the road. Our steps quickened as we headed toward the source, at once fearful and hopeful. We approached an uninteresting, light-blue house with a glaring light bulb over the door. The shades were closed, and the TV was on. "Act friendly," I reminded Joe for no reason, as if I feared he would be an asshole. The door opened and a wrinkled, long-faced man peered out into the darkness. He didn't say anything.

"Hey! Sorry to bother you, but our RV broke down about a mile from here and we need to use a phone," Joe said exuberantly.

The man paused for a moment and then replied without emotion, "You can use my phone in the garage. I'll get the key." He disappeared into the house for a few minutes, then emerged methodically and silently beckoned us to follow him.

"Is there a town near here?" Joe asked, trying to start a conversation while the man unlocked a side door of his dark, paint-peeled building.

"Carrabelle," he replied. No conversation opportunities here.

"What's with all those destroyed homes on the beach?" Joe tried again.

"Hurricane five years ago."

"So your house was OK?"

"Yep."

We entered a place spookier than any Halloween haunted house I'd toured as a child, or any place I'd ever seen, period. Our only light sources were the moon—barely piercing through the dirty windows—and the man's flashlight tossing its beam around the musty, dank room. At first, all I could make out were little pairs of reflective eyes along the walls—hundreds of them, all peering down at us. Just before horrified screams escaped my mouth, my eyes adjusted to see a massive collection of stuffed birds, all placed on shelves against the walls, from floor to ceiling. They apparently hadn't received much attention in recent years; they were covered with dust, and spider webs stretched from one to the next. The wide-planked floor creaked and was littered with rusted tools, antique paint cans, and mildewy cardboard boxes. The smell of mold and death bore into our nostrils like ammonia. I quit breathing through my mouth and tried to conceal my look of terror, in case Fright Man accidentally flicked his flashlight my way.

He led us back through several rooms, each one darker, smaller, and smellier than the last, all with dead, staring birds peering at us. Joe pinched my leg hard but I couldn't see his face. Finally we stopped in a tiny, low-ceilinged room where all the butchering and taxiderming went on. Birds still surrounded us. Fright Man bent down in the corner, mumbling something about looking for a phone, and my first desire was to grab Joe and run like hell all the way to Miami. I convinced myself he was digging up a crowbar with which to bludgeon us. We had no weapons, we couldn't possibly see our way out of this maze of deceased fowl, and our getaway car was, well, Lucy. I nearly burst into tears of relief when he pulled out a real telephone—an old one like my grandparents used—but a phone.

He phoned a towing company and with the least possible words, communicated our need for help. His flashlight sat on the table, its thin beam focusing on a single bird, its eyes half-glowing beneath a veneer of dust.

"You better git back to your car," he said after he hung up. "The tow truck'll be here in 15 minutes or so." We followed him out of the darkness, this time more curious than scared, wishing we could see the haunted place with the lights on. I still can't understand why we didn't ask a single question about bird-stuffing or who did all that work. He must have thought we were completely at home in the world's weirdest place.

"Hmmm," was the only reply we received for our goodbyes and thank yous.

Bubba, a big man with glasses, towed us easily to the garage of an ACE Hardware store in Carrabelle. His accent can best be described as Late Gomer Pyle; his dress, Early Beverly Hillbillies. I'm not making fun here—just the facts. We slept here in the ACE Garage last night and spent today asking-and-answering a million questions about Lucy. It will take three days to fix her bearings because a part has been ordered.

## February 19, 1993

Today's Events:

1) Read all morning inside Lucy, who is parked in the   garage.

2) Left Joe by himself and walked down to The World's Smallest Police Station—a phone booth with a phone as old as Fright Man's. Town residents are proud of their claim to fame, which is featured in the *Guinness Book of World Records*.

3) Kept walking, wound up at the marina. Met a cross-eyed woman with four teeth (I counted), her glasses so thick her eyes looked like floating eggs, and on her pimply chin, a light orange beard. A beard! Across her neck traced a long red scar with matching orange fur growing out of it. She was selling junk out of the back of her 30-year-old station wagon. I'm sure I was the only passer-by all day; I hope this isn't her way of making a living.

4) Came home and read some more. Joe's reading the *Ultra Van Manual*; I am reading a two-year-old *People* magazine I found in the john here.

I am scared to death about our circumstances, but try not to complain too much about it to Joe. When I do, he gets scared and we end up in a downward spiral, forecasting doom and wishing we had never been born. We're running low on money and this auto repair bill, however reasonable at $115, will just about do us in. I feel like a nutcase for ever trying to make this journey, and I hear punishing voices in my head saying, "Who do you think you are, cruising around the country like a couple of happy tourists when you don't have the means?" Other times I beat up on myself for thinking that our art will ever sell, since it hasn't so far. It keeps going like this until I become despondent and crawl into our bed area and stare. Then I get out my journal and write about being despondent and staring.

## February 20, 1993

Spent the day painting in Lucy. The lighting was not optimal inside the garage, and the mechanic's regular clanking on the rear of the vehicle would throw our paintbrushes off track, causing cussing and sometimes laughter.

We've been painting from photographs we took of Derick's in San Diego. Painting someone's house makes us focus solely, and for long periods of time, on that particular person. It's almost as if I have spent the day with Derick, and have concentrated—without meaning to—on his personality, his habits, his likes and dislikes, his mannerisms, his choices, his relationships—his whole being, I guess. I don't think that people realize that when we paint their home, we are really painting them. They also might not be comfortable about the fact that we think about them so intensely for so long. We are always surprised when we finish a painting at how much of that person we see in the work.

All the ACE hardware employees love Ruby and she loves them back.

We are headed to the Tampa area tomorrow.

## February 25, 1993   Lake Seminole State Park, FL

The end is near. We possess only $38 to our name. The Gasparilla Art Festival is two weeks away! We don't have enough food in the refrigerator to last until then, so the money will have to be spent mostly on groceries. Our gas is near empty, but we plan on remaining stationary at this nice State Park during the day, and driving to a nearby church parking lot for the nights. (This plan worked well last night). Ruby has enough food because we stopped at a garage sale on the way through Florida a few days ago and bought an old bag of stale cat food that had been ripped and taped back together. It was only fifty cents, a bargain, unless you consider the fact that Ruby hates the stuff and makes a terrific scene while eating it. She glares at us, then picks up one tiny piece of cat food with her teeth and spits it on the floor. She then moves slowly over to it and gags it down with a grimace, all the while eyeing us with a look of loathing and animosity.

Our propane is low too.

The only way to take our minds from our plight is to paint. That's what we did today from 6:00 a.m. until midnight, and unless a millionaire happens to pass by and drop a few hundred dollar bills on the ground near us, that's what we'll be doing everyday. We took a few breaks to ride our bikes along the paths of the park, through the forests of pine, vines, and palms, and by the blue lake with its *Beware of Alligators* signs every 100 yards or so. Ruby loves to run alongside our bikes no matter how fast we go. Near our parking spot there are open fields where Ruby can chase us and play Frisbee, and a water spigot across the way will be our early morning shower spot when we get desperate. Cold showers taken on a grassy surface are nothing new to us, but are never to be looked forward to with relish.

The church at which we park for the night is an active one. Meetings there last until after 11:00 p.m. There are some dedicated Christians around here.

**February 26, 1993**

Setting up our indoor studio is a pain in the butt. We must first move the bulky stack of flea market frames that are strapped to one of the front seats, so we can move the seat to face our pop-out worktable. The frames, which we eventually paint and use to frame our art, are tied with a rope to the seat for safety when driving, and must be carefully moved, one by one, to our bed. We then lay out our drop cloths and all of our art supplies and squeeze into painting position. If we want to stop for lunch, we have to clean out the area enough to fit our plates, which involves moving all of our supplies onto the dash and pushing back the drop cloths. After lunch it all goes back again. God forbid one of us might need to take a nap, in which case all the frames would have to be moved to still another place. At the end of the painting day, which is usually 9:00 for me, and midnight for Joe, the whole mess has to be tucked away in its proper place all over again. If someday I ever have a studio in my own home, I will leave my mess exactly where it is when I'm through working and enjoy it.

With all its pitfalls, our mobile studio is not bothersome to other people. The satisfaction of not taking up anyone's kitchen table or living room floor is worth the effort.

We paint constantly. We'll have a good selection for Gasparilla.

### February 27, 1993

I tried not to think about money while we painted today, but it didn't work. If we don't sell paintings at Gasparilla, we will have no choice but to find a mission for the homeless. There are no baseball cards to sell, nobody we know east of the Mississippi, no way to earn money right away. And asking family for money is not our thing. I've never been inside of a homeless shelter before. I'm sure we would fit right in because

a) we haven't had a shower in five days
b) we're getting used to making friends with perfect strangers right away
c) we truly are homeless
d) we could commiserate with all the drunks about needing a long, tall, cold one.

But this is no joke. This is frightening. The only reason I don't start cracking up (which I have before) is that Joe acts so calm about it. He says he's just as scared as I am, but keeps on painting and conversing as if we are fine. "What else can I do?" he says. Well for one, I think, you could run naked around the park screaming about little green men trying to shave your head with an ice pick.

### February 28, 1993

Paint. Getting a little sick of 18-hour paint days. Want to launch paintbrushes into the bushes.

### February 29, 1993

Painting too much isn't only hard on our hands, eyes, and backs. It's also hard on our minds because we are constantly inside the heads of other people—trying to portray their persona with our paintbrush. If that isn't difficult enough, each painting isn't just about the person who lives there. It's about middle-America in general—its hopes and secrets, its humor and its pathos. It starts to get heavy when these people hang around in your psyche from dawn to midnight. Nature hikes are essential to purge our brains of humanity.

## March 1, 1993

We got so burnt-out on painting by noon today that we decided to go spend money. We were out of food and propane, a good excuse to throw cares to the wind and relieve ourselves of 33 of our last $38. Our grocery-shopping spree didn't last long, though, and we found ourselves back in the camper painting by 1:30. Thirty-three dollars doesn't go far these days.

## March 4, 1993

We are officially insane. I am sure we could get certified somewhere, if we tried. We have $5 left to our name and guess what we spent it on? Movies. That's right, movies. We'd been painting everyday from before sunrise until long after midnight, getting extra ready for the show this weekend, and trying to forget about poverty. The night before last we finally lost our minds. We were parked at our little church, watching conservatively dressed people arrive and depart with regularity for their nightly meetings, while we begrudgingly shoved our paintbrushes around our canvases. (Everyone associated with the Church is used to us by now, but no one has waved or come over to ask us what we're doing). Finally, feverish with claustrophobia, stiff-necked, and fed up, I announced, "I'm getting out of here!"

"Where are you going?" Joe asked, weary and  sick-looking.

"Anywhere. You can sit there and paint, and I'm going to drive this rig over to that tacky shopping mall a few blocks down and see if I can find some action."

"What kind of action?"

"Anything. I'll give blowjobs for fifty cents apiece. Or maybe I could just window shop. Which one sounds better?"

"I'll pay you fifty cents..."

"OK, OK, I saw that coming. Anyway, here I go. I'm packing up my paints."

"Well, I need some action too, you know."

"Then come on. We'll think of something."

## The Freeway    145

We drove hurriedly to the mall and knew exactly what kind of action we'd be partaking in the minute we pulled up. A marquee listed six movies that were showing and below the sign, in big, lit-up letters read ALL SHOWS $1.00. We looked at each other and grinned.

Unfortunately, we had no three-hour epic sagas to choose from, so we ended up watching *Matinee*, a movie set in the Florida Keys during the Cuban Missile Crisis, in which the entire cast thought the world was coming to an end. I couldn't say whether under normal circumstances I would have liked the movie, but in our condition we soaked it up. For almost two hours we were *free!* Free of paint and Lucy and stale cat food and art shows and money problems and arguments over trivial things, and boring vegetarian food. We left the theater feeling like real people.

We rose at 5:00 a.m. today, rejuvenated and alive from our previous wild night of fun, and began painting immediately in the church parking lot. A few rays of sun later, we hurriedly drove to the park to wash in the cold water spigot before anyone would see us. No one came along until the end, when I was clothed and shampooing my hair. Some passers-by took a picture of me. Now I know how hobos and Amish people feel when others want to photograph them. They go about their lives as usual, and normal people find them fascinating and charming. I wonder what those folks were thinking: Oh look, honey, how cute! A starving artist in its natural habitat!

It's amazing what a movie and a shower will do for morale. We were sunny and content all day, not one word about money between us. Feeling better than ever, we painted until dark and returned to the church.

"So," Joe mumbled as the clock neared movie time, "We don't need all of those three dollars, do we?"

Tonight's movie pick was *Home Alone Two*, which we chose only because Tim Curry starred. The first *Home Alone* movie is on our Top 10 worst of all time, but we loved the hell out of the second one because we needed to. And Tim Curry was great, as usual.

Now we have one dollar left to our name. I can barely write the words.

**March 5, 1993**

Show this weekend. Today some old folks came over to ask questions about Lucy and our art table. But really they came to talk about themselves, like most people. After they left, Joe lost his temper.

"Me, me, me! Is that all anyone can yak about? We talk to new people all the time and does anyone know a thing about us? NO! They're too busy blabbing about themselves. Tell me if I'm wrong here when I say we have a slightly interesting life. We live in a giant marshmallow, we have a romantic career, we see and do the strangest stuff everyday, and what do people want to jack their jaws about? Their own hum-dee-dum, humdrum boring lives. Great. Your second cousin's dog groomer was an artist? You don't say? Oh! You sell corrugated cardboard for a living. Fascinating! Stellar! You saw a purple motor home once? Whoop-tee-do! One of these days I'm going to just walk away from someone like that. Just turn right around and go the other way while they're in mid-sentence. You watch, Dori. I'm going to."

"OK, honey," was all I could say.

Then, later, he went on a tirade about Ruby's hair.

"Shedding season sucks!" he yelled. "Everything we own is covered in dog hair. I've swept out ten bushels today. I found some on my toothbrush this morning and then at breakfast there was one in my oats. I washed my face and found dog hairs in my mouth afterwards from the towel. She should be bald by now."

"Are you O.K. honey? You seem a little uptight today."

"Uptight? Why would I have any reason to be uptight?" His voice escalated. "We'll be dead of starvation next week, but who's uptight about that? Not me!"

Silence.

"You're sexy when you're scared," I said quietly.

"Yeah, well..."

Silence. That was the end of the diatribes for the day.

I'm glad I'm not the only one who's nutty around here.

**March 8, 1993   FESTIVAL OVER!**

The past few days have left me in an emotional stupor. With one dollar in our possession, we pulled up to the Gasparilla Art Fair area scared out of our minds. Our gas tank registered below the empty line, our refrigerator was barren, Ruby's food ran out the night before, and even our propane was nearly gone again. My eyes felt like they were bugging out of my head and I was shaking. Joe was even quieter than usual. That morning I would burst into tears without provocation and Joe would curse about the most trifling of things. Only Ruby remained the same—playful and oblivious.

As we set up for the festival—the same circus-like routine as for the shows out West—we noticed that the art of our fellow exhibitors rated substantially higher on the talent and technical scale than in San Diego and Tempe. In fact, the competition worried us a little; the art was that skillful. We even saw several artists that attempted something approaching conceptual, which we hadn't known to exist on the outdoor festival circuit. Whether this was a good or bad thing for us, we didn't know. We'd been sick with anxiety for too long.

We sat down for the artist's meal (rice and beans, free this time) and felt out of place among these obviously seasoned festival vets who all knew each other and sat in little groups, drinking beer and telling stories about other festivals and how much money they'd made here and there. We returned to the camper and stayed up until 1:00 a.m. finishing frames and mounting hangers. I was so nervous I had to step outside Lucy regularly to catch my breath and sometimes puke.

The next morning spectators started wandering the festival at 9:00 a.m. Joe manned the booth while I lay in bed back at the camper, with a mild headache and not-so-mild nausea. I dreaded going to check on Joe, of hearing that we weren't selling anything again.

At 11:30, I knew I had to face the music. I shuffled feebly over to our booth space, still sick, my heart pounding with fear, through the great crowd of spectators, occasionally sidestepping strollers and leashed doggies. I was embarrassed that I was so fearful and was sure that everyone was whispering about how neurotic-looking I was as I passed them.

Joe practically sprinted up to me when he saw me coming, grabbed both my arms and jumped up and down whispering, "We're rich! We're rich! We're rich!"

"What the hell are you talking about?" I said, annoyed that he wouldn't just tell me what happened when I was about to pass out from nervous sickness.

"We sold four paintings already! And everyone really likes our work. I swear!"

"No sir."

"Yeah! Come look!"

I suddenly had bundles more energy than I had one minute before and bounded over to the booth with Joe.

"See! Look which ones sold! *Goldilocks, Tremors, Mayhem, and Pot o' Gold.* Can you believe it?"

"Oh my God," I moaned with relief. "We're not going to starve." I could feel every muscle in my body melt as my mind absorbed the idea of $400. "I think I need to throw up."

"Why don't you go back to Lucy and lie down. I'll be OK here today. Just make sure you take care of Ruby. And here's $5 to get yourself some lunch at one of those kiosks. Live it up, man!"

I spent the rest of the day sleeping or reclining, still sick but knowing I would be well soon. Even though my lunch, a chicken pita sandwich, was not the fanciest food of all time, it was ambrosia after weeks on a starvation budget, and best of all, I got a real live stomach-settling Coca Cola.

We sold even more paintings. We kept selling all weekend. If our paintings were a little more expensive, which several artists commented they should be, we would have made even more money.

Prizes were given out to several artists, judged by some museum curator from Cincinnati Ohio, but we didn't receive anything. The art that won prizes was big and mildly cutting edge, from a festival perspective. I watched the grand prizewinner at the award ceremony accept his $15,000 and wondered what I would feel like with that much money. I would just tinkle on the spot if they gave me a check like that. We'll probably never have that happen to us.

We felt proud to be a part of a quality festival such as this and after begging information from several festival artists, ascertained that Gasparilla is a very hard show to get into, and is one of the best in the country, especially because of the big prize money.

Monday morning after the festival, before we'd decided where to go next or what to do with our millions, we sat dreamily eating our breakfast of cold cereal (another treat after oats, oats, oats), and kept repeating over and over, "We're going to make our living from *art*. We're going to make our *living* from art. We're *going* to make our living from art. We're going to *make* our living from art. *We're* going to make our living from art," and so forth. After years of doubts and dashed hopes, we've finally realized that we can make it happen! In one weekend our lifelong yearning has been satisfied, and it couldn't possibly feel better than this. We are the luckiest people in the world!

Sometime later, after breakfast dishes were washed and put away, we constructed a plan for the next month and a half. We are scheduled to be in an art show in Gainesville, Florida in mid-April, so we'll drive there tomorrow and paint until the show.

One more thing. We smell. We still have a long way to go before other people will agree that we are the luckiest people in the world.

## March 10, 1993  Campground 30 miles south of Gainesville

Before heading to Gainesville, we opted to partake in the sun and sand for the afternoon. I can't remember the name of the beautiful Gulf beach where we played, but the weather was ideal. By evening we decided to set out, figuring we'd stay at a Wal-Mart along the way.

We were sun-worn, dirty from the beach, hungry, and growing testy, but we forged our way northward, hoping to land somewhere close to Gainesville for the night. While we drove, the skies grew darker from the combination of nightfall and the black clouds that were beginning to build up in the west. At nearly 9:00 we pulled into a rest stop where I announced I could not drive another inch. We still hadn't eaten, the weather looked more and more threatening, and we were exhausted. Joe said OK.

I stepped out briefly to use the facilities and passed, on my way to the restroom, four mangy young transients sitting on the curb near the restrooms, staring at me like a vulture. I hurriedly used the toilet, anticipating a dirty, teenage hand reaching around the door and strangling me when I exited the stall. This didn't happen but I nearly ran out to the motor home when I was through. The kids were standing now and staring at Lucy like vultures.

"Did you see those kids?" Joe asked when I climbed back into Lucy.

"Did I see them? I thought they were going to kill me."

"They're up to something. Everyone tells us to watch for suspicious characters at rest stops. Well those guys might as well wear a sign that says, 'I'm going to rob and kill you in about 15 minutes'."

"Oh my god!" I groaned. "What are we going to do? I can't keep driving! I'm half dead!"

"I promise I'll drive from here. You just sit and relax. We'll go just a little farther. We'll find the next Wal-Mart or McDonalds and stop for the night. I promise."

Joe remained, as always in crisis situations, calm and determined. I stared out the window wondering what was going to happen to us next. The wind picked up gradually; the frequent gusts jerked Lucy to the right, making it difficult for Joe to drive. I scanned the pre-exit signs for indicators of an upcoming Wal-Mart or McDonalds, each time becoming more demoralized. I didn't say much, just sighed occasionally. Finally, up ahead, we saw a yellow beacon in the distance, a shimmering sign of wonder and comfort. The Golden Arches. I screamed with melodrama, "We made it!"

We obtained a parking spot in the fluorescent glow of a streetlight in McDonalds lot and ate leftovers like starved animals. The temperature had dropped significantly, and we bundled together on Lucy's front seat under our coats. I wished so much that we could sit inside that warm, lemon-colored interior and get a fresh, hot Quarter Pounder with cheese. We're still too worried about money to splurge. Those carloads of lucky high school kids—running in and out of the restaurant shouting obscenities, all on their way south for Spring Break—don't know how good they have it.

We prepared for bed right after dinner while Ruby munched happily on her fresh, new dog food. It was beginning to rain, but we passed out in seconds, and Ruby joined us directly, curling up at our feet.

At 1:00 a.m. we were awakened by what sounded like a hurricane. Lucy was swaying back and forth in the howling wind and rain was coming down so hard on her aluminum we had to shout to hear each other. We opened the curtains facing McDonalds and saw palm trees bent over sideways in the wind, like you see on TV in footage of hurricane weather. Lightening was flashing so often it seemed as though a million photographers were taking our picture at once. The blinking did not let up for a second.

"The weather guys never said anything about this," I shouted to Joe.

"This is bad," he yelled back.

We sat up for nearly half an hour, looking worried but not knowing what action to take. Ruby curled up in the corner, wincing and shivering every time the wind would slam against Lucy. Finally, the blasts became so violent, we realized we would topple any minute if we didn't do something.

"What are we going to do?" Even my loudest shout could barely be heard.

"Let's open a window and we if we can get the wind to blow through. Then maybe we'll have a chance," Joe yelled.

We opened one tiny window in the bedroom, just one little crack. The rain, which was coming sideways with the wind, came pouring in the window as if someone had thrown a five-gallon bucket of water at us. Joe hurled the window shut again, and I rushed to get towels to soak up the mess.

"We've got to move," Joe hollered at the top of his lungs. Lucy's hull intensified the sound of rain to a deafening crescendo. I made the okey dokey sign with my fingers, unable to be heard or think of anything better. Lucy started easily and Joe, the smarty pants, drove her into a position that faced her rear to the wind. I realized the ingeniousness of his ploy after he turned off the engine. Lucy's teardrop rear end is perfectly aerodynamic, so the wind flowed right around us. We could hear the wind now, and see its effects out the window (boxes, signs, etc. flying by) but we were no longer pummeled by it.

We didn't sleep a wink all night. Our hearts raced and we clutched each other every time we heard a flying object hit the McDonalds or one of the streetlights. It is a miracle nothing hit Lucy. Joe and I have never ever been in a storm this violent before. Nothing remotely close.

By the time we were ready to move out this morning, it had passed. Temperatures have dropped at least 50 degrees, but the wind has died and the rain has stopped. Across the street from McDonald's is an RV park, and that's where we are now. We were too tired from our fitful night to move more than 20 feet. We don't care if we have to spend a whole $11. We just can't go any further.

We slept all morning and then ventured out into the almost freezing temperatures for a breath of fresh air. The first person we encountered in the rustic RV park was an elderly man who said, "You survived the storm I see."

"Yep," we said.

Soon a lady in a coat, mittens, hat, and boots approached us. "I'll bet you're glad you're here and not down south, eh?"

"What do you mean?" I asked.

"The Storm. Haven't you heard?"

"Heard what?"

"The Storm hit the Gulf from Tampa down to Fort Meyers with coastal flooding, power outages, and high-wind damage. They had to evacuate thousands of spring break tourists to inland shelters. And nearly fifty tornadoes touched down all over the state. Some of them are just north and south of here. Millions of people are without power and it's supposed to get down to 22 degrees tonight."

"Are you serious?" Joe asked.

"Yep. They're calling it The Storm of the Century."

We thanked her for her information and walked away stunned and thrilled. We couldn't wait to get to a newspaper to see more about the damage! Unfortunately, the storm kept the newspaper trucks from filling the machines, so we'll have to wait until we get to Gainesville tomorrow for the morbid details.

"We could have been in big trouble if we'd stayed south of here" I reminded Joe back in the camper, snuggled up next to the heater.

"Yeah, I'm glad we didn't stay at that rest area. Someone was really watching out for us."

"It's a good thing. We need it."

It's night now and I'm huddled under the covers, writing with one hand and holding my flashlight with the other. I didn't believe that lady when she said it could get down to 22 degrees in Florida. It can.

**March 17, 1993　Gainesville, Florida**

As more stories about the Storm of the Century have been reported, we are more amazed that we survived intact. During the past week, we have read articles in the newspapers about homes, cars, boats, and especially RVs that were destroyed all over the state—from coastal flooding, high winds, and tornadoes. One hundred and fifty people were killed in various gruesome scenarios; some froze to death during the week-long power outage. Scientists reported that lightening struck 59,000 times in one night, some sort of record. Just after the storm, on the front cover of one Florida newspaper, was a picture of the beach where we'd played on the day the storm hit, being enveloped by a giant wave nearly as high as the condominium it was ready to destroy. On our way north on I-75 to Gainesville we drove by at least ten different areas that had been flattened by tornadoes. Trees and houses were splintered to pieces or uprooted; road signs and billboards were twisted and mangled. There were many places in Florida we could have been that stormy night where we'd have lost a lot more than a night's sleep.

Our first mission after arriving in Gainesville was to find a home for a month. We toured the typical college town, with its abundance of trees, pizza restaurants, and rude drivers, to look for an RV or trailer park that would: a) be cheap, b) allow pets, and c) be close enough to town so that we could ride our bikes everywhere and not spend money on gas. (We discovered upon arrival that we can't find the keys to our bike locks and have been trying to concoct a way to break that unbreakable Kryptonite). This list of requirements left us one choice: a place called RV PARK, according to the peeling, vine-covered sign out front.

We entered the park from a four-lane parkway via a skinny dirt road littered with knee-deep potholes and swallowed up by trees. Our suspension was tested to its limits on the crater-size ruts, and we did a number on our paint job on the claw-like branches that scraped Lucy's sides. At the end of this gauntlet, the park opened up into a clearing in the dense forest where a motley arrangement of decrepit RVs and makeshift homes were parked satisfactorily apart from each other. It's creepy, but perfect. It's quiet, Ruby-friendly, profoundly cheap, and best of all, there's an alligator pond on one side. We can look out any of Lucy's clean windows and see nothing but palms, live oaks, or pine trees hung with Spanish moss and vines. The sun never really penetrates here; only a few speckles of light make their way into the interior of our nature enclave, which will keep us cool if it decides to get hot soon.

Our next mission: jobs. Our precious money will not last us until the Gainesville show, thanks to those lousy student loan payments we have to make. (The bankruptcy couldn't relieve those debts because they are government loans.) Hours after setting up our new residence—which entailed plugging us into an electrical outlet, hooking up a water hose to our pump, and inserting our holding tank tube into their septic tank—we walked down to Wal-Mart a half a mile from here and surveyed the classifieds. Our first idea was to become "traffic coordinators for a major automotive event" (in other words: "parking lot scum for the drag races"). We applied that very day, requiring us to unhook Lucy all over again and drive out to the Gatornationals speedway. We then cruised over to the Gainesville Hilton where we applied as night waitpersons. This evening, we called both places from a pay phone and were told, "You're both hired." We chose the Hilton because it pays more, and it's within walking distance. We start working tomorrow.

So far Gainesville seems like a wonderful place. It offers a smidgen of culture due to the large university; the abundance of trees makes it picturesque; it's a reasonable size; it's affordable; and it hasn't been overrun with pretentiousness like Colorado has.

SIDE NOTE: I was just looking through my journals of days-gone-by and came upon a laughable side note that I'd written in the margins:

> *Joseph is my husband. I allow him to read my writings. I extremely resent, let me say here, his paltry, ridiculous criticisms of my profound and meaningful words. He is a speck. I am a genius of the highest caliber. Of course, we all know that if he would take the time to apply himself to his own writings, he too would ascend to greatness and therefore stop his jealous critiques that stab me like a butcher knife.*

**March 18, 1993**

It's beyond fantastic that we can make a living from our art. Joe and I keep grinning at each other twice an hour, and we both know what it's about. The question is—now that we've settled down a bit—can we do this outdoor festival thing well? What are the possibilities? Could we really make over $2,000 a show? And if so, could we eventually afford a real life with a home and car and lawnmower? Imagine a baby to go with it all! Really, the home thing is a little too dreamy to entertain. But it would be amazing to get good at this festival business and be able to bring in some generous cash.

Should I feel guilty for wanting more instead of being overjoyed that we didn't end up at the homeless shelter?

**March 19, 1993**

We went next door to the Suburban Propane/Sprint Mini Store today to fill up on propane. The price of propane here is outrageous! Joe, of course, had to notify the counter lady of this fact, to which she replied, "We've been charging that price for two years." As Joe walked out the door he answered, "Yeah, and it's still twice as much as the whole rest of the country charges. I guess two years ago you really screwed people."

**March 20, 1993**

Working a job is hell so we bought a lottery ticket. The pot is $88 million, and hoards of people are lining up for this week's tickets, because $88 million is so much better than last week's measly $77 million. With our money we will buy a ruby-studded collar for Ruby, some new paintbrushes for me, and a less smelly pair of sneakers for Joe and a timing light for the Ultra Van. I wrote a poem in honor of my new gambling spree.

The Lottery

The passage through life makes me drowsy
I falter and strain, my posture lousy.
Hope's departure has desecrated my spirit,
I've taken misery's shackle, and I must wear it.
But the Florida Lottery affords strong chance
To whip poverty's butt without even a lance.
When Joe my husband sees this poem
He'll demand a request that I'll surely owe 'im,
To never attempt at poetry again
And I will cry but then I'll refrain,
But deep in my heart a true poet lurks,
As sure as our Lottery win, I'll create great works.

**March 21, 1993**

We didn't win the lottery. Probably some rich people did. I have to rise at 4:00 in the morning to wait tables and walk a mile and a half to that godforsaken place that's run like a hot dog stand instead of a Hilton.

Yesterday, as I gathered my things at the Hilton after my shift of drudgery, the manager, Mark, asked how I was getting home without a car. When I answered that I was walking, he said, "Not without this!" and handed me a steak knife. "Gainesville is the serial killer capital of the United States. Ted Bundy was here. Last year the police found body parts in the Steak n' Shake freezer just three doors down from here. You carry that knife like this, see? And if anyone comes along, AARRRGGHHH! Right in the gut. OK?"

**March 22, 1993**

I quit. My third shift at that place and I quit. The asshole manager scheduled four brand-new waitresses for a morning breakfast shift with no one to train us and no manager on duty. We stood around like idiots, trying to help customers with no knowledge of the workings of the restaurant whatsoever. I walked out in the middle of my shift, something I have never done in all my 15 years of jobs. What will I do for money now?

At least Joe still has his job. For now.

**March 25, 1993**

Joe's off working at the Hell-ton Hotel while I look through the want ads again. My search has produced two most delightful opportunities: 1) Get paid to have my private parts experimented on by college students or 2) Give blood. Tomorrow, Joe and I will go in for our first blood donation (it's plasma, actually, whatever that is).

While I paint for the upcoming show, I look out upon the homes of our neighbors, who could all be generously described as candidates for the Island of Misfit Boys. Some would say they are white trash. But I think these people probably wish they were white trash. They are all strange, eccentric loners—not necessarily poor and definitely not of this world.

OUR NEIGHBORS:
1) A deaf man who lives in an abandoned orange Greyhound Bus. He stays inside most of the time but occasionally has visitors who, instead of fruitlessly knocking to announce themselves, must rock the bus back and forth to get the guy's attention.

2) Living in a moldy, putrid, once-silver 50s trailer is Zanzibar, the skinniest, scariest-looking man alive. His dark eyes sink way back into his wrinkly head, and every line of every muscle on his arms shows through his gray, saggy skin. He has wild, black curly hair and wears practically shredded clothing. But he's nice, believe it or not, and is always offering us food, which we politely decline. His three year-old son Pierre comes to visit him every other day, and Zanzibar spends the whole day scurrying through the RV park looking for him because Pierre always hides. I'd hide, too.

3) David is a 30-something nurse who lives under a U-shaped piece of corrugated tin. He has a door, but no windows. Every night he turns on his Christmas lights, which are strung neatly around his area from palm tree to palm tree. He keeps his sight tidy and has a graveled driveway on which to park his van. He keeps an orderly little garden and feeds the resident birds every day. Once he asked us to smoke some weed with him, but we declined in favor of pumping him for information about his weird home. He told us that he used to live under a big tarp suspended over a collection of refrigerator boxes, but the park owners asked him to build something more permanent.

4) Gary. A man in his forties. Lives in an itty-bitty camper with thirteen cats. Enough said.

5) In a skuzzy trailer lives Bob, another nurse. (There are lots of hospitals in Gainesville). He has a miniature grass-covered yard bejeweled with all sorts of lawn ornaments. In the midst of his plastic yard paraphernalia he leaves his minuscule dog, Blondie, tied up all day while he works at the nearby mental hospital. Blondie stands on her petite hind legs and howls all day long. When we first moved here, we thought her wails to be the mating call of a tropical bird. The next day we changed our guess to a maniacal human scream. Days later we laughed uncontrollably when we found the perpetrator of the savage cries to be a mangy, bug-eyed, yellow critter, small enough to fit in the palm of my hand.

6.) Betsy is a super sweet woman in her 60s who has been waiting tables at the Holiday Inn for 30 years. Her husband/boyfriend/partner hides in their ugly little 60s trailer and drinks out of a paper bag *all day long*. He's been rushed to the hospital in an ambulance twice now with delirium tremens. He returns home after a few days, and resumes his vigil at the window, nursing his paper bag again. One time Joe took pictures of the paramedics hauling him away. Betsy didn't like that one bit.

7) Betsy's nephew lives a few campers away. The only time we see him is when the cops come to bust him for drugs.

## March 26, 1993

We broke our bike locks with a car jack, an evil lesson Joe learned from Mark, the Hilton manager. Joe still works there and hates it, but we need the money. Mark tried begging me to come back, apologizing for his lame scheduling, but I declined, as I can easily make more money donating plasma. At least I thought I could until today.

We rode our bikes through the attractive University of Florida campus to a little clinic on the other side. We were told we could make $20 a session and could both donate twice a week. *That's $80 a week!!* We can get by on that, provided that we eat little, don't drive Lucy, and stay away from the movie theater.

Well, everything went fine with our interview. Have you slept with any homosexual males lately? No. Have you used any intravenous drugs in the past year? No. Had any blood transfusions? No. Great, you're in. I wish all job interviews had easy questions like these. Then a nice man, appropriately named Drew, drew our blood. Here's where I came up short. They declined my blood. Drew told me that my iron count was too low to qualify, that I was anemic. I feel like such a loser! I can't even get a job that entails lying on a cot for forty minutes. My husband supports us with his job at the Hilton and has good blood. Drew told me not to worry, though. If I take iron caps and eat lots of raisins I will probably qualify next time.

We're back at the camp now, weighing the pros and cons of buying iron tabs. It's a risky venture, throwing away a perfectly good $5 in the hopes that it will help me make more money in the future. Oh, wait—news flash—it looks like Joe has made the decision. He's insisting I buy them no matter what, since I'm anemic. Well, that's over with. Let's go spend money.

## March 29, 1993

Joe and I are now a few pints of plasma lighter but forty whole dollars richer. I passed my iron exam this time, barely, and we were both allowed to give. First, we sat in a waiting room and watched All Star Wrestling on the overhead TV with fellow plasma donors. The group consisted of two types of people—college students and street people. I don't know which we qualify as, but I hate to admit we're probably closer to being the latter.

We were soon ushered together into a large commons area packed with hospital beds, each hooked up with tubes and bags of colored liquids and blinking lights and gauges and needles and arm bands. My nurse (we each had one) explained how our plasma wouldn't be used for ten years, just to make sure it was AIDS-free, and how we'd feel a strange taste in our mouths, like a peppermint patty, caused by the additive that runs through our veins during the process. The machine somehow takes our blood, whips it around a centrifuge to remove all the red blood cells, and replaces it, minus the plasma—a thick, urine-colored substance. The process would take from twenty to forty minutes, depending on how much water we drank the night before. The more dehydrated one is, the slower and more painful the suck procedure can be. Don't ever, we were told, drink alcohol the night before giving. Several of the regular donors are gutter drunks and have a miserable time on the machine because they are constantly dehydrated.

My water content must be fine because my procedure took the minimum time. Joe's too. It hurt, a little, but was the easiest money I've ever made. Lie down, read People magazine, watch TV, and be treated with kindness and respect by pretty nurses. My only complaint is that I am worried about having a drug addict's needle trail up my arm, by the time we're through. Joe's only complaint is that the peppermint patty liquid made his mouth feel like a dead man's.

SPECIAL NOTE

Gainesville is a dangerous place for bicyclists. Car drivers here are psychopathic. Every venture out onto the mean streets is a flirtation with death. We have nearly been killed several times by speeding, oblivious, rude, and mostly crazy drivers. I've never seen anything like it.

**March 31,1993**

Joe works at the Hilton only two nights a week now. The
management keeps switching the schedule around without
warning and Joe ends up with two shifts. I told him he doesn't
have to work, that our blood will get us through, but he says
the extra money won't hurt and although he despises the place,
he can put up with it. I have to respect him for that.

Mostly we just paint.

Zanzibar, the scary-looking nice guy, came over to see our
artwork today and introduced us to his Indian friend, Gopal.
While Zanzibar was very friendly and complimentary about our
artwork, Gopal was an asshole. He is in town for the
Gainesville art festival, too, and he wouldn't say a word about
our paintings. He did, however, manage to get in plenty of
words about how much he hates Americans, how Americans
are only interested in money, how tacky Americans are, and
how Americans are so stupid and uneducated. After he left, we
secretly changed his name to "Goatballs." Zanzibar returned
later to apologize for his friend's rude behavior and told us that
Goatballs is one of the greediest people he knows. He will do
anything for money, Zanzibar reported, even screw his friends.
Zanzibar should know, because Goatballs stole some of his
new jewelry designs and claimed them as his own. When
Zanzibar confronted him, Goatballs replied, "That's business".

They could make a soap opera about our trailer park called
*Days of Our Lowlifes.*

**April 3, 1993**

It's my sister Debi's birthday. I am so thrilled to be able to
send her a present. I bought her a 39-cent muslin bunny at
Wal-Mart and mailed it in a little envelope. Knowing Debi, she
will love and appreciate it and probably keep it forever.

**April 5, 1993**

HERE'S WHAT'S HAPPENING:

1) Plasma donations going well. A remarkable way to make a
   living.
2) Hilton Hotel job a joke for Joe. Managers don't care about
   any of the important inner-workings of restaurant service
   but reprimand the wait staff if they don't use the word
   "sumptuous" when describing the food to patrons.
3) Ruby's happy to be settled in one place. Betsy told us to
   keep Ruby inside at night so the alligators don't eat her.

One night, a year ago, the gators crawled out of the pond and ate two poodles off their leashes. So far they've left Ruby alone.

4) Art making is progressing swimmingly. Back in my conceptual art days I never would have dreamed that painting could be so fulfilling all by itself, without cunning, up-to-the-minute ideas behind it to shock the art world. It's just gratifying to get lost in paint.

5) We're not so sure we like Gainesville anymore. The drivers are consistently bloodthirsty. And there's something else, an unnamable creepiness about it. Maybe that's why the serial killers like it here.

**April 7, 1993**

Joe almost died today. A wicked Gainesville driver finally accomplished the ultimate Gainesville goal—to hit and injure an innocent bicyclist. Every day that Joe goes out on his bicycle, I worry and wait to get that fateful phone call from a hospital emergency room. At 2:00 p.m., I was outside painting under our EZ-Up canopy when Joe sauntered up with his bicycle over one shoulder. "I got hit," he uttered, out of breath. His bike was a twisted wreck, and one of his legs was covered with blood.

"Oh my God, are you OK?"

"I guess. My leg's scraped up pretty bad. Some fucking idiot came flying out of a parking lot in his big van without looking or stopping. He slammed on his brakes at the last minute, but he still hit me and I went flying out into the street. Thank God there weren't any other drivers coming or I'd have been squished like a melon."

"Did somebody call the cops?"

"Yeah," he said wearily. "They didn't care much. The asshole didn't even get a ticket. I just took his insurance information. Hopefully I'll be able to get a new bike."

"Yeah, but how long will that take?"

"I don't know but this sure sucks. We need our bikes everyday."

"I hate Gainesville," I stated.

**April 8, 1993**

Joe called the guy's insurance company yesterday and found out that all the information he gave us was phony. We must have our bikes to get over to the plasma center, so Joe spent hours trying to untwist his bike. It runs now, but the front end wobbles. Now, when out riding our bikes, our middle fingers automatically spring up as a reflex to any drivers in our vicinity. Since almost all Gainesville drivers are born-killers, flipping off everyone seems reasonable. I don't know how we missed it before, but we've suddenly been noticing that there are posters all over town condemning Gainesville drivers and their disregard for bicyclists. One poster tells the story of a typical driver who swerved and killed one of the University of Florida champion bicyclists. He had no excuse for his crime and was only given a $500 fine! Other posters call for legislation and awareness of the issue; if I lived here, I'd join in, but I would *never* want to live here. I hate this place.

## April 9, 1993

Joe had a good story to tell about his plasma suck experience for the day.

Sean was his nurse. While Sean was poking Joe's arm and hooking him up to the machine, an old fellow in a fluorescent orange hunter's cap waved his free arm frantically from across the room. "Sean! Sean! Over here!" Sean excused himself, walked over to the old man, administered to the guy's seemingly desperate needs, and returned to Joe, shaking his head.

"What's wrong with him?" Joe asked.

"Oh, that's just Harold." Sean said.

"Is he one of Gainesville's loonies?"

"Yeah. He's always calling me over there for something. Most of the time I'll be walking by and he'll go 'Pssst. Hey Sean. Come over here. I've got something to show you,' in this secretive crazy man's voice. I'll go over and he'll open up his magazine like it's something he only wants me to see. And you know what it'll be?"

"Naked ladies?"

"No. Food. He's always showing me these full-page spreads of fancy meals and gourmet banquets. 'Hey Sean, look at this. Doesn't that look good? Mmmmmmmmmmmmm'."

Joe finished his story adding that, in a few months, we'll probably be staring at the centerfold of *Gourmet Magazine* with lustful eyes, too.

**April 10, 1993**

Joe quit the Hilton. Got sick of it like I did.

**April 11, 1993**

We've had to stop working on the same painting at the same time. Lately we've been choosing smaller canvases, and if we try to work on the same piece simultaneously, our brushes will clank together. So now I'll start a painting and Joe will finish it, or the other way around. We discuss color, composition, and choice of object placement as we go. I think it's pretty obvious why we are working on smaller canvases. We just plain don't have the room.

Most people that comment on our collaboration say that they could never work that closely with their spouse. Zanzibar asked us today, "Do you fight over art?" We usually don't, but we have developed a good rule in case we do disagree. Whoever started the painting gets final say. It works! No arguments can build when one person knows they can't win. But quarrels rarely happen anyway. Collaborating seems to be our thing.

**April 13, 1993**

It hasn't been often in our travels that we've run across bad people. Brent and Page Fox of Marina Del Rey, California are two. This afternoon we met another. His name is Ralph Farnsworth, nicknamed "Farney", and he lives in a cheap, nondescript house on the road to campus from our trailer park. We've seen the old guy working outside on his numerous old vehicles, and a few times Joe has stopped to converse with him about the mechanical aspects of owning a pre-1975 vehicle. I watch and smile. Joe has mentioned before that Farney is a pompous know-it-all, but we haven't many friends, and any extra knowledge we can acquire that might help Lucy run well is worth putting up with a few idiosyncrasies. Farney's suggestions have so far helped us correct a windshield wiper problem at least.

This afternoon, as we rode by his place on our bicycles, Farney poked his old head out of the engine of a not-so-cherry 1966 Mustang and waved.

"Do you want to stop?" Joe asked.

"Sure," I said. We were on our way to the natural foods store and, as always, had no schedule. We pulled into his half-grass/half-dirt yard with our warmest greetings.

"How are you, Farney?" Joe asked.

"Not great," he grumbled.

"What's wrong?"

"What's right? I've got more ailments than I can count. You see me out here working on these cars all the time. This isn't easy for me, you know. I haven't got long to live."

"Really?" I asked, concerned. He'd never mentioned his health problems before.

"Oh yeah, you have no idea. You come on inside." Neither of us had ever entered his house, and we weren't sure if we wanted to. For lack of a good reason to decline, we reluctantly consented.

He opened the screen door, unlocked the main door, and let us in to the dark, air-conditioned interior. The decor was brown and orange, all '70s. The curtains were drawn. I expected to smell that over-cooked green bean and bacon smell of this sort of home, but instead was met with a fresh-scrubbed Pine Sol odor mixed with fresh baked something.

I nearly jumped when an old woman stepped out of the kitchen. Was she here in the dark all the time? Why was the outside door locked?

"You're just in time for cookies," she said. "My name is Grace. I'm Farney's wife."

"Nice to meet you," we said as we shook hands. She seemed like a sweetie.

"Sit down and watch television while I get my stuff out," Farney said. Grace went to the kitchen and brought out a plate of chocolate chip cookies. *Days of Our Lives* was on, but not loud enough to hear.

"Farney says you have an old vehicle," Grace said as she sat down in one of the brown vinyl La-Z-Boys opposite us. "You know, the government is trying to pass a law that outlaws all vehicles made before 1980. For the environment, I guess."

"That would be bad for us," I said.

"Yes, it's unconstitutional, don't you thi..." She stopped mid-sentence when Farney walked in the room with his shirt off (YUCK), dragging an oxygen tank. He sank down in his La-Z-Boy and stuck two tubes into his nose, to connect himself with his tank. His pasty, hairy, blubbery belly had a long, red, protruding scar running from his neck down to his belly button.

Little white circles were pasted all over his chest, with wires growing out of them, hooking him to the contraption on his oxygen tank cart. Before I could start feeling sorry for him, he opened his mouth.

"You kids shouldn't own an older vehicle. You haven't earned the right." This came out of nowhere.

"What?" Joe asked.

"I worked my whole life so I could retire and then have the luxury to tinker around and travel a little. I get to tinker, but traveling is too hard now. I worked with chemicals for 30 years and look what it did to me. Now I can't even enjoy my retirement. You kids think you can just run away from life, jump in an old van, and live off the land. Then you come around here expecting an old man to give you advice and help you out, so you can have the advantages I never got."

"Farney, stop it," Grace cut in, clearly upset. "Don't listen to him, kids. He just gets riled up sometimes."

"Hush up Grace. They need someone to tell them. They're just lucky they have me being honest and not someone down the road less understanding. You aren't going to find people everywhere who are willing to help out a couple of kids who have nothing to give in return."

"Are you saying we're freeloaders? All you're giving us is advice," Joe said, angered. I was on the verge of tears.

"Time is money. Advice is costly. I worked for fifty years to get my knowledge. You said freeloaders, I didn't. But if that's the word you like, OK."

"Farney!" Grace cried

"You know it's true, Grace," he barked, getting louder now. I started crying. I was afraid to leave, but I don't know why. He couldn't exactly chase us.

"You're making her cry," Grace pleaded.

"It'll do her good."

"We'll be leaving now," Joe said, getting up. His face was red and I could tell he was ready to blow. I think he felt some debt to Farney for his motorhead advice or he would have strangled the guy by now.

"Now, now, hold on a minute. If you can't take a little constructive criticism. Looky here. This is what I brought you in here to show you. This is my payback for all the years I worked with chemicals. Hooked up to all these gadgets. But I should show you something really interesting. Watch this." As I

dried my tears, still horrified, and Joe sat reluctantly back
down, seething, Farney pulled up the leg of his pants. As if he
wasn't naked enough already.

"Oh, Farney," Grace grimaced. "Don't pull that thing..."

"Hush up, Grace. Now look at this," he said, pointing to his
lower leg, a bloated, deformed, white mass with blue veins
making termite-like trails all over it.

"Oh, boy," I moaned, ready to puke.

"That's right, oh boy. These are what you call varicose
veins. You ever heard of those? This is just like the elephant
man. It hurts me every day, all day long. Sometimes I have to
go lay down in the middle of the day, it hurts so bad." He went
on to tell about how he got each of his health problems and
how long he'd been suffering, the details of which I was too
stunned to pay attention to, after our ass-kicking. I sat staring,
feeling like a loser, a freeloader, a good-for-nothing. Maybe we
should just get real jobs and quit bothering people all over the
place. We don't deserve to live this way, I thought. Joe was
quietly sitting next to me, waiting for a break in the lecture to
duck out the door.

"We've got to get going," he said, when Farney stopped to
breathe. All worked up from his sermon, sweat was rolling
down his bluish face. "Thanks a lot for the cookies, Grace." We
started for the door, praying that the old fart didn't start up
again.

"Just stop by anytime," he said from his mechanical rodent
trap. "Enjoyed having you."

"Don't you listen to him," Grace whispered as she escorted
us out the door. "He just gets worked up sometimes. He
doesn't mean it. He's a good man."

"Thanks again for the cookies, Grace," I said.

We hopped on our bikes, in a daze. Somehow I expected
the world to be different when we came out of that hole. But
the sun was still bright and people were driving their cars like
maniacs, being normal.

"What a psychotic asshole," Joe said as we drove away. We
pedaled quietly for a bit.

"Do you think he's right? Are we freeloaders?"

"Maybe. But who the hell is he? We really need to be
listening to a disgusting blowfish like him."

I started crying again and pulled into an empty campus
parking lot out of sight from Farney's dreaded place.

"I feel terrible. Like I did when I was a kid."

# The Freeway **167**

"Don't let it get to you, honey. He's wacky. He's the biggest fucking asshole you'll ever meet in your life. It's not us."

"Are you sure? We are freeloaders, you know."

"So what. At least we're nice people. Even if we don't have money to give back to people, we're appreciative and respectful. We don't run around shitting on people who help us out".

"Yeah, I guess. I just wish we could be rich and famous right now so we could pay back everyone who's helped us out."

"Maybe the people who help us out feel good about it without getting anything in return. Remember those cross-country bicyclists that stayed with your family in Steamboat for a few days when you were in high school? Did they pay you anything?"

"No."

"Do you resent them?"

"Hell, no. It was the funnest thing to happen to our family in years."

"Did they eat your food?"

"Yeah."

"Did they spend the night?"

"Two."

"Were they freeloaders?"

"God, no. They brought a little adventure to our lives."

"Do I need to go on?"

"No. I just hope the people we impose on feel the same way."

"Some won't. Look at Farney. Can't win them all, right?"

"Right. You're right. Yeah. Thanks, honey. Let's go get some snacks."

"Thanks for crying."

"Why?"

"Because I felt the same way you do. I just talked myself out of it."

"Let's change his name to Farty."

"Good call."

We made jokes all the way to the store and all the way home about Farty's hideous monster leg and his gross house and his whiny health complaints. What a gargoyle.

(Why are my stories about my enemies ten times longer than the ones about good people)?

**April 14, 1993**

   Is it ever hot.

TODAY'S SCHEDULE:

| | |
|---|---|
| 6:30 a.m. | Arise and argue about how to cook French toast. |
| 7:30 a.m. | Tie up Ruby and depart on bicycles. |
| 7:35 a.m. | Stop to tickle Blondie and say hello to Gary, who's off work today. |
| 8:00 a.m. | Have blood sucked at plasma center. Someone yelled at the nurse when she turned off All-Star Wrestling. |
| 9:00 a.m. | Take perilous trip to grocery store. Dodge and flip-off reprehensible drivers. |
| 10:30 a.m. | Return to camp, fall asleep. |
| 12:00 p.m. | Eat leftovers and stare. (Still recovering from yesterday's incident with Farty). |
| 1:00 p.m. | Install door bug screen (another Vaughn Gizmo) and admire its artfulness and utility. |
| 3:00 p.m. | Begin working outdoors on ingenious masterpieces, pondering their influence on Western Civilization. |
| 5:30 p.m. | Devour delectable salad, listening to Bob Dylan. |
| 6:00 p.m. | More painting, lots of bug slapping. |
| 7:00 p.m. | Reluctantly show artwork to snoopy neighbors. Betsy's quote: "I really like them, but why don't you put a little kitty curled up on the couch?" |
| 7:30 p.m. | Swat bugs and clip fingernails. |
| 8:30 p.m. | Paint more, still outside, Dori covered with bug bites. |
| 11:30 p.m. | Clean brushes, plow through carnivorous insect mob, and retire. |
| 1:00 a.m. | Dori finally drifts off after husband takes a long LOUD shower. |

**April 17, 1993**

   Goatballs came by today. What a butt wipe. We told him that we'd been accepted into the Ann Arbor Street Art Fair in Michigan this summer; our notification just arrived this morning in the mail. "What?" he said. "You got into Ann Arbor? Did you hear that, Zanzibar? They got into Ann Arbor. Dave Perry can't even get into Ann Arbor." He looked at our paintings up close and continued, "Well, I guess I don't know much about painting. Anyway, you better get to work. Your whole booth

will be bought out on the first day. You can make ten or
twenty thousand dollars there."

We're not sure we believe him, about the money, but his
remarks are a good indication that we did well to be accepted.
Ten or twenty thousand! Sure!

## April 18, 1993

For a change of pace, I took a few hours to peruse books at
the university library. Curled up in a cubbyhole in the far
reaches of the fiction section, I enjoyed the poetry of William
Carlos Williams and the imagery of People magazine. The best
reading, though, I found carved into the wooden cubicle
separator:

1)  Visualize the Hippies Starving to Death
2)  (Next to a confederate flag): Burn Baby Burn!
3)  I love Black People
4)  Lee mighta surrendered but I never will! (And it's
responses):

> a) Will never surrender what?  Your truck? Your chew?
> Your hound dog?
> b) That was 100 years ago you ignorant backwards
> redneck fuck.

## April 19, 1993

My last day at the plasma center, a fiasco, at least brought
in enough money to propel us, alive and breathing, to the
Gainesville show this weekend. As Joe and I rode our bicycles
down to the plasma center, we looked forward to our last day
of donating with pleasure.

"Let's get you hooked up in a hurry," a gruff nurse said as
she led me to my machine. "We've got a lot of people today."

Never had a nurse been even slightly curt with me before,
so I was taken aback. When she stopped at the machine that
would be sucking my blood today, I froze. Just the week
before, I had watched from my nearby plasma bed while a
young black man moaned in agony from this very machine,
which kept beeping and seemed to be malfunctioning. His
nurse tried everything to remedy the situation, repeating,
"There's too much pressure" as the poor guy tried to conceal
his pain and maintain his composure. After 15 minutes of
button pushing and pouch squishing, the nurse pulled him off
the needle, apologized, and let him go.

"I don't want that machine," I said to my nurse. "It was broken last week and I saw it hurting someone".

"There's nothing wrong with that machine," she barked. "We service these things every week. It's probably not even the same one."

I knew it was, but succumbed to her meanness. "OK."

As she searched for a vein in which to plunge her needle, she looked puzzled and asked, "Who ever told you you could give plasma?"

"I do it all the time."

"Well you shouldn't. Your veins are too small. I'm surprised anyone ever got a needle in you before."

She did find a vein in a jerky and rough manner, while I cringed. From the beginning of the suck process I could tell something wasn't right. My arm started hurting right away—a dull pulsing pressure at first, increasing to a throbbing pain, as if my arm were going to explode. Panicking, I waved at my nurse, who was administering to one of my fellow victim/donors.

"Just a minute," she yelled impatiently. The pain continued, increasing slowly. I waved again.

"Please help me," I pleaded from across the room.

"I can't just leave at the drop of a hat," she said. Eventually she came over, in no hurry that I could see.

"What's the problem?" she asked without emotion.

"It hurts my arm. It feels like pressure," I said.

"That's not supposed to happen. I don't see anything wrong with the machine." She treated me as if I were lying. She massaged my arm, pushed buttons on the machine, and, to my horror, smacked the machine with the palm of her hand like it was a pop machine that wouldn't give her a Coke.

"Does that help?" she asked.

"A little, I guess."

She went back to her other patients. It didn't take long before my arm flared up again, worse this time. Tears erupted over my face. I called to her in a crybaby voice, "It hurts." Again she slowly finished up with her other people and walked over absently. "It hurts," I said again, my face wet by this time.

"I'll try to get you off, but I can't until the pressure goes down," she said, a little more concerned. Using the coke machine method and repeatedly spouting, "What's wrong with this thing," she seemed to be making progress. My arm pain decreased little, but I sat quietly, my tears slowing at the prospect of freedom.

"Sometimes people pretend they're hurt so they can get out of here without giving and still get their money," she explained, supposedly to make up for her rudeness. "You don't seem to be faking it."

"No ma'am," a previously unnoticed African American man piped in. He was huge and tough looking, like a bodyguard. He was propped up on the bed next to me, apparently watching the whole scenario.

When the needle was finally taken from my arm, I breathed a sigh, and the black man leaned over to touch the nurse's arm and said, misty-eyed, "The whole time she was over there dying, I was dying right along with her." He winked at me and smiled tenderly.

I never told anyone at the front desk about the faulty machine; I guess I forgot to blame someone in all the commotion.

NOTE: The very first day we gave, the nurse told Joe what big beautiful veins he had—that he was the ideal plasma-giving specimen.

## April 22, 1992   Gainesville show over

We can make it to Birmingham. Next weekend we have a show there—recently decided upon because it's free and it's on our way up to the Midwest, where the summer shows are. We can also buy a timing light for Lucy. Six hundred dollars is hardly a killing but I feel like a prosperous businessperson.

The festival art selection at Gainesville paled compared to Gasparilla's high quality extravaganza, and the buying public consisted mostly of college students and just-lookers. Our artist neighbors were of more interest than the crowd.

The woman across from us must have made double our yearly income at this show alone. She sold watercolors of baby blocks and teddy bears in soft pastel colors to everybody on Earth, it seemed. Eager Moms waited in line for up to 20 minutes to buy her sappy, Kmart-ish pictures. (I will surely burn in Hell for making fun of other people's art). Her assistant, a younger guy, came over to our booth for a break, complaining that they never stopped selling all day and that instead of paying him a commission the artist lady offered only minimum wage. I didn't feel too sorry for him after the way we've made money the past month.

The artist to our left was a friendly Peruvian woman with little command of the English language. Her paintings were large and abstract—a watered down, doctor's office version of Willem de Kooning with a touch of Helen Frankenthaler. Her sales were minimal so she had plenty of time to converse with us, mostly about the difference between Americans and South Americans. To sum up her comments: Americans are pretty tacky, excluding me and Joe, of course. Later, as we broke down our booths, she asked, "What does it mean when something sucks? Is that good?"

"Why?" I laughed.

"A man came to me and said 'This show sucks'. Is that good?"

"No," I told her. "That's very bad. He hated the show."

"OK, yes. I understand. This show sucks. That is true," she stated solemnly.

### April 24, 1992   Oak Mountain State Park, Birmingham, Alabama

1) Lucy made the trip. People gawked and whistled and laughed and pointed and saluted her all the way.
2) We will set up for the Magic City Art Connection tomorrow.
3) We're worried about going into Birmingham. The only thing we've heard about this place is that racism was big in the 60s. Will there be police swinging billy clubs and young African American men with crowbars on every corner?
4) We saw a big red billboard just south of here. A horned devil with a pitchfork and a long arrow for a tail warned, *Go to church or the Devil will get you.*

### April 30, 1993   Wal-Mart Parking Lot, Birmingham, Alabama

We have been pleasantly surprised with Birmingham, Alabama. Amazed, actually. Ever since we crossed the Mississippi, we've seen nothing but flatlands. Suddenly, just coming into Birmingham, there are mountains (hills by Colorado standards) covered with pine and deciduous forests, even in the city. The dogwoods and azaleas are in bloom, and the streets are scented with perfume. Downtown Birmingham is clean, the old architecture wonderful, with no sign of race riots anywhere.

Our festival was held in beautiful Linn Park in Downtown Birmingham. The crowd that attended was the best-dressed bunch of people we'd seen anywhere—classic, understated, and stylish without being too trendy. Their attire was exceeded only by their manners. At first we didn't know what to make of their unbelievable niceness. "They must want something," I told Joe, but nixed that idea when it turned out to be the first city where no one tried to talk us down on the price of our paintings. Almost everyone that visited our booth made thoughtful compliments and treated us like good friends. Several Birminghamians: Kathy McGuire, a show coordinator; Ricia Neura, the artist across from us; and Ben Burford, one of our new collectors, went far out of their way to befriend us and make us feel welcome. Of course, we've heard of Southern hospitality, and I guess this is what they're talking about. The Southern accent in Birmingham is the deepest we've some across since Carrabelle, Florida, but somewhat more gentile sounding. More *Designing Women* than *Gomer Pyle*.

Several less positive occurrences took place this past weekend: 1) Our first automobile accident, 2) the crazed gunman threat, and 3) the Horny Hippie incident.

The money poured in for two days, a whopping $1700. I shook with excitement, barely able to contain my glee, so much so that when I went to move Lucy for pack-up afterwards, I rammed her into the back of another artist's new suburban. His name was Banister Pope. He wasn't happy about the basketball-size dent, but when my pent-up emotions burst into tears, he turned sweet. Insurance will cover it, he said. Lucy survived unscathed.

After I exchanged insurance information with Banister, Joe and I began the unglamorous job of dismantling the booth. Joe was loading the van over on the street while I pulled down the hanging strings from the booth near the center of the park, when my neighbor artist said to me casually, "There's a crazy man waving a gun over there." I looked across the grass to see an old man running through the park yelling obscenities and brandishing a handgun. I instinctively hit the dirt without so much as a peep, waiting to hear gunfire. Three police ran by my feet in the direction of the lunatic and within 30 seconds had talked him out of his firearm and handcuffed him. I half expected a Rodney King battle, but the officers calmly walked

the man toward their squad car chatting and smiling with him
as if they were old friends. It's the Birmingham way.

Another person we met during the festival, Craig, a
longhair, guitar-carrying sort with arms as big around as my
index finger, offered us a place to take a hot shower. Being
adventurous and naive, we accepted, and showed up at his
apartment after dinner on the last day of the festival. We talked
a little with our new acquaintance about music and the hidden
wonders of Birmingham before I ducked into the bathroom for
my shower. I so looked forward to my much-needed shower
that I didn't imagine that anything could upset it. I flicked on
the light switch of the not-so-clean bathroom, undressed, and
pulled back the shower curtain to find an open, curtainless
window overlooking the crowded area of Five Points. People
were milling around below, while I stood naked and stunned in
the bright light for all to see. I immediately dropped to my
knees and crawled on the cold, dirty tile floor back to the light
switch. I'd have to shower in the dark. It wasn't easy or fun,
especially since I was worried that someone could still spot me.
My coveted hot shower turned into a paranoid attempt to get
clean as quickly as possible.

Joe's turn. I warned him of the privacy problem but, being
a man, he was undaunted. I collapsed on a beanbag chair to
converse with Craig. Ten minutes of small boring talk. Next,
this pasty, spindly, granola-boy was standing in front of me,
rubbing his hairy bony feet on mine and saying, "Can you read
my mind? Do you know what I'm thinking?"

My lightening-speed answer was, "Joe!!"

Seconds later Joe popped his head out of the bathroom
door and asked, "What?"

"Are you almost done?" I hollered, hinting with my eyes
that something was wrong. He didn't get it.

"Almost," he answered casually.

"I'm ready NOW."

"OK. I'll be out in a minute." Still no clue that he had
caught on. Maybe he knew and was just remaining calm as
usual.

The Horny Hippie had quit his foot maneuver right away
because I had jumped up and stood near the hallway to the
bathroom, but he still looked at me like a wolf from across the
room. I acted normal, talking about the springtime plant bloom
as if nothing had happened, attempting to take any sexiness
out of the situation. I wondered how the doofus could think I

would ever be attracted to him! He continued his goofy/lewd staring until Joe came out of the bathroom and I announced, "Gotta go!" I grabbed Joe's arm and dug my nails in as I dragged him to the door. As we left hurriedly, Craig called out, "Y'all come back now!"

## May 5, 1993 Louisville, Kentucky, home of Norb and Dolores DeCamillis

On our way here this morning, we pulled off the road in Ethridge, Tennessee, to explore Amish country. Lucy would probably have fallen apart if we had attempted to drive her down the dirt road that led to the highest concentration of Amish farms, so we unhitched our bikes and rode. My Stump Jumper mountain bike easily traversed the country roads, but Joe's rickety ten-speed was still fragile from the Gainesville accident. He cussed every half-mile or so, if no Amish people were riding by in their carriages. The fields were singing with yellow flowers; the day brilliant.

A festival artist in Gainesville taught us a simple way of buying goods from the Amish. He'd said that if you see more than one Amish carriage riding around in an area, just drive out into the country there and you'll find their farms. He warned us that the Amish are very private but they like to sell their homemade goods.

The first farm at which we stopped was white, like all the others, with indigo blue Amish clothes hanging in an orderly fashion on the clothesline out front. A teenage girl came out of the farmhouse wearing a long blue dress, a bonnet, a thin, dark mustache, and combat boots. She didn't smile but brought with her an armload of handmade potholders for us to chose from.

The girl held out the potholders without conversation. They were made from soft wool fabric—just two pieces sewn together with the most crooked hand-sewn seams imaginable. Fifty cents apiece, she said. We bought two, just so we can say we have Amish potholders.

As we rode up to the next farm, four young boys all in dark blue and straw hats stopped their chores, walked to the front porch, and stood in a line, side-by-side. Joe waited on his bike while I walked up to them in my shorts and lipstick, suddenly feeling like a brazen hussy. They stared at me as if I was naked, which I nearly was, in their estimation. Their mother came outside and looked at me, nothing to say.

"Do you have any straw hats?" I asked.

"And sorghum," she replied flatly. After she reentered the house, I got my camera ready to take a picture of the boys. I centered them in my viewfinder and was ready to shoot when the mom opened the screen door and said, "No pictures." That was the end of that. She held out two-quart-sized metal cans of sorghum molasses—more than we would ever use in our lifetime. We had no room in Lucy for them, and all heavy things such as these should be avoided, to save our suspension. We bought them. We can barely make a living, and we bought two heavy things we'll never use, just to make some Amish people happy. I carried the sorghum over to Joe, smiling, and walked back up the stairs to the porch; the little boys' eyes never left my legs for a second. "What's your dog's name?" I asked the boys. Their black and gray-spotted sheepdog had been licking my feet.

"Sport," the littlest one offered. His next oldest brother poked him for talking to a slut.

Now, the woman came out holding out a short stack of straw hats—the reason we came. Only $6 apiece for quality hats that would cost $40 at Banana Republic. I took two, in our sizes, to be worn at the festivals to keep the sun off. Since I had no more $1 bills on me, I gave her $15 and told her to keep the change. The previously dour woman's face lit up and broke into an ear-to-ear smile.

Joe and I pedaled away, waving and saying goodbye to the five leaden faces watching from the porch. No response, not even a smile. After they filed into the house, we backtracked a bit and took pictures of their clothesline and old plow, this time not asking for permission, so as to avoid being told "No."

We will be staying at Norb and Dolores's home until our next show, in Chicago, in a month. We are becoming professional houseguests. Dolores has set us up in their basement where we sleep and paint. There isn't much light, but there is a television. I had forgotten what TV was all about. The only shows that aren't awful are *I Love Lucy*, *The Andy Griffith Show*, and *Star Trek*.

Dolores bears a resemblance to Grace Kelly and Catherine Deneuve. She scoffed when I told her this, saying she had lost her looks when a golf ball hit her in the eye a year ago, leaving it permanently bluish. I hadn't even noticed. Norb has that heavy-lidded Italian DeCamillis look. We sit around the kitchen table in the evening and gossip about family happenings over the years. We've never been privy to the Louisville DeCamillis Grapevine, so we inhale the juicy tidbits of dysfunction with fervor. Births, deaths, successes and failures, squabbling, backstabbing, side-taking, trips abroad, children in college, criminal behavior and humdrum life—a family like everyone else's.

## May 8, 1993

The basement is inspiring us. I'm working on a dark painting with a glowing television radiating from its center. Joe's recreating a corner with a high window and pink and black floor tiles below. Our private enclave has given us ample time to converse about art. We rarely like to get into art discussions, but today we did.

We talked about how it must seem peculiar to others that our paintings depict interiors of houses when our life is lived for the most part outdoors, without a home. The various landscapes and people around us must seem a more obvious subject matter than brightly colored rooms. But interiors have been an object of my creative interest since college, and Joe seemed to merge with my sensibility when we began painting together. Home, to us, is the most important of all places, because it is where our joy and our pain begin. It is where we learn to fear and where we learn to love. No other subject matter can pull from us the passion of vision as strongly as rooms can.

From the comments we've received at the festivals so far, we've learned that people see warmth and humor in our paintings, while also pointing out a pervading emptiness. Our years as house painters have had a profound influence on our work as we witnessed in the neighborhoods of suburbia the lack of human life during the workweek. The only sign of life, most of the time, is the barking of lonely dogs from the fenced-in backyards. But this literal emptiness is only a part of the dark side to our work. Most of the menacing qualities are suggested in twisted angles of walls and floors, shadows that don't quite fit their object, and a collection of objects that suggest an enigmatic narrative. A hint of something lurking in a dark corridor gives rise to questions about secrecy and danger.

Some people see absolutely no dark side to our work. We hear comments such as "These are hilarious!" "They are so

charming and humorous!" "What beautiful, happy colors!" We
are just as pleased with these interpretations. We have a strong
aversion to forcing ourselves to make art that has "an edge."
We have heard from the more art-educated people that see our
work that they like our more twisted paintings, that our
figuratively lighter paintings are too cute. The word cute is a
huge compliment to us. For one person to see horror and
another to see cuteness is the goal of our work because it
means we've conveyed one of our ultimate, perhaps cliché
beliefs—that there is good and bad in everything.

We love the people we meet on the road, and our paintings
are tributes to them and to all average Americans. In no way do
we seek to poke fun at them or show only their pain. We've
had more than a few supposedly cool people say things like,
"That's great! Where do you find all these tacky homes? What
kind of weirdo lives in this house?" or "I love it because it's
everything I hate about America." We find our homes to be
everything we love about America, and no home is ugly to us.
Our travels have taught us how good people can be, and how
their secrets and pain only make them more interesting and
human.

Painting is our medium, because we love to paint, but it
also rides in perfect harmony with the rest of our quest as
artists. We want our work to appeal to a broad audience, and
we've found that oil painting is the most broadly accepted
medium of all the fine arts. Many other artists working in
mixed-media, photography, print-making, even pastels and
sculpture, complain about the fact that when they announce to
people that they are artists, they are asked the question, "What
do you paint?" This has nothing to do with why we paint, but it
works out nicely.

The following may sound a bit too poetic, but describing
why we love paint could only come out that way.

The buttery feel and earthy smell of it. Its ability to
transform a real scene into a fantasy seen only through our
eyes, with our emotions and beliefs imprinted in it. Putting
down that pure white and immediately seeing the glaring day
beaming through a window. Laying down Van Dyke Brown in
the corner and seeing anthropomorphic images peering from
the darkness. The pain in your hand bones and the Prussian
Blue under your fingernails at the end of a day. Taking days to
work on one little area that never quite looks right or taking

just minutes on a huge, complicated area that comes out like magic.

These are not reasons for painting that you can explain at an art festival.

## May 13, 1993

We get out occasionally, to see the light of day for health purposes. Louisville is, unquestionably, the friendliest place we've been. Even friendlier than Birmingham. As we ride down the street on our bicycles, everyone outside on their porches or working in their yards stops to wave and smile. And this is not a small town. In the supermarket, when I say excuse me, people say, "Oh, no. Excuse me. It was my fault." Even men. Employees of businesses treat us like they want us to come back, a rarity elsewhere. I told this to Dolores who said, "Really? Well, I'm glad to hear that. A friend of Norb's who came in from out of town said that same thing. That people here are so nice it seems suspicious."

## May 25, 1993

. North to Chicago tomorrow. We made arrangements to stay in Deer Point, Indiana, with Joe's (Great) Uncle George and Aunt Toni. We are learning to give people notice.

## May 27, 1993   Home of George and Toni Smith, Deer Park, Indiana

Just after we arrived last night, Uncle George treated us to dinner at his Country Club. Aunt Toni is sick with the flu and has been in bed ever since we arrived, poor lady. Over our fancy dinner of steak and baked potato we coaxed Uncle George into telling us some World War II stories. The best one was when he to  got see Mussolini's dead body after he was hung. When we got back to the house he pulled out a shoebox full of black and white photos with white borders. Most of the shots were of WWII bomber planes in flight, taken from the bomber on which George was a gunner. He thumbed through piles of them, until he found Mussolini and silently handed us the photo. There he was, a bloated white naked corpse. I saw Mussolini's weenie!

We used two rolls of film photographing their home. They have a stuffed bobcat, just like the Herrmans in Texas!

## June 7, 1993  Home of Jim and Alida Zamboni, Melrose Park, Illinois (A suburb of Chicago)

I have much to catch up on. I'm laying on a pink flowered bedspread in the room of Gina Zamboni, Joe's teenage cousin. We've had a huge share of Italian neighborhood stories and outrageous Italian food, but only at dinnertime because we've been at our festival everyday until 7:30 or so.

The 57th Street Art Fair in South Chicago: We made $3,000. We made $3,000. Three thousand dollars!!!! I can't stand it! Our dream is coming true! I'm even getting a little used to this money thing. We never have any left over after buying art supplies and basic living expenses, but at least we have enough to pay bills, and we don't work for someone else. This is a fascinating experience. I hope I never take this for granted.

The festival was held near the University of Chicago, an oasis in the middle of a bad neighborhood. The crowd was mostly yuppies. Many buyers made exclamations about how inexpensive our paintings are; I told another artist, Kathleen Eaton, about this, and she definitely agreed. She was sure we'd sell more if we raised our prices, even doubled them. She explained that people would take our work more seriously if we charged higher prices; they'd assume our paintings are worth that much. I understand what she means, but raising our prices is a scary thing. What if suddenly no one wanted to pay the higher price and we couldn't sell and we had to go back to work at the Gainesville Hilton or give blood for a living and live in a trailer park next to an alcoholic and a man who liked living in a refrigerator box? It could happen.

No unusual characters to report at the 57th Street Fair. We were too excited about selling to pay attention.

Tomorrow we are driving into the city with Alida and the girls to the Taste of Chicago and the Chicago Art Institute.

## June 8, 1993

Our day in Chicago:

Joe and I couldn't afford more than a few bites at the Taste of Chicago but we had fun joking around with Alida, Gina, and Lisa. They are like family should be—casual.

The Chicago Art Institute went too quickly. Alida had to be somewhere—not that I'm complaining—so we only had one hour to see everything. Given the time restraints, we were forced to choose only our most coveted art destinations. In museums, our definition of sculpture is: that which acts as an obstacle in the path to the painting galleries.

First we ran to see the Old Masters. Trying to whiz by the paintings of the greatest artists of all time is no easy job, and I cried out each time Joe yanked my arm to pull me away from a Vermeer or Ingre. With little time left, we took in some of our favorite American artists: Hopper, Wyeth, Whistler, Sargent, Turner, the Pre-Raphaelites. In our final minutes we stared in ecstasy at the Van Goghs (only to be truly appreciated in real life), and the Toulouse-Lautrec painting of the partying drunks at the Moulin Rouge.

We happily skipped the most contemporary section, reasoning that we would do better to just grab the museum pamphlets about that collection and read about the art. Conceptual art's merit usually ends after the work is thought up.

Tomorrow it's off to Michigan, where we will stay somewhere near Ann Arbor until the show there.

### June 13, 1993   Apple Creek Campground, Grass Lake, Michigan
EVENTS THAT LEAD UP TO THIS MOMENT:
1)   Our first try at finding a home was a crappy primitive campground in Hell, Michigan. (Real name!) Blistering hot, humid, no level camp spots, no showers, and the first night we were up until four in the morning listening to two drunken rednecks in the neighboring spot talking about auto parts—a sore subject for us. Their campfire smoke drifted in our windows that we couldn't close because it was hot as HELL. And we couldn't ask them to shut-up because they had asked us nicely to join them earlier. So we experienced a night of choking smoke, sticky heat, an angle to our bed that made all the blood rush to our heads, and two rednecks yelling "No, make that Quaker State!" We left the next day to find another home.
2)   Found the Apple Creek Campground outside the tiny town of Grass Lake. The world's bumpiest road led back into the woods, and there, next to a small lake (more of a swamp, really) we found our home for the next month. We have a quiet, dirt camp area under majestic pine trees. The camping facilities here include a swimming pool, a freezer full of popsicles that we'll never be able to afford,

somewhat clean showers, a miniature golf course, a big field for Ruby Frisbee, and walking trails into the woods. It sounds fancy but it's fairly primitive. Once we arrived, we set up our canopy and wobbly art table, explored our new home and inspected its advertised features, then plopped down on Lucy's denim seats for a hot dog feast.

3) To bring us up to the moment, we are in bed. I am trying to write and Joe is poking me with his cold feet and laughing like an evil villain.

## June 16, 1993

Is it possible that we've actually found an everyday life, a grind, a humdrum existence? For three days we've been on our own, not freeloading off unsuspecting relatives, on solid ground, with no place to be for a month. Gainesville was the last time we settled down for any length of time, but I will never call that place my home, not even temporarily. I feel so secure, which shows one how very relative security can be. I want to paint and cavort about with abandon.

Bill and Mary, who run this place, are friendly enough. We hardly ever see them unless we're using the pay phone by the office or trudging over to the pool in our swimsuits. They've conscientiously asked us to let them know if we find anything unsightly or otherwise displeasing in the campground. This is a switch from the Gainesville campground where not a soul ever checked on the place. It could have blown sky high with all of its inhabitants in it and the owners would still expect their weekly rent check.

## June 19, 1993

We paint and paint. Get up at 6:30 a.m., paint until 10:30 at night. One break for swimming, three for eating. Our skill at painting keeps improving and our interiors are gathering even more furniture, objects, and personal touches. We are concentrating more on detail. We don't plan these changes, but we can't help being influenced as we stay in more middle-class homes. As we grow more inspired by them we become more interested in becoming better artists, and portraying the homes with more care and realism.

## June 21, 1993

I went to take my shower today, in the usually well-kept shower building. I walked into a shower stall, which, as in most

RV parks, has a plastic curtain leading into a small, private dressing area with another plastic curtain in front of the actual shower. I began undressing in my little cubical, my toiletries all laid out, when I noticed a strong and stinky smell. I sniffed, disgusted, and wondered where it was coming from. I wasn't sure if I could stand taking a shower if it persisted. So I curiously pulled back the shower curtain and to my horror found that someone had taken a five-pound steaming dump in my shower! Some idiotic lady or an uninformed little girl with a long colon must have entered the showers thinking it was the restroom and thought, "Well, I guess this is all they have!" I decided I'd rather be dirty myself for another day than deal with a stranger's poop. I told the RV park managers about it and then came back to the camper to tell Joe. Joe, of course, thought my Cultural Encounter at the showers was the funniest thing he'd ever heard. As I've been writing about it, I've heard him crack up three times at his vigil at the painting table.

## June 25, 1993   New camp spot, Apple Creek Campground

We asked if we could move into a prime spot on the "lake" (as I said, more of a swamp), that previous campers just vacated. Our new home is picturesque, but we have visitors we hadn't anticipated—loud bullfrogs and more mosquitoes.

## June 26, 1993

Art Art Art. Paint Paint Paint. I had a dream last night that an army of little paintbrushes was marching around the camper getting paint all over the ground, and all I could think about was catching them and getting them cleaned before the paint dried in their bristles.

In the interest of time and money our paintings just keep getting smaller. To keep up with the demand for paintings, we need QUANTITY. But we're not willing to give up quality, so we make smaller and smaller paintings. We were hauling big ole frames—the size of a door sometimes—around in our tiny living area, and now we think they are too big if they won't fit into a breadbox. Considering the size of our working space, this new format is awesome! In the past we would have cringed at making an artistic decision based on practical considerations, but now we realize what bozos we were. Were we masochists? We barely had any room to move!

I can't believe how hot it is. It gets more miserable everyday.

## June 27, 1993

Here are the good things about our hike on the Apple Creek Campground Nature Trail:
1) We found some fluorescent cobalt blue dragonfly wings in the trail and filled our pockets with them.
2) Joe caught a tiny tree frog as small as his pinky nail.
3) We took pictures of me in a field of purple flowers up to my neck.

These are the bad things about our hike on the Apple Creek Campground Nature Trail:
1) The pollen count was a kachillion particles per square inch, so we sneezed and spit phlegm the whole way.
2) Sticky, thorny plants grabbed our ankles and made us complain the whole way. Our ankles looked like pizza when we got home.
3) I accidentally trudged through a puddle of black mud in my thongs.
4) I had to go to the bathroom.
5) Kamikaze-attack deer flies were dive-bombing our head and shoulders. I screamed a lot.
   We're glad our Nature Hike is over.

## June 30, 1993

An elderly couple from the next-door campsite invited me over to show me their video collection today. They have every movie starring Jeff Daniels because Jeff Daniels is originally from Chelsea, Michigan, which is half an hour from here. When I entered their camper, the woman was watching *The Butcher's Wife* starring Demi Moore and Jeff Daniels. She paused the movie to point out their special shelf, solely dedicated to their Jeff Daniels movie collection.

## July 1, 1993

Still painting day and night. It's hot and humid. We paint outside under the E-Z up as much as possible, but sometimes we have to move the whole studio inside to keep the mosquitoes away. We sit inches away from our three-speed oscillating fan and still I moan. My legs are covered with big red swollen bites, and I'm coated with sweat all day, everyday.

Today I broke out in tears—temporary insanity from overwork, heat, bug fever, and lack of exercise.

"Heat EEEEEEEEE!" I cried, dropping my wet paintbrush on the linoleum floor. "I can't take it anymore! I need air conditioning." (Full-blown blubbering by now). "What are we doing here? This place is awful! I'm dying."

"Let's go swimming," Joe offered.

"We already did, twice. I'm still hot," I sobbed.

"How about a popsicle?"

"We can't afford it."

"Right." Joe sat thinking, helpless.

"Don't you feel awful? Don't you want to scream?"

"Yeah. Mind if I join you?"

"Sure," I smiled.

Joe began a bad imitation of me crying. "Goodbye, cruel world, it's over. Dori, you go on without me. I'm all washed up. You're strong. You're a survivor. You'll be better without me." He fell on the floor, clutching his heart. "Don't forget to feed the dog, and give my sweaty shoes to charity."

I was laughing by now, kicking him on the floor. "Shut up. I don't sound like that. You only wish you could cry like me."

"Well, are you ready for a popsicle? Just this once? It's an emergency, after all."

"You're right," I said, enlightened at his reasoning. "I am almost losing my mind. It's for medicinal purposes, right?"

"Come on."

## July 2, 1993

The Fourth of July camping frenzy has begun. Motor homes, trailers, pick-up campers, van conversions, and tent campers have all converged on our quiet home for the long weekend. Toddlers and teenagers, old folks and dogs, seedy types and plain middle-class human beings are here to keep us company for the duration. There are firecrackers popping here and there, loud screaming games at the miniature golf course, men and women arguing over how to pop up the pop-up camper, and the swimming pool is packed. I certainly took for granted the pleasures of peace and quiet before. When they leave I will never complain again.

**July 4, 1993**

FOURTH OF JULY FESTIVITIES

1) We celebrated with the Nelsons, a family from New Hampshire camped near us. We watched Ruby attack the Nelson's fireworks and singe most of her whiskers off.
2) Danced around howling with sparklers for a few minutes.
3) Sat on lawn chairs facing the swamp with the Nelsons and talked about slot cars (whatever they are) and different types of fireworks.
4) Couldn't sleep most of the night due to carousing rowdy pubescents and hellish heat.

**July 6, 1993**

As usual, the temperature reached the high 90s by 11:00 a.m., and humidity near 100%. Mosquitoes swarmed about us, even with our skins' toxic barrier of Deep Woods Off. My painting progressed slowly; I was too busy swatting bugs and wiping sweat off my face to be very productive. I became more frustrated with each paint dollop I'd dip into.

"Stupid paint. It dries too fast in this heat. I can't even move it around on the canvas."

Minutes later: "Damn Bugs!"

Soon after: "Great. A big sweat drop on my console TV. How am I going to fix that?"

At last: "Take that!" I launched my medium-sized, wet painting into the woods, Frisbee style. It flew like a bird.

"What the hell? What did you do that for?" Joe yelled, running into the woods to find my poor masterpiece. I sat at our art table with a scowl on my face, no reply. I'd always wanted to do that. Joe yanked the smeared living room scene out of the bushes, and carefully examined it. "We might be able to save it," he said. "I can't believe you did that. Are you going crazy?"

"HA! Going crazy! Of course I am! What kind of a stupid question is that? Who wouldn't go crazy under these conditions! I can't take it anymore! I demand that we go into town tomorrow and go to two movies, and anywhere else where we can get air-conditioning for long periods of time. I demand it!"

"OK, OK. You're right, you're right. We'll go tomorrow. Just don't do that again, OK? Sheesh!"

The promise of a reprieve settled me some, for a while. But still, there was a whole day to live through. Even the pool was warm, due in no small part to the Fourth of July mob that probably tinkled in it. But it was Joe, not me, who started the next hullabaloo.

"It's late. Why haven't you started dinner yet? I'm starving, " Joe barked.

"I can't. The oven will get hot."

"Well, I'm starving. We've got to eat something. Can't you find anything cold?"

"Not that you'd eat. We'll have to get stuff when we go to town tomorrow. Maybe we can be super naughty and drive down to that little hamburger place in Grass Lake. They have malts there".

"I can't wait that long to eat!" Joe snapped. "And we shouldn't spend the money and you know it!"

"What am I, your doormat? Here, asshole!" I pulled cold hot dogs and raw broccoli from the fridge and dumped them on his lap, and jumped out of the camper. I ran as fast as my out-of-shape legs would go, swatting mosquitoes from my ankles and tripping all the way, fighting back the tears. There were no suspicious smells in the showers today, and no people in sight so I ducked inside a dressing room cubicle and sat there. That jerk, I thought. Who the hell does he think he is, my boss? I won't speak to him for three days. (Like I could go more than fifteen minutes without talking.) I waited for a little while,   then began taking deep breaths. I told myself I'd be much better able to assess the situation if I took care of my needs first—eating especially. I walked back to the campsite, calmer now, still slapping bugs off my legs.

Ruby waited at the perimeter of our campsite, her eyes sad, her ears perked with expectation. She knew we were fighting and wouldn't be happy until we fixed it up. My Vow of Silence never had to be tested. Joe walked around from the other side of Lucy to meet me with a sheepish "I'm sorry" look, his arms outstretched.

We drove into Grass Lake, four miles from here, and had hamburgers and malts in the air-conditioning. And tomorrow we're going into town! We talked at dinner tonight about deprivation's dramatic effect on the brain.

## July 7, 1993

I don't think we'll be seeing two movies in one day again, because they tend to cancel each other out. We saw *The Firm*. and *Sleepless in Seattle*, two movies I would have rather had a couple of days to go over in my head separately, to savor every dramatic or romantic moment while suffering out at the swamp. But the air-conditioning was too fabulous to pass up, the next trip to town too distant to resist walking right back into another theater.

**July 10, 1993**

I wrote Joe a song. It's not very romantic, but it made him laugh so that's almost as good. (Sung to the tune of "My Favorite Things" from The Sound of Music.)

> Nimoy on Star Trek and not working jobs,
> Winter in Florida and Crystal doorknobs,
> Clean bathroom floors and Joe when he sings,
> These are a few of my favorite things.
> American flags and soap by Clinique,
> Old forties music and playing all week,
> Art made by Hopper and clothes that don't cling,
> These are a few of my favorite things!
> When the dog farts, when the checks bounce,
> when the music's rap,
> I simply remember my favorite things
> And then I don't feeeeeeeeeel like crap.

**July 11, 1993**

Today we discovered Speed Golf, the most important discovery in sports history since round balls. To remedy our heat craziness and painting sickness, we paid $1 to play Miniature Golf. We bored quickly of regular mini-golf and thus attempted to spice up the game by making it a timed competition rather than one of accuracy and least times hit. Both players must tee off their respective golf balls simultaneously and *anything goes* to get your ball in the whole first, as long as you don't touch it. This includes ordering your dog to drop it in the hole, pushing and yelling at the competition, and using your golf club like a hockey stick. I believe we made more noise playing Speed Golf than the entire Fourth of July camping crowd. Bill the Campground Man came out of the office several times, probably ready to scold us, but would watch us for a few minutes and then walk back in with a smile on his face. This is the most fun I've had since the Dune Buggy Encounter.

## July 14, 1993

We're addicted to Speed Golf. It is the light of our lives, our fix that gets us through the day, our exercise, our nourishment, our love.

## July 16, 1993

Painting, eating cheap food, swimming in the morning before the kiddies come to swim/tinkle, explaining our paintings to inquisitive campers and kids, listening to bullfrogs, and watching the fireflies as the moon rises over the swamp—it's the same every day. Only Speed Golf (make the sign of the cross when you say it) stands out in our lives.

## July 17, 1993

We thought we'd brave the wild woods again for something different to do. We prepared for the onslaught of deadly attack deer flies by wearing baseball caps, Off!, and clothing that covered everything except our face. Twenty feet into the woods, they ambushed us. At first we tried swatting them, but flapping arms had no effect on them. We kept our cool, still swinging and slapping at them but determined to continue with our little hike. Soon I turned to Joe, ready to ask him what he thought our next move should be, when I saw the look of terror on his face. "They're all over you!" he shouted, and started furiously slapping my head and back. My goal to remain calm was slipping from my grasp. Now the flies were covering Joe and swarming around him like mad hornets. I kept walking, holding in the panic, certain we could overcome this minor obstacle, while Joe flailed about, trying to keep walking, too. Finally the insect horde got the best of us. A swarming sea of black surrounded us like a cloud, many of the flies clinging to and biting through our clothes.

"Oh my God!" Joe cried, "Run for your life!"

We took off running toward the campground like those screaming school kids in Hitchcock's *The Birds*. We sprinted toward the swimming pool with the swarm all around us; we were too slow to outrun them. We dived in with our clothes on and stayed underwater as long as possible but when we came up for air, they attacked our heads until we sunk back under. After a few minutes of this hiding game, most of the beasts gave up and flew back to the woods. We're safe now, back at

the camp, never to attempt such a foolhardy risk again. I think
our adventure would make a good IMAX movie.

**July 18, 1993**
    Leaving for Ann Arbor Street Arts Fair day after tomorrow.
Lots of last minute, framing-mounting-varnishing-etc. to take
care of. We have about $11,000 worth of paintings to exhibit.
That's a lot of paintings when you consider how inexpensive
they are. We've raised the prices slightly, as other artists have
instructed us. I lost a few hours of sleep last night worrying,
and probably will tonight, too.

**July 20, 1993   Wal-Mart Parking Lot, Ann Arbor, Michigan**
DAY 1—ART FESTIVAL
    We suck. This is supposed to be one of the top five shows
in the country and we didn't sell a thing today. We heard that
Bannister Pope, the artist we crashed into in Birmingham,
Alabama, made $12,000 in the first three hours! We're scum.
The worst ever. Why did we ever decide to be artists? It's 4:00
in the morning and I haven't slept a wink. I'm too upset to
even cry. Do other artists ever feel like this?
    One tidbit of interest at the show: I made friends with an
artist named Holly Ambrose, who sells gorgeous found-object
jewelry and wore a bright red 50s dress and a hat adorned with
four life-size cardinals. I wanted to hate her because she made
$9,000 today, but she was funny so I spent some time
swapping on-the-road art stories with her.
    One extra bad thing, to add to our extra bad day of sales is
that it's hot and humid (big surprise) and we can't use our
shower for fear of filling up the holding tank with water and
putting too much weight on Lucy's suspension. So we're hot
and sticky and dirty, on top of being bad artists who can't sell
anything.

**July 21, 1993**
DAY 2—ART FESTIVAL
    We really suck now. Not one thing sold today. Not one
thing. Maybe it's because our booth looks like a Parisian flea
market vendor's with paintings of many sizes in every style of
frame imaginable dangling on strings from pavement to ceiling.
    I'm just lying in bed scribbling on my journal to the light of
the Wal-Mart street light, hot, filthy dirty and sticky, and scared

shitless. If we don't sell anything, we are in get-a-job-quick trouble.

All the other artists are doing great—making money, smiling, looking clean and fresh—it's hard to watch. Holly Ambrose was on the cover of today's *Detroit Free Press*, with her fancy cardinal hat and everything.

The last time we felt this bad was back in The Hood. Well, maybe we don't feel that bad.

## July 22, 1993
DAY 3—ART FESTIVAL

We sold art! I have no idea why everyone waited until today to buy from us, but just after dark, when all the strollers and dog-walkers went away, the festival was stormed by a wine-drinking, dressed-up crowd who liked our stuff. We sold $3,500 after 6:30. I am so relieved and excited I can't sleep. Joe and I sat up talking for hours about the people that bought our work, (mostly executives and higher-ups in the automotive industry) and what their comments were, who was nice and who was snobby, what they wore, how long they spent in the booth before they bought, how old they were.

We still have one more day at the show, and even if we don't sell anything more we'll be OK. We'll make it to the next show, in Charlevoix, Michigan, and we'll probably be able to buy a small covered trailer to pull behind Lucy and carry our art supplies and booth. We can barely move with all that stuff packed up front.

I met another artist who hand-paints photographs of funky, tropical scenes of Central America. I'd seen and loved her work at Gasparilla this spring, but was too shy to introduce myself. (I was petrified of everything then.) At four feet, eleven inches—a full foot shorter than me—she commands attention with her booming voice, her short platinum blonde hair, and the eccentric, colorful clothes she wears. I loved her the minute I met her.

Among the many things we spoke of, she recommended I see her psychic, who lives in Florida, the next time we're down there. Although very skeptical, I think I just might do it, because I trust her.

I'm exhausted. And I can't sleep. Although I'm delirious with happiness, I think this emotional zigzagging will leave me in a state of collapse after the show. Do other artists have these highs and lows, all dependent on whether or not their work sells? I'll look like I'm 74 after a few more years of this.

**July 24, 1993   Apple Creek Campground**
It's over. I survived. I feel like a Mack Truck has just hit me. The final day of the festival we earned enough to boost our earnings to approximately $5,000. We are so proud of ourselves!

**July 27, 1993**
We bought a trailer today. We drove to Ypsilanti, Michigan, a suburb of Ann Arbor, and paid $900 for a 5' x 8' covered aluminum trailer. Although it seems like a lot of money, we've looked around at trailer prices for days and have determined this to be a good buy. After getting it back to Apple Creek, we immediately loaded all of our art baggage into it. We are free! We have tons of room! Lucy feels like a mansion inside now! We can sit across from each other at our kitchen table/studio table instead of cramming together on one seat! We are moving up in the world!
Tomorrow we head north for the Charlevoix area. We will find another campground until our show.

**July 31, 1993   Thurston Campground, Central Lake, Michigan**
Life just keeps getting better and better. Our new home on the beach of Central Lake, maybe ten miles inland from Lake Michigan, is Utopia compared to the Grass Lake Swamp. Although a small campground with less spacious camp spots, it has reasonable prices, clean showers and an actual lake fit for swimming.
The first day we pulled into our allotted space, road weary and in the mood for privacy, a "mentally challenged" woman ran up to the Ultra Van and started belting questions at us.
"Wow! Nice trailer! What's in it? Bicycles? It's the same color as our camper—tan and black. Yep. Tan and black.  Same as our camper. What's in it? Did you just get here? Are you going to stay here? I've been here a long time. Yep. Long time. I've been here a long time. That's my trailer over there. See? Tan and black. Yep. Oh, you have a dog. Nice Dog. Is he nice?"
"NO!" we replied in unison.
"She bites," Joe added.

She ran away. We looked at each other guiltily and then shrugged. Too worn out for guilt.

Later we walked by her camper and saw the obligatory retired people name sign that announces the owner of its occupants, hanging over the door. The top sign says Roger and Ethel Stevenson (her guardians) and a sign just below it says *Oompa Loompa* (that's her). For once we don't have to make up a stupid name for someone.

## August 1, 1993

Painted from morning until 5:00. Then took a long swim across the lake. Paradise. And I wouldn't say this out loud to anyone, but we are just getting better and better and better at this painting thing. Sell, sell, selling your art requires you to have to make, make, make more of it and how can we do anything but get lots of practice and improve? Those blab, blab, blabbing professors in colleges should send their students out for a year of this festival stuff and then see how someone gets better at making art. All those lousy critiques do for you is make you question everything you do.

## August 2, 1993

Cute kids come over to ask about our paintings and see what we are doing. We loan them art supplies and clear a space on our picnic table so they can join us. I get a little sad because they remind me of how much I want to have kid.

## August 4, 1993

Oompa Loompa walks completely around the campground to avoid setting foot by our campsite. Ruby senses Oompa's fear and barks at her like rabid Old Yeller.

## August 6, 1993

At the end of our row of campers, a heavy-drinking, over-tan riffraff couple have been here as long as we have. They are super friendly and always super drunk. Late this afternoon they offered us a boat ride and we, of course, accepted. We had our doubts when they tried in vain to start their ramshackle 70s boat decorated with orange and brown racing stripes. Gasoline dribbled into the lake, and blue smoke bellowed from the tail. They wiggled this and that mechanism to coax it into running, while pouring beer down their necks and laughing about polluting the lake. Feeling adventurous, we climbed in, noting the husband's happy red face and the wife's nipple hanging out of her bikini. A little slurred pre-boating conversation informed us that they are in their 40s, live and work in Detroit at a car factory, and make it a point to spend their two weeks vacation every year at this same campground, where they can stay as drunk as possible the entire time.

Our two flights around the lake took us a little too close to a boat dock once, but other than that we stayed safe. Most campers were having dinner or lighting their campfires, so we faced no boat traffic. Even above the roaring, spattering old boat motor, I marveled at the peacefulness and grace of the lake at sunset, and felt  a gratitude I've not experienced in years—for my life, my experiences. I smiled at Joe several times, imagining that he must feel the same way. Then Gary stopped the boat in the middle of the lake. "Turn the other way folks. Time for me to use nature's biggest toilet."

**August 7, 1993**
New neighbors: two fishing buddies. Dwayne and Terry. Bass Masters, they say. Both work at the GM plant in Grand Rapids. They have invited us for fresh fish a la campfire tomorrow night. "What if you don't catch any?" we asked. "We will," they said.

**August 8, 1993**
PMS POEM
I always want more
I'm sick of everything
Everyone else has nice stuff
I have nothing
I'm too fat
I have no money
I have ugly clothes
I'm lazy
I'm mean to everyone
Nothing good ever happens to me
My husband hates me
The dog is repulsed by me
I tell dumb jokes
I can't cook
I eat bad food
I always look frumpy
I better eat some chocolate.

That was the story of my day until Dwayne and Terry pulled their shiny metallic red Bass Master Fishing Boat up to the dock, holding a string of big fish high in the air. I needed something, anything, to distract me from moping around and hating myself.

We closed the camper curtains and exchanged our paint-stained, ripped clothes for non-paint stained ripped clothes (we have two kinds) and joined our new friends. While Dwayne prepared the fish with cornmeal and wrapped it in aluminum foil with poked holes, Terry started a fire and opened a can of baked beans. They talked politics through dinner—a right-wing politics in which Rush Limbaugh is considered liberal.

After dinner Terry pulled out his harmonica; we listened to the old standards for hours ("Polly Wolly Doodle," "My Darling Clementine," "Camptown Races"). No reason to talk. Other campers nearby turned their campfire seats to face us. The small group of roughhousing kids came out of the woods. The yellow glows from inside several campers were extinguished as old-timers stepped outside. Aside from the crickets and the crackle of fire, Terry's sweet, whining harmonica was the only sound drifting through the camp and out over the lake until we all went to our beds.

### August 11, 1993

It's show time! We'll drive the 30 miles up to Charlevoix, stay there while we do the show, and come back to recuperate before leaving for good.

### August 17, 1993

Where has the time gone? The Charlevoix show—a one-day event—is over; not a huge money pay-off, but worth it. The crowd consisted only of well-to-do yacht owners who were chiefly interested in purchasing pastel watercolors of boat scenes. Some artists fared well.

On the last day, a high-strung young man in a three-piece suit—completely out of place at an art festival—suspiciously offered to be our agent. Mr. Business marched in, glanced only briefly at our work and after introducing himself, and launched into an overzealous barrage of ideas for "making us a household name." He could put our images on T-shirts, mugs, bookmarks, etc. Mr. Business took my arms and stated with passion, "I'm going to rock your world! You two are a marketer's wet dream." UGH!

Disgusted but interested in the man as a character, we humored him and asked a bundle of questions pertaining to what he actually does and what he could actually offer us. It turned out, as we suspected, that he had never really represented an artist, had no idea of the inroads and connections it takes to promote an artist, and had no knowledge or love of art in general. He was basically a pretender who thought he had come up with a new, easy way to make a buck. A short amount of time in the art industry will cure him of that illusion.

Speaking of selling, we often get  well-meant but irritating suggestions from other artists to "get in there and sell." When they find out we are new at this festival thing, they assume we are in need of some advice. We thank them sweetly, then turn around and roll our eyes. Our sales policy is to be at the booth, smile, answer questions, be attentive and friendly, and generally make ourselves available. After that, the customers are on their own. We'd like to think our work is good enough to sell itself, which so far it has been. I hate dealing with high-pressure salespeople and would hate even worse to be one.

EARTH-SHATTERING IMPROVEMENT MADE:

We've learned how to get rid of our art-on-strings. One of our artist neighbors taught us that if we stretch a huge canvas tight around our booth poles, we  can hang our work directly on it with drapery hooks. This will be easier, and it will look better. No more art swinging around the booth like Tarzan!

We returned to Thurston Campground to new neighbors—an alcoholic Canadian and his two teenage sons. The boys sit around camp all day and complain and fight with each other while the Dad drinks beer, wine, or hard liquor all day.

## August 21, 1993

We are ready to kill the Canadians. Here is a list of our grievances:

1)  The oldest boy taunts Ruby when we aren't around. Other campers have told us about it and have scolded the guy while in the act. He continues. One day I caught him red-handed and yelled, "Quit teasing our dog!" His reply: "I wasn't! I don't know what you are talking about!"

2) The boys stole our towel. When Joe marched over and grabbed it, saying, "This is our towel!" They replied, "I don't know how that got over here."

3) The Dad, drunk as usual, knocked on our camper door one morning and said, "Do you like Canadian bacon?"

"Sure," we answered.

"No, you don't. You don't even know what Canadian bacon is. You Americans eat glorified ham and think it's Canadian bacon. I'm going to bring you some real Canadian bacon." He left and returned minutes later with a wax paper package of "real" Canadian bacon. Then he left. It looked like thin strips of raw, fatty, uncured pork. We cooked it up. It was terrible—bland and a little rotten. "How did you like the real thing?" he asked later. "Sure beats that American crap, doesn't it?"

"Yeah, it was great," we smiled. He offered us more. Our excuse was that we were on a special diet and couldn't eat too much meat. He was drunk enough to readily accept this explanation from two people who eat meat at practically every meal only four feet away from his campsite.

4) We figured the boys have had a hard life. We wanted to make an effort at kindness—the only bit of good treatment they'd probably get for a while—so we wandered over to make conversation. We also thought it might keep them from continuing their encroachment on our rights as citizens.

"So what's it like where you live in Canada?" I asked.

"Just like here," the older one said.

"Really? Isn't it colder?"

"You stupid Americans. You all think that Canada is The Great White North. How could you not know that there are parts of Canada that are South of some parts of America? Don't you people learn anything in school?"

I pointed at him directly in the face and said, "You're an asshole," and walked off. So much for making friendly with the underprivileged.

**August 22, 1993**

We've decided to take the northern route over Lake Michigan to get to Chicago where our next festival will be held. If Lucy breaks down, help stations will be few and far between, but most Michigonians have highly recommended that course for the scenery and cool weather.

I will miss this place. The weather is refreshing, our daily lake swims have given us a little exercise, and the people have been a flowing source of entertainment. I haven't even craved a movie or dinner out.

### August 23, 1993

BAD NEWS. I called my mom from the pay phone across the street and she told me that my Dad was in a terrible accident. He was crushed by the boom of a crane. He was an hour away from civilization with no other people around except for his new girlfriend, Sunny. She ran to flag drivers down on the highway nearby, but Dad lay helpless and barely breathing under the boom for hours before an ambulance arrived. He was flown to the hospital in Grand Junction where he will remain for months, probably. His back is broken, his kidney crushed, a lung collapsed, and other things I can't remember. I called the hospital after I hung up with Mom and spoke briefly with my Granny, who told me Dad was too drugged up to know whom he was talking to. I feel so helpless. I wish I could fly out there right now, but I guess we'll have to settle for a long slow trip in Lucy. We'll need the money from the Chicago festival next weekend to get home. At least it will feel good to be moving in the direction of Colorado.

### August 25, 1993  Deserted Beach, Upper Peninsula, Michigan

We drive. I've been having a hard time writing the past few days. Our little lives seem so...little, after Dad's accident.

### August 27, 1993  Quiet street, Marinette, WI

We have fallen in love with the Upper Peninsula. (U.P. they call it). Once over the Mackinac Bridge, which connects Lower Michigan with its upper region, the temperature drops at least ten degrees. The area is sparsely populated, and tourists are few and far between. Its foliage—pines and open fields of wildflowers—remind me somewhat of the high country of Colorado, only without the mountains. The few towns along the Northern edge of Lake Michigan seem to have stopped in time about 30 or 40 years ago—interesting to look at but no reason to stay.

I can't believe it's come to this, but Joe and I have both admitted we are actually yearning for a home. A home home, as in a house that we own in a place that we love. We still need the road, but we've recently confessed to each other that we've been scouting each place we see for its potential as a settle-down headquarters. The cost of living on this side of the Mississippi is so much lower than out West that the possibility of home ownership could be in our reach someday, as opposed to never back in Colorado or California. The U.P., with its home prices starting in the $10,000 range, would be on the top of our list if it weren't for the cold winters. Of course a baby would be an added bonus to our little dream, but I try not to get my hopes up.

We are now stopped for the night in Wisconsin. Day after tomorrow we look forward to a Great Event: Dori and Joseph DeCamillis will stay in TA DA! A hotel room! Yes, we have procured lodgings for one night in a hotel just north of the Chicago suburb, Highland Park, where our show will be held. We have recited again and again all the fantastic benefits of our upcoming hotel jubilee, including long showers, a ceiling high enough to raise our arms, a bed that one can walk around, television, total privacy, a stationary room that will not rock or creak during intimate moments.

### August 28, 1993   Hotel, Highland Park, Illinois
Need I say anything about our hotel experience? Some things are just too sacred to write about. We are the happiest non-campers on this planet.

### September 4, 1993   Driving, I-80 East of North Platte, Nebraska
Homeward bound. I've called the hospital every day since Dad's accident, and he is finally coming out of his drug-induced stupor enough to carry on a coherent conversation. He will be able to walk, but he'll be in physical therapy for some time.

The Port Clinton Festival of the Arts was positive. We made reasonable money: $1,500. How funny that just months ago, at Gasparilla, we thought $1,200 was the end of all things. The big news from Port Clinton: WE WON A PRIZE! At the awards' dinner when the show director announced, "And first prize in painting goes to Dori and Joseph DeCamillis," we thought there must be some mistake. We never win prizes. I have since been, of course, joyful, but have regarded the incident as a fluke. Joe, however, has become obsessed with the prize idea. He's talked non-stop as we've cruised across America, questioning why we never won a prize before, why we won this time, how we could win more. His competitive side is emerging, which could be a good thing since he usually wins when he makes up his mind to. I've told him to shut-up about the prizes several times already; he apologizes and then retreats into a fantasy world out Lucy's window, where blue ribbons cover our bodies and we roll in a pile of Best-in-Show cashier checks.

Our only complaint about the Port Clinton show, about all outdoor festivals, is that almost all of the artwork exhibited is lacking in inventiveness and soul. Unlike in the galleries in Los Angeles, where art is prized for its voice, its differentness, its ability to provoke thought, or its rebellion, festival art is geared toward its ability to make money. Skillful and aesthetically pleasing, festival art appeals to a broad audience, which is no crime. But most of the conversations we've overheard between circuit artists concern money: how to get into the best festivals, who's selling the most art, how to best present your work, etc. I rarely hear circuit artists mention creative concerns. I have even had artists tell me outright that they have developed a formula (a naughty word to most artists) that they've stuck with in order to insure their marketability.

I'm not saying that the contemporary art world of L.A. and New York is without a bad side. Art valued solely for its shock value and lack of skill is tiresome and frankly, not art. Joe and I call most of it Philosophy Art or Phart, for short.

I'm not sure that Joe and I fit perfectly into either venue. Our work is broadly appealing, but has a dark side not common on the festival circuit. This could mean we fit into both worlds...or neither.

After the show, we hit the freeway toward Colorado.

We've seen a lot of corn. Green cornfields from Wisconsin to Nebraska, against a late-summer-blue sky. I may not want to move to the Midwest, but I love driving through it. Gentle hills roll past whitewashed farms with their quiet silos and country dirt roads. Later, in Nebraska, where the landscape flattens to vast prairie expanses, sunflowers beamed at the sky, with butterflies fluttering among them. The butterflies got a little out of hand through one stretch; yellow, white, or blue butterflies, or Monarchs, streamed from the fields across the freeway, flitting and weaving between cars like the flight of a million ballerinas, continuing for miles. Then this evening a fog rose from the dark fields and collected in low patches along the freeway, just as the evening's profusion of fireflies began blinking. The fireflies' twinkling blended with the mist, and for thirty minutes we drove through this, silently.

### September 10, 1993  Home of Joe's parents, Nancy and Deek DeCamillis, Denver, Colorado

We decided to stay with Nancy and Deek until we leave in January for the Florida festival season. Through a friend, we have a part-time job at the Logan School for Gifted Children teaching art to juvenile geniuses. We are so looking forward to some time off the road—to hang out with family, to rest, eat healthier, sleep more peacefully, enjoy heat and air-conditioning, get some exercise, and, best of all, go to Wal-Mart for supplies instead of a spot to sleep.

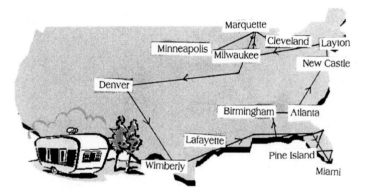

# PART 4

Finding a Home

## January 12, 1994   Home of David and Kim DeCamillis, Denver, Colorado

Some people who have a job, kids, and a mortgage dream of chucking all of their responsibilities and setting out into the world for adventure. We, on the other hand, are as full as ticks with adventure and have come to yearn terribly for the staid life. Being settled for five months has been so refreshing we have decided we need to find a home now. Six people we met at a party last night asked us why we are going out there to do it again. The answer is obvious to us. We have no other way of making a living. Our skills and experience give us two career choices—make art or work at McDonalds. But this year our focus is very clear. We must find a place to settle down.

Teaching at the Logan School has been a valuable life experience, and the means to survive until now. We spent most of our spare time painting in  Deek and Nancy's guest bedroom—our quarters for the duration—excluding a few trips to Steamboat for visits with my family and repairs on Lucy, courtesy of Duckels Construction.

HIGHLIGHTS OF LAST FEW MONTHS:
1) The most embarrassing thing I've ever done: I mistook Deek for Joe and grabbed my father-in-law's butt.
2) Dad: he's home, in bed mostly, or walking very slowly. The accident didn't keep him away from work long; he's back running the company, although a little slower.

3) The replacement of Lucy's engine: Again my Dad generously donated the services of his mechanics to replace our old Chevy 308 with the equally weighted but more powerful 350. If Lucy's suspension and body could handle it, she could probably reach speeds in excess of 85 mph.

4) The infamous "James Brown Soul Center of the Universe Bridge" Controversy: On the same trip to Steamboat, we were witnesses to a town scandal of great magnitude. The story began a few years ago, when my Dad was the contractor on a bridge in Vail, Colorado. Upon completion of the project, the City of Vail named the bridge Bob, a gesture that attracted media attention from all over the globe. This year Duckels Construction finished another bridge, this time in Steamboat, and a citywide contest was held to name the new concrete masterpiece, a promotional ploy on the part of the City Council to gain media attention, I was told. After all the nominations were in, the titles to be voted on were The New Stock Bridge and The James Brown Soul Center of the Universe Bridge. Here's where the controversy began. James Brown won, but received more votes than there are people in Steamboat. My family and other Steamboat natives and old-timers were in an uproar because they hated the name and blamed the City Council for ballot stuffing so Steamboat could get some press. Needless to say, Steamboat did get press. Newspapers all over the country and as far away as Japan reported the affair. There were some very upset people in my hometown, and the night before James Brown himself came to town for the ribbon-cutting ceremony, some hideously backwards rednecks spray-painted *Coon Crossing* across the side of the bridge. City workers were out at dawn blasting the words away to prevent this little part of the story from making the papers. It didn't. But perhaps my humble journal pages will leak the story someday.

5) Teaching: after five months of teaching art to kids, we have determined the occupation to be among the hardest jobs known to man, even though our kids were superior in every way. We barely had life to live after leaving the classroom; we were zapped of energy and creativity and patience and thought. The kids were so eager and quick to learn that we were constantly challenged with keeping them busy and stimulated. Other teachers told us that they had to acquire an ability to pace themselves, but we weren't

involved long enough to learn it. I don't know how we
accomplished any of our own art on top of that job.
6) BIG DEAL: Joe's brother, Mike, an herbalist, prescribed a
strict natural healing program to promote fertility. I was
diligent and faithful with my regiment for five months. His
program included a varying combination of herbs and
vitamins, meditation, and exercise. Hope it works.

In only eight days we depart for Miami. We are very low on
money, as usual. We have enough to make it to the next show
(barely) but are stocked with plenty of paintings to sell.

Our last days will be spent with Joe's brother, David, and
his wife, Kim, in their million-dollar home. The staggering
difference in the comforts of our living situations makes me
extremely jealous, sometimes even depressed. Once again, I
resort to the question of the ages, "Am I white trash?"

David and Kim don't leave me time to ponder such a pitiful
attitude; they know how to have fun, just like us poor folk. We
play games, watch movies, drink good wine, and talk about
everything. Kim, although a vegetarian, is a gourmet cook and
a perfect hostess. After dinner tonight I asked her, "Did I thank
you for that great meal tonight?"

"Ten times," she said.

## January 19, 1994

The temperature has been below zero for days. I am so
happy to be heading south. Yet I will miss our private room
with a king size bed and our very own bathroom.

## January 21, 1994   Home of Robin and Dave Maus, Wimberley, Texas

We left Colorado at 5:00 a.m. yesterday morning, in order
to travel as far south as possible in a day to insure a night in
Lucy without freezing temperatures. Before Kim and David
awoke, we bundled in our warmest paraphernalia, trudged
through the snow, and threw our few things into Lucy, cussing
and banging our mittened hands together while Ruby ran
circles around the camper to keep warm. We drove into the
rising sun, joyous that we wouldn't see temperatures like these,
or snow, for a long time. About 10 miles down I-70, we
stopped for gas and I asked the gas station attendant what the

temperature was. She replied that it was just warming up to about 15 degrees below zero.

Our route took us east, then south straight down to Texas. We got to pass through that little sliver of Oklahoma called the panhandle. That was pretty much the highlight of the first 500 miles.

We spent last night on the side of the road in Texas—no rest area or pull out, just the shoulder. Today we rose early again, eager to visit Robin Maus—the cute, short gal I met at the Ann Arbor festival—and her husband, Dave. After months of interacting with regular people, we looked forward to a meeting of like minds—loner crazy artistic vagabond hermit outdoor festival nuts like ourselves.

Robin and Dave live in a red ranch-style house under a yard full of pecan trees and across the road from the Texas River. When we drove up, we were greeted with a Southern welcome: a) They came all the way out to our vehicle to give us big hugs, b) They offered us water immediately, and c) They politely asked us every imaginable question about our trip. I think I'll adopt the Southern greeting myself if I ever have a home.

The interior of the Maus's home wins. The rich wood walls are well-adorned with vivid-colored art by artists from all over the country, including us. Circuit artists always have amazing art collections, by virtue of their easy access to fellow artists, and the possibility of trading art, Dave says. We photographed their home, but knew we wouldn't get many paintings out of the pictures. Their home is too cool—not "normal" enough.

"So what are home prices like in Wimberly?" I asked Robin after we sat in the living room to relax. The guys were throwing rocks in the river.

"God, they used to be reasonable. We bought this house for under $200,000. But prices are going up like crazy. People from Austin are heading for the hills because Californians have taken over Austin. Why? Are you guys thinking of moving here?"

"Well, not if it's that expensive. We've got to find a place that's super cheap."

"The only places in the country that are still cheap anymore are the South and the Midwest."

"Well, we'll probably be seeing both this year. We have to come up with something."

## January 24, 1994

We depart tomorrow. I will hate to leave this place. We've had peace and good friends for days. Walks by the river and through the woods, talks around the fireplace, a look into another artist's way of working, delicious but vegetarian food.

## January 26, 1994 Home of Dick and Mary Herrman, Tomball, Texas

The Herrmans, last year's perfect strangers, indulged us with the prescribed Southern welcome of hugs, water, and questions when we glided late-morning into the driveway of their English Tudor home. We had to stop on the way from Wimberley to fix the gas pedal with duct tape, so Joe and Dick are out in the garage jerry-rigging a more permanent gas pedal cure—a door hinge. Mary and I are preparing chicken-fried steak, fried okra, mashed potatoes, and peach cobbler for dinner.

I already know we couldn't live here. Houston is too huge.

## January 27, 1994
SERIOUS REVELATION

When it happened I am not sure, but Joe and I have changed dramatically in our approach to painting. Our collaboration has become almost psychic! Today we were taking pictures of the Herrmans house for our paintings. Up until now we'd have to discuss our choices about which corner to shoot or which angle to take—the stuffed bobcat on the hearth or the flowered bedroom with stuffed animals on the bed. Now, without saying a word, we hand the camera back and forth, only nodding at the other's choice, knowing we agree with each other.

Then back in the camper, where we were painting from photos of our family's homes, I noticed that after I'd finish working on a piece, I'd hand it to Joe for him to work on and completely trust that he would only improve it. We used to have to say, "Now what are you going to do with that?" or "I want you to emphasize this." There is no arguing, no discussing, no questions. When the painting is finished we admire it knowingly, as if we both knew all along how it was going to come out.

I wonder if the Herrmans realize how little money we have.

### January 28, 1994   Home of Byron and Eleanor Elliot, Lafayette, Louisiana

After leaving the Herrmans we kept to freeways, which we will continue to do for this trip. Not once have we complained about missing the back roads and side stops of our last trip through Texas and Louisiana; the freeway's smooth tour through the country, although wanting in variety, has less potholes, more part stores, and gets you where you're going the fastest.

We stopped for the day at the Elliot's fancy condo. Gracious Eleanor took us on a tour of Lafayette. We went to a park with historical buildings, a Mardi Gras store, and through swamps. But driving in her Mercedes 450 SL made us happiest.

HIGHLY INTERESTING PIECE OF TRIVIA:

At the historical park where tour guides dressed in traditional peasant-type clothing explained Cajun customs and ways of life, a tour guide explained the reason for the exterior stairway, commonly attached to the small, rural shacks of Louisiana's backcountry. In this predominantly Catholic, very isolated country, it was common to have upwards of 10 or 15 children, and little contact with other families or the outside world. The outside stairway was allegedly designed to keep the brothers' and sisters' bedrooms completely separated. The sisters' room was usually only accessible through a door in the back of the parents' bedroom, and the boys' room was at the top of those exterior stairs, making familial nighttime meetings next to impossible.

In bed before Joe fell asleep we talked about the possibilities of making Louisiana our home. It's cheap and beautiful and has character and a mild climate. I don't know, though. It doesn't seem to speak to us, whatever that means.

Mission: to get to Miami in two days. The odds are against us ever arriving there because of Lucy. Also, we have barely enough gas money to get us there, let alone food money. People have asked, "Why not get a credit card for these tight situations?" After bankruptcy, I tremble at the thought. Some ask, "Why not ask your families to wire you money?" This option is even less desirable than credit cards. We made it through the past few years without asking relatives for loans; why in the world would do it now when we aren't even in debt? Besides, I'm getting used to not having money. Why can't constant fear be an acceptable way of life?

## February 1, 1994 McDonald's Parking Lot, Kissimmee, FL

Lucy breakdowns are as natural as breathing to us now. Today at a rest stop she wouldn't start so a nice tourist drove Joe to *seven different towns* to find a carberator gasket. We were back on the road in two hours.

## February 2, 1994   Home of Walt and Marilyn Davison, Coral Gables, Florida

Hardly any money left! I'm afraid! I'm afraid!

We were finally lucky enough to meet Walt and Marilyn Davison, the interesting retired airplane pilot and his wife that Warren Suckow of Phoenix had told us about. We were warmly invited to come directly to their house, after we phoned them from a local library.

Only Walt was home when we arrived at their 1920s home in gorgeous Coral Gables, a neighborhood with old homes of Spanish Architecture, exotic tropical landscaping in every yard, majestic entrance gates and tree-lined avenues.

So far Walt hasn't been unusual at all. Only friendly and hospitable. He has offered us their spare bedroom for the duration of our show. As we conversed with him in his eclectic living room, I felt odd knowing that we have $20 left to our name and are pretending as if we are friendly out-of-town guests with not a care in the world.

## February 5, 1994   Miami Beach Arts Festival Over

Why the hell do I worry about stuff? I've been shaking with fear of starvation for days. The show was a howling success. In addition to our second biggest moneymaking show yet, we made new art friends, and encountered the most unusual crowd of spectators yet. Let's just say we saw a lot of skin and silicone.

NEW COLLECTOR: A woman dressed like a bag lady came into the booth and poked around for a few minutes and then left without saying anything. An hour later she returned and asked Joe if she could rest in one of our director's chairs for a few minutes. Joe reluctantly agreed, fearing our rickety chairs might not hold up under her large body. She sat for over 15 minutes, her foul odor and stained clothing gathering looks of contempt from other booth visitors. Joe confesses now that he was just about to ask her to leave when she turned to our largest, most expensive piece and said, "I'll take that one."

Joe just stared at her.

"I'll take that one," she said again, more forcefully. "Do you take checks?"

Later she came to pick up the piece in a brand new Lexus, easing our fears that the check might not be good. This is a big lesson for us about treating people equally.

All in all, we have never partaken in a festival where we were so inundated with praise. While I was mostly aware of people's manners and way of dressing, Joe concentrated on more important matters. Joe had this story to tell:

In the middle of the hot day, when the crowd was at its thickest, someone's wiener fell out of its bun. It lay in the middle of the street for only seconds before someone accidentally kicked it, and then someone else kicked it again. Soon it was darting about the street like a mangled soccer ball. Few of the players of this greasy game realized that they were participating, but the ones that did usually bent down to wipe off their shoe after their play. The wiener became gnarled and tattered, then it split in half, and then it was squashed; its destroyers either oblivious or disgusted. Joe was just about to give up wiener watching when a leashed poodle, recently groomed and being escorted by an over-clad, overweight woman, came sniffing up to one half of the squished weenie. The woman recoiled from the treat as if it were a dead animal (I guess it is one), and tried to drag the pooch away, but the fine scented frank got the best of the dog, and he yanked his owner's arm nearly out of its socket to get at it. The treat was gone. The weenie's second half was eventually smooched into a reddish brown splat on the pavement—still interesting to doggies, but not enough to sink a fang into.

This is Joe's idea of entertainment.

The Davison's have, without any help on our part, arranged our accommodations until our next show in Boca Raton in a few weeks. We will stay for two weeks with another Ultra Van couple here in Miami—Lane and Jean Guthrie, who own a five-acre tropical fruit orchard. The Davisons will take us to visit the

Guthries in a few days to certify to our new landlords that we're not dirty drug-addict nutcases.

**February 6, 1994**

We were awakened this morning by the sound of a lawnmower. We peeked out the pink gingham curtains of our guest room to see Marilyn Davison in a tiny, pink bikini, mowing the yard. Her long blonde hair was tied in a little bun at the base of her neck and she glided happily around the yard.

"Wow," Joe said.

"I hope I have a bod like that when I'm in my 70s," I said.

After we got dressed, we scrutinized the Davison's home for future painting material. Of all the homes we've visited, this place cries out to be painted by Dori and Joe. We ran around snapping pictures, fighting over the camera.

"Look at this brass 70s lamp with that velvet tiger wall hanging and that bowl of candy on the table!"

"Yeah, yeah, give it to me. I've got this hamper in the bedroom with a bra hanging out and a fire extinguisher next to it, and the bedspread's killer."

"I can't wait to start a painting of this place. Let's develop our film right away."

We took four rolls of film, a record.

We went into the kitchen to find Marilyn in a flowing transparent yellow robe with a feather boa trim, making breakfast. Over breakfast, we talked Ultra Vans.

Walt is known throughout the Ultra Club as The Man With The Light Coach. He is, on his own admission, obsessed with making his coach as-light-as-possible by stripping down every item possible, including such insignificant amenities as the toilet, the dash and all its gauges, the stove, and all the over-head cabinets. It's not that he never uses the van either; he leaves Florida six months out of the year to escape the heat and travel out West. Marilyn decided some time ago that life with a five-gallon bucket for a toilet and a tiny camp stove on which to cook is not acceptable living conditions for long periods of time, and she lets Walt gallivant around the U.S. at his leisure, while she stays at home in the summer and volunteers for organizations such as the Garden Club. Their arrangement suits them both, but I can't imagine it for myself; I would miss my honey so.

**February 8, 1994**

Today's tourist discovery was Miami's famous South Beach, where movies are made, models are photographed, and beautiful people from all over the world sip umbrella drinks at tables outside art deco cafes. Glamorous, willowy women parade the street wearing almost nothing (I mean that), while dark men in sunglasses stare at them. I gazed longingly not at the perfect bodies but at the menus of the restaurants. Oh, how I would have liked to sit at one of those shady tables and order a tropical salad and a margarita! But no, Joe and I had to go back to Lucy and eat corn chips and peanut butter and jelly sandwiches with our jug of warm, distilled water. Sometimes we get in short arguments over whether or not we should splurge on a special treat. Whichever one of us is stronger and wiser that moment says the dreaded bankruptcy word and we both agree to forgo pleasure and walk dejectedly away from our temptation.

**February 10, 1994   Home of Lane and Jean Guthrie, Miami, Florida**

Last night we met the Guthries, 80 year olds who take care of their own fruit orchards. They are also parents to Janet Guthrie, the first woman to race in the Indianapolis 500. Walt drove us over to their house to allow them to scout us out .

I think they approve of us. We are settled tonight in Lucy under a sky full of stars, nestled with the smells of sweet tropical fruits.

SEMI-INTERESTING SIDE-NOTE INVOLVING CLELBRITY NAME-DROPPING:

I told Lane that my father used to be married to Johnny Rutheford's sister. Lane said that his daughter Janet, in her years of car-racing, spoke very highly of the famous car racer. She said that Johnny was a gentleman in an industry of pigs.

**February 13, 1994**

Joe had a terrible stomachache from eating too many star fruit. The Guthries told us to help ourselves to the fruit, but to be careful not to eat too much or we'd get sick. You'd think a thirty-year-old would understand this advice. Poor Joe. He just couldn't help himself. He is so excited about being surrounded by fruit that he made a list of all the produce in the orchard while he moaned about his poor tummy:

Mangoes (of many varieties), Bananas, Oranges (King, Navel, and Pineapple), Lycee, Cashews, Allspice, Avocado, Orange-fleshed Limes, Monssera, Papaya, Coconut Palms, Macadamia Nut, Carambola (Star Fruit), Pomello, Grapefruit, Persimmon, Lemons, Limes, Pomegranate, Cheimoya, Sapadillo, and Jack Fruit (which fetches over $100 apiece).

## February 15, 1994

We're making art and eating fruit. We introduced the Guthries to microwave popcorn, which they found fascinating and delicious.

And about our paintings:

When we began the outdoor festivals, our aim was to make money. We never intended on being deeply creative or passionate about our paintings. But life seems to have been playing a joke on us. Without trying to come up with a catchy gimmick or thoughtful concept to get some attention in the art world (that was the way we used to do things), we've found a way to make money and follow our creative instincts. As our paintings get smaller and more detailed, they come closer to expressing the vision about home and everyday life that we've always had but could never convey properly. In earlier sarcastic moments, when we were still half in the grips of the world of art academia, we joked about how, in doing these festivals, we were setting out to fool some suckers into paying money for un-smart trinket paintings. Now we joke about what snoots we were.

By accident we've also come up with an artistic project that involves more than our paintings. Our life—the act of living on the road, showing our art to regular people, seeing their homes and immortalizing them—is like one big anti-cerebral performance/installation. How could we ever have come up with a new and different concept to enthrall the art world when we were immersed in it, still trying to use the same visual language? Now that we follow what truly inspires us and interact with all different sorts of people, we have been enlightened to ways of communicating artistically that we never imagined.

## February 18, 1994

Too busy to write. Last minute prep for the Boca Show.

**February 20, 1994**

We gave the Guthries a case of microwave popcorn as a thank-you gift.

As we left Miami for the Boca Raton show, we discussed whether we could make it our home someday. We love its cultural diversity, beautiful scenery, and mostly non-snooty people. We decided we didn't want a big city, though. It's got to be smaller.

**February 24, 1994   KOA Campground, Pine Island, Florida**

With the Crocker Museum Art Show in Boca Raton now behind us, we have less than one week to prepare for our second year in the Gasparilla Festival of Art in Tampa. Before I recount how we ended up on Pine Island, I will give the Boca update:

Great sales. Perfect weather. Crowd consisted of 400,000 very wealthy people.

Now that we can be considered real circuit artists, we've noticed that festival-goers pretty much ask the same questions. Each festival artist has a selection of questions that are always asked, and some of the questions are super annoying. About her photos of third world countries, Robin Maus gets, "Have you been to these places?" (No, someone else takes my photos for me and I put my name on them. DUH!) Because the mixed-media work of Paul Andrews has sinister connotations at times, he gets asked, "Is this about the holocaust?" even when it's a picture of Midwestern farm children. We now have our own selection of dumb questions. "Are these 3D perspectives?" I didn't even know what it meant until someone pointed out that they are referring to those perspective exercises you do in high school art class. I want to tell them that our perspectives are completely askew but I just say sure. We also hear, "Are these miniatures?" What am I supposed to say? Yeah. They are small.

We chose a camp spot sort of close to Tampa; after scouring the southern gulf coast all day and seeing the most expensive RV parks in Christendom, we finally found a KOA campground on Pine Island, a barrier island near Fort Myers. It's the cheapest place around, and it still costs a staggering $20 a night! This place is extra fancy—the roads are paved!!!

**February 26, 1994**

Painting and painting. And painting and painting. The photos we took of the Davison's and Guthrie's homes are ideal for our purposes. Old folks have collected a lifetime of objects with sentimental value and have lived in their place long enough for their consciousness to have seeped into the walls. It seems like we could paint an entire series of the Davison's home alone.

We saw a bald eagle today, sitting atop the campground American flag. Almost brought me to tears.

**February 27, 1994**

Saw the shuttle launch from all the way across the state. Just a barely-visible white pointy cloud, shooting from the horizon. Almost brought me to tears.

**February 28, 1994**

Today we took advantage of the free manatee boat watch that is offered by the campground. We saw manatee! I'd never heard of the friendly walrus-like creatures until today. On the trip, we met a senior couple from our campground who invited us to lunch with them at a local seafood restaurant. Afterwards the gentleman gave us his card, which stated that he was an Admiral in the British Navy.

"Admiral. That's pretty high up, isn't it?" Joe asked.

The man replied in his wonderful accent, "Well it isn't at the bottom of the heap".

After the couple were out of earshot I said, "Joe, you dunce! Don't you know what an Admiral is? They're like a General in the Army!"

"Well I didn't know."

I've been secretly smirking ever since. I usually don't one-up Joe in the military vocabulary area.

**March 5, 1994   Campground, Winter Garden, Florida**

We left Pine Island, did the Gasparilla show this past weekend, then drove here. We didn't win one of those monstrous prizes at the show, but we made a lot more money than we did last year. I'm getting to be like one of those artists that never reveal how much they make. The dollar amounts used to be fascinating to me, but I'm getting used to saying, "Good show", OK show, bad show, etc. It's hard to believe

we've only been at this show business for a year. Seems like
we were born on the circuit.

"Why do you guys paint homes?" a guy asked Joe while he
sat at the booth.

"I'm not sure," Joe answered. "Maybe it's because we don't
have one."

"What do you mean, you don't have one?"

"We live on the road, in a motor home."

"Permanently?"

"Until we find a home. We're looking."

"That's why you paint homes. Because it's what you desire."

"Could be."

"No, I mean it. I read this story about Andy Warhol. He
asked some guy what he should paint and the guy said, 'Paint
what you want the most,' so Warhol painted money."

"Hey, that's pretty good. You're probably right."

HORRIBLENESS:
We stopped in a parking lot somewhere in Tampa to look
at our AAA book for camping ideas and let Ruby run around a
bit. After a little while, Joe caught Ruby eating a mound of
human feces that had been deposited in the nearby bushes.
Because Joe's stomach is 100% stronger than mine, he cleaned
out her mouth with various soaps and lots of water. We still
wouldn't let her lick us all day, and she was quarantined to five
feet from us, even while inside Lucy. Joe made up a short song
about the incident, to the tune of the *Scooby Doo* theme song.

> *Ruby Dooby Doo, you eat poo*
> *We know because we've seen you.*

Our AAA guidebook led us here, to the loveliest setting for
a campground we've ever seen, just outside Orlando. We will
be attending the Spring Ultra Van Rally near Cape Canaveral in
two weeks and this will be our home until then. We are nestled
in a peaceful forest of brilliant green fern beds and towering
live oaks, surrounded by vast meadows of bellowing cattle.

As always, our arrival was followed by the now time-
honored tradition of popping up our canopy, the unrolling of
our green turf yard, and setting up our studio. This time a
wooden picnic table was put to use in our outdoor workshop.
Fellow campers strolled over as usual, asking if we are with the
circus (HA HA). The typical Ultra Van questions are put forth

and answered, and obligatory invites exchanged for later
campsite visits, and any pertinent information regarding
campground amenities dispensed. The only need-to-know info
we received pertained to the cattle; we were told to always
watch for the bulls when entering the pastures and make sure
we stayed close enough to the fence to dive over in case one
might mistake us for a wayward matador.

Within hours of driving in, we were already painting, our
bright indoor scenes contrasting sharply with the dark, natural
outdoor heaven around us.

## March 8, 1994

For the past few days, our nearest camping neighbor has
been a retired Canadian (not retired from Canada, just work).
Today he noticed us trying to hand-saw a large sheet of
Masonite into thirty little canvases for our paintings and dashed
over with an offer to do the whole job himself with his power
saw. We would have been completely batty to turn him down.
While he slaved away at his campsite-turned-sawmill, insisting
he was having a great time, we tried to look busy at other art-
related projects. Had we sat in lawn chairs drinking lemonade
while a man twice our age did our heavy labor for us, we
would surely be going to Hell.

After the canvases were cut, after we coated them with
layers of gesso, after we sanded them several times, we stared
at their blank faces with wonder. To think that within a few
months they will all be finished paintings hanging in the homes
of people all over United States!

Painting began just after dark. Our little table lamps were
the only means of seeing our work. Oil paints don't dry very
quickly, which leads to the inevitable congregation of matter on
the painting surface; here in Winter Garden we are plagued
with dust particles, cow hair, gnats and no-see-ems, broken
leaves and pieces of eagle feathers. I'm tired; more on eagles
tomorrow.

## March 9, 1994

Two majestic bald eagles have built their nest in one of the
live oaks on the edge of the campground. At various times
during the day, campers position themselves so as to catch a
glimpse of the huge birds perched regally atop their home, or
bringing twigs or rodents to the nest. A retired couple not far

from us is not as happy about the birds as the rest of us,
however. Boogers, their old cat, must be kept inside the motor
home at all times, because when he is let out for even a few
moments, one of the eagles sweeps over to a tree just above
Booger's campsite, ready for kitty victuals.

**March 19, 1994**

We've decided lower-Florida won't make a good home for
us. We like the warm weather and all, but need to settle down
in a place where winter actually exists.

As our stay in Winter Garden draws to a close, we feel
remorseful that we have to leave. We've walked daily through
the sunny open meadows among the cows, gazed quietly at the
morning mists that rise in the fields, painted easily and without
complaint for days on end. Some of the old-timers have
planned a potluck for tomorrow—our last day here.

**March 20, 1994**

We contributed chocolate chip cookies to the geriatric
extravaganza, which were promptly finished off before the
festivities even began. A carbon copy of every old-fashioned
potluck that ever was, the menu consisted of over- mayonnaised
macaroni salad, over-mayonnaised potato salad, over-sugared
baked beans, Kentucky Fried Chicken, Marshmallow-Coconut-
Mandarin Orange Thing, Three Bean Salad swimming in
Vinegar Sugar Syrup, and other fattening but strangely
comforting delights. We all sat in a circle of lawn chairs
surrounded by pink flamingos and American flags. Several
snoopy picnickers asked us about our art-making setup. As
usual, our simple, direct answers were returned with intensely
uninteresting stories about someone's second cousin's
hairdresser who was a real good artist. We've honed our
conversation redirection skills to focus on more interesting
subjects, such as stories about the person we're talking to.
Nothing goes better with post-potluck indigestion than tales of
winter in Canada and other natural disasters. We ended up
waddling back to Lucy, our hearts light, and our minds slowly
shifting back to on-the-road mode. Jack Kerouac only wishes
he was us.

Joe's brother Tony will soon be moving to Orlando for a
new job, and he happens to be house-hunting in town right
now. We will be visiting him tomorrow.

## March 21, 1994   Orlando, Florida

Tony's new job entails raising money for the business interests of Lou Pearlman, an Orlando millionaire, whose businesses include several TCBY frozen yogurt shops, a company that makes blimps, an airline, and a new teen band called the Back Street Boys, among other businesses. This morning we met Tony and Lou Pearlman at the local airport for a free ride on the Gulf Blimp. Normally this adventure would have cost us $100 apiece.

We waited on a grassy field at the airport while the Gulf Blimp finished another trip over Orlando. Lou Pearlman is a red-haired, freckled, heavyset man, friendly but somewhat distracted, probably by his uncountable goings-on in the business world. Tony was his usual excited and talkative self, telling us about the huge potential of the airship company, and about the Pink Floyd Blimp that is presently touring with the band. Then the Gulf Blimp came into sight over the trees.

The blimp tour was very much like a ride in a low-flying airplane except that we were outside breathing fresh air. The passenger part of the blimp is like a bucket, as on a hot air balloon, only bigger and with airplane-like seats. Joe and I decided Orlando is probably the best city anywhere to take a blimp tour, due to its abundance of amusement parks. Disney World, Sea World, Universal Studios, Adventure World, Gator World, Epcot Center, all look like a children's toy village, with small gray race tracks, bulbous parsley trees, mirror ponds with minute water falls, and colorful plastic molds of miniature castles and towns.

We also decided Orlando would be one of the last places we'd like to live. We haven't seen a place this plastic anywhere in the country.

Back at the airport terminal, we met members of Lou's new adventure, the teen rock band, The Back Street Boys. Tony explained that these young men, ranging in age from 14 to 22, had been recruited by Lou in a nationwide talent search to be members of a pop band that theoretically would appeal to young teenage girls, much like the 80s group, New Kids on the Block. They have just recently moved from their various homes around the country to Orlando.

Tony asked us to show Nick and Brian the Ultra Van. We led them to our space in the parking lot, and when Nick poked his head in the front window, Ruby nearly bit his face off in a fury of rabid, teeth-bared barking and foaming at the mouth. I nearly collapsed from heart failure, but the rest our group (all men) laughed wildly. Then they came up with an ingenious plan to scare the life out of one of the dark haired Back Street Boys. (Forgot his name).

"Look at this cool camper, man," Nick said as he led his victim to the Ultra Van.

"Wow. Cool."

"Look inside that front window. It's awesome inside."

Unknown Back Street Boy strutted without hesitation up to the window, while I shivered in anticipation of a lawsuit. Ruby lunged out the window in his face. He promptly jumped four feet in the air. I had to laugh, now that I was sure no future pop stars would lose an appendage, but the poor guy got teased the rest of the day.

"Do you guys have time to take a ride on Lou's yacht?" Tony asked.

Joe said, "We have time to do anything in the world."

Lou and most of the gang piled into his baby-blue Rolls Royce, while Tony, Nick, Joe and I followed in Lucy. We arrived at the marina of a quiet lake just as the sun was setting, and boarded Lou's big boat, the measurements and specs of which I am not familiar. I do know that it hosted all the necessities of seafaring voyages, such as a full-size bar, three televisions, a massive stereo system, a pastel mauve and teal decor, and several bedrooms.

Joe and I seated ourselves on the front deck with some Back Street Boys and their girlfriends. While Lou guided the boat around the lake, we told stupid jokes and watched the crimson sun set behind the distant horizon of moss-covered oaks and palms. Just yesterday we ate mushy food in a trailer park!

The Back Street Boys, I must say on their behalf, were impressively well-mannered, friendly, and clean-cut. Somehow I imagined that a group of teenaged, future pop stars would be the last people I would want to hang out with, but our day was a welcome change from weeks of hermit-like existence in the woods. We'll see what they act like if they meet with success.

After the boat ride, we stopped at a TCBY for yogurt, where Lou entertained us with stories about his cousin, Art Garfunkle. Our two-vehicle caravan then drifted to Lou's house, where Lucy may not have been a welcome sight in this neighborhood of circular drives and fountains. Tony proudly gave us the tour of the "villa," a brand-new pillared and balustraded stucco home of 9,000 square feet, with an Olympic-size swimming pool completely surrounded by lush tropical vegetation. I eventually stopped counting the bedrooms and bathrooms, which were identically decorated in splashes of pastel mauve and teal, each with a glass sea mammal sculpture. Lou's bathroom alone could park four Ultra Vans and still have room to take a bath. We ultimately found ourselves in the billiards room, where Lou's extensive collection of entertainment paraphernalia was proudly displayed. He owns a platinum copy of Michael Jackson's Thriller, a real C3PO suit from Star Wars, the original model of the U.S.S. Enterprise used in the first Star Trek movie, and other signed trinkets.

After watching a few home-movie type videos of the Back Street Boys practicing their act, Lou grabbed his guitar and broke out in song. Art Garfunkle's "Bridge Over Troubled Water" was followed by a song that Lou had written himself, hopefully to be included on one of Art's upcoming albums. We listened enthusiastically until Brian the Back Street Boy convinced us to play a little pool, which we did until the wee hours. Of course I didn't say this, but Joe and I have little faith that The Back Street Boys will ever be successful. They are great kids and all, but starting up a pop group this way will never work.

Although Lou has plenty of room for us, we have opted to sleep in Lucy tonight, to avoid any boisterous Ruby encounters with morning joggers. (If we are with her, she will keep her trap shut.) The neighborhood is quiet but I am having trouble sleeping to the sound of concrete dolphins spewing water four feet in the air. If we were flanked by fourteen rumbling semis I would be sleeping like a baby.

## March 22, 1994  Spring Ultra Van Rally, Titusville, Florida

This is our first real Ultra Van Rally. Our Ultra get-together at the Craig's in Joshua Tree was only a mini-rally, a great distinction in the minds of Ultra Owners. Here, official Ultra Van business will be transacted, tech sessions will be held, craft sessions will be available for the ladies, and coach owners will walk around with their chests puffing out, full of importance.

We paid our fees upon entry and inched our way into the shady, unpaved camp area that has been reserved by the Ultra

Club. This was our first glimpse at over twenty coaches in the same place, all in a neat row and shined up for the occasion. A sense of pride permeated our souls as we pulled into our designated slot. We were greeted warmly by Walt and Marilyn Davison and a few club members we'd heard about but never met. This particular rally is for Eastern Ultra owners, and some of the attendees here have come all the way from Canada just for the occasion. A few members eyed us suspiciously, as if we were crashing a senior's only party.

**March 23, 1994**

The past few days have been a whirlwind of events, transporting us into the bewildered stupor we've become accustomed to. Who are we? Where are we? We've gone from an old folk's potluck in the woods to a yacht ride with a teenage pop band to shooting pool in a millionaire's mansion, to a tour of Cape Canaveral—in only a few days. Am I losing my identity? When am I going to have a life of waking up in the same town each morning, with the same friends to call?

I woke this morning and scurried over to the showers to beat the morning shower rush. I hate it when you have to wait in line to shower in a campground restroom. The concrete floors are freezing cold and usually dirty, the rust-stained shower curtains are always too small so you have to pretend not to see the naked senior citizen ladies doing their shower thing, and by the time it's your turn, the entire dry-off area is three inches deep in water, and the drain is clogged with gray hair. Today I did not have to wait and was fortunate enough not to have someone waiting for me to finish, all the while pretending not to see me doing my shower thing.

We spent all day chatting over old times with old-timers. Norm Helmkay, a Canadian Ultra owner with a V-8 Ultra like ours, convinced us to take a short trip to *New Jersey!* to have vital rear suspension work done by the Hull family—excellent mechanics who charge a fair price. We have no festivals scheduled in the month of May, and we can visit Joe's sister, Julie, in Delaware along the way. How strange that we can, on a day's notice, decide to change our course by some 500 miles. I can think of places I'd rather see than New Jersey, but Ultra repairs are serious business. We freeloaders have to go where the next cheap deal takes us.

Tomorrow we leave for St. Augustine, Florida for our next festival.

### March 26, 1994 Dirt parking lot, St. Augustine, Florida

We set up a day early for the Saint Augustine Art Fair (or some such title). Until a week ago, I was unaware that St. Augustine is the oldest city in the United States, founded not long after Columbus discovered America. (What did I learn in college, anyway?) Much like a European city, it hosts different architectural styles from the 16th century to the present, and old bridges, fountains, cobblestone streets, and statues. Horse-drawn carriages clop over the cobbles, echoing down the thin alley-like avenues and through the grassy squares. These carriages break the spell of olden times, for heaps of Midwestern tourists lean over the carriage sides with their cameras, listening to their over-enthusiastic tour guides belt out their memorized speech. As they passed the wax museum, which is situated directly across from our festival booth space, the zippy tour people would yell, "Life-like and life-size replicas of Elvis Presley, Adolph Hitler, Sylvester Stallone, and more!"

### March 29, 1994 Dirt parking lot, festival over

Damn it. The festival is over and we only made $180 lousy bucks. Barely anyone came to the silly show, where the artwork was reminiscent of that at the San Diego and Tempe shows.

Now that our paintings are more time-consuming and detailed, we always get asked, "How long does it take you to make these?" We tell them the detailed ones can take a week or two, but it's so hard to say when the piece passes back and forth between us, and several paintings are going at once. I know why they ask it. They want to see if the labor makes it worth the price, since it's so small and our prices are going up. Most people tend to want to buy their art by the square foot, it seems. Little do they know how many other things go into the price of a painting. The time spent painting it is a fraction of what goes into it, and a small one! Let's see. We have to prepare the painting surface, draw out the image, frame and varnish paintings, create and maintain resume and an artist statement, buy art supplies, buy office supplies, buy film, shoot and develop photos, apply to festivals, document art work, pack for, attend, and unpack from festivals, recover from festivals, keep a mailing list, address and mail festival invites and thank yous, do bookkeeping and filing (a picnic basket is my file cabinet), keep up on art tax laws and do taxes, take trips to the bank, keep records of artwork and where it is, title and price artwork, look at art books and go to galleries and museums to look at art, and, occasionally, clean and organize our painting area. We have to pay for our booth and all its supplies, as well as fork out hundreds of dollars for booth fees. This does not include the most expensive, time-consuming, heart-breaking, thank-less job of all—Lucy.

I know the "how much time" question is well-meant, and I often ask it myself, but just one time I'd like to reply, "Eat me."

## March 31, 1994   Ocala National Forest Campground

Here in the woods I will have time to recap the past few days.

St. Augustine proved so enticing that we actually looked into real estate prices. This is the first time we've actually considered settling down somewhere, but of course the home prices were far from our grasp, as no homes were being offered for $180. But we dreamily imagined what it would be like to live in a charming, historical beach town with nice people and even better weather. This place is a possibility!

We walked ourselves ragged on the cobblestone streets and saw examples of several centuries of architectural styles on our tour of nearly every school, church, hotel, restaurant, and civil building in town. Ruby left her mark in front of several of these landmarks, as if to say, "I'll show you something historical!"

Now we are camped among the pines and palmettos of this lovely central Florida National Forest.

SIDE NOTE:

Back at the Ann Arbor Street Fair, when I met Robin Maus, she told me about a psychic that lived in this area of Florida. Robin visits Marie Lilla, a certified medium, and swears she can tell you amazing things. For a Cultural Encounter and out of curiosity, we are going to take a daytrip to Cassadaga, Florida tomorrow to see what Marie Lilla is all about. I am very skeptical but a little excited.

## April 1, 1994   Still at Ocala Campground

After breakfast sausages over a campfire while listening to bratty kids racing by, we left for Cassadaga. We exited the freeway onto a skinny road through a thick pine forest, and soon passed a large sign reading *Spiritualist Camp* before entering the very small, secluded town. Cassadaga was founded in the late 1800s by a man of psychic abilities who was told by spirits in his dreams to build a camp in the middle of the Florida woods as a haven for soothsayers. Ever since it has been the home of many mediums and a place where people from the world over come to see the psychic of their choice.

The unpaved streets are lined with cute cottages, and each has its own sign bearing the name of the medium who resides there. Most of the medium's names are precluded by the title, "Reverend." There is also a large old hotel with a quaint restaurant, a bookstore with New Age-type books, and a church.

We approached *Villa Lilla* expecting a haunted-looking old home covered with devilish wind chimes, but instead encountered a plain brick suburban-like home with a Wagoneer parked in front. Marie is a fiftyish, rail-thin woman with short, blonde, curly hair who came to the door dressed in blue jeans and a pink sweatshirt, and smelling like cigarettes. She led me into her sparsely-decorated, wood-paneled office—no crystal balls, velvet drapery or black-light posters. We sat down and she began.

MY FORTUNE
1) I am going to have a baby within one year (HA HA)
2) We will own our own home within one year (BIG HA HA)
3) She said I am a workaholic and should take a day off more often. (She got me there.)
4) She mentioned my brother-in-law, Mike, by name and gave me specific information about his life, which I shouldn't reveal to anyone but him.
5) She described our artwork in detail, without knowing that we are artists. (I became more amazed at this point.)
6) She said we'll be going to Delaware and Georgia and will have a great time at both places. (How could one ever guess Delaware and Georgia of all the places to travel in the world? She is right, we are going to both!)
7) She said we have a very important business venture taking place in California and should not miss it. (We've been wondering whether or not to apply for the Sausalito Art Festival; I guess now we'll risk the $25 jury fee.)
8) She said Joe, who she's never met, comes across on the outside as very calm and reserved and quiet, but he's actually very intense, and he needs to lighten up a little. (I am sure she is the best psychic in the world now.)

After the session, I rattled off the details to Joe, who listened with amazement. "She's for real, isn't she?" he said.

"Yeah, all except for the home and the baby."

"What do you mean? It could happen."

I rolled my eyes. "In our wildest dreams. How long have we been going without birth control? Four years? And all of a sudden, within three months from now, we're going to get pregnant."

"You never know. Maybe Mike's herbal healing program did something."

"Uh huh, and a house. We have no credit, no town to live in, and no money."

"I guess we'll see."

Secretly, I am filled with hope that these things come to pass within a year—our craziest, wildest dreams come true. To think that our wildest dream three years ago was to be media superstars!

We drove back here to our woodsy campsite in Ocala National Forest, glassy-eyed and filled with talk of future possibilities.

### April 6, 1994   RV Park Outside Ocala, Florida

This campground, our waiting place before the Gainesville show, has proved to be an adequate, temporary home. There are always open shuffleboards for relaxation breaks, and there is dirt road for walking Ruby. The only annoyance is the groundskeeper who, three times a day, cruises loudly around the park on his old lawn mower to check on things, while his three-legged dog limps behind him, barking furiously. If the spectacle wasn't so loud, I might think it was funny.

### April 14, 1994   Bad Gainesville, Florida (Wal-Mart)

If I can help it, I will never come to Gainesville, Florida again, as long as I live. I hate this place. My memories of it are bad enough; I had no idea my opinion of it could get worse.

We didn't make much money, and in a place where serial killers make up a good portion of the population and bicyclists are used as target practice, I got stopped twice by the police—once for drinking a non-alcoholic beer and another for wanting to walk Ruby across the festival.

We leave tomorrow for the Florida panhandle. I welcome the thought of anyplace other than Gainesville.

## April 20, 1994   Emerald Beach Campground, Navarre Beach, Florida

It's almost impossible to think that a full-time life on the road could get to be humdrum, but it has, to me. If I brought this up to Joe he'd say, "What are you talking about? How'd you like to worry about Lucy breaking down every day? You call that humdrum?"

Each time we pack up our stuff to leave, each time we arrive at a new place—no matter how thrilling it's supposed to be—I do it begrudgingly, as if I am a factory worker doing the same monotonous task for the umpteenth time. I think of normal people in their comfortable homes, with their new-model cars, their kids asking them questions, and their regular hot showers. I think of having a checking account with a branch just down the street, a full-size ironing board just in case, and mostly, a little studio. Oh, I do want a home.

## April 26, 1994

Leaving Navarre Beach soon. Having large mood swings. One minute I'm throwing the Frisbee to Ruby on the beach with pleasure, the next I'm sulking in Lucy's bedroom, staring at the ceiling. Wish I had a home. Any home.

## April 27, 1994

Last day here. Conversation today:

DORI: They're watching *The Sound of Music* in the camper next door. I can hear every word of it.

JOE: Are you jealous?

DORI: Of what?

JOE: That they get to watch it and you don't.

DORI: I'm jealous of dead people.

## May 1, 1994   Deserted street, Birmingham, Alabama

Days have passed. The Magic City Art Connection is over and we almost doubled our sales from last year. I practically had a heart attack last year when we made a paltry $1,700 and now it's run of the mill to make twice as much.
BIG STATEMENT:

I think we want to make Birmingham our home. We love it here, even more than the last time we came through. The only doubt we have about moving here is why we would pick Birmingham, Alabama. Before we came here, we would have said that it could have been the last place on Earth we'd live, just from the things we've heard about it. But we've fallen in love with it, even more than we did with St. Augustine.

We've listed some pros and cons:

PROS:
Beautiful
Inexpensive
Mild climate
Central to festivals
Super nice people
Small-town atmosphere
Semi-cultured
Great botanical gardens
Easy to get around
The right size (one million people)
Fantastic architecture
We have a good feeling about it (most important reason)

CONS:
Because of Birmingham's reputation, people would think we are crazy for moving here.

Of course this is only talk. We'll see if we find a place we like more.

Joe and I just had an argument over which is better: Regular Oreos or Oreos with Double Stuff. I like regulars because double stuffs are like cake with too much frosting. Joe *likes* cake with too much frosting so we see where he is coming from.

### May 27, 1994  The Hull's House, Layton, New Jersey

Yes, a long time has passed since my last entry. My road-weariness is affecting my desire to write. Much has happened since Birmingham:

1) Distant suburb of Atlanta: We visited Joe's cousin Kathy (the queen of hospitality). We painted in the basement all week while she waited on us hand and foot *and* supervised her two children. This must have been the Georgia destination Marie Lilla foretold.

2) Atlanta: We attended Aunt Judy's (cousin Kathy's mom) wild and crazy Kentucky Derby Party. I wanted to like mint juleps but detested them. I expected a fresh, minty green

frozen thing with an umbrella in the top, but instead got a shot of gasoline with a hint of Wrigley's Spearmint gum. After watching the Kentucky Derby, with all of its weirdly named racehorses, I decided that if I had a racehorse, I'd name him James Brown Soul Center of the Universe.

3) Hollywood, Georgia: We stayed at the home of Joe's Uncle, Tommy Grundy and his family, not far from where Deliverance was filmed or supposed to have taken place. We listened to dozens of stories about their Southern existence, including the one about their local firefighters. If someone in their county needed to get rid of a dilapidated home or out-building, all that's necessary is to call the fire department. For the simple payment of a case of beer, volunteer firemen will make the house go away by setting it afire, putting it out, setting it afire and putting it out until it's gone or the firemen are too drunk to continue safely. This is how they train new firemen.

4) Smoky Mountain National Park: The Smokies surprised this Colorado Rocky native by being substantially bigger than molehills. We stopped frequently to take our picture with majestic backdrops, which will come out great, I am sure, because the humidity made my hair look fantastic. We discovered the reason the Smokies are called Smoky when we reached the highest point on the road and saw nothing but fog.

5) New Castle, Delaware: For two weeks we stayed with Joe's sister, Julie and her husband Anthony. We had nothing but fun, sitting around talking, watching movies, touring historical New Castle, going to the beach, and sitting in the Jacuzzi. Although I am terribly accustomed to goodbyes, I shed real tears when we left.

6) Layton, New Jersey: Today we met Ed and Betsy Hull, an elderly couple who have owned several Ultra Vans and own The Layton Garage, where Ed and his sons do excellent work on any kind of car. We are parked in their rural, countryside backyard, with a view of a stream, an old weather-beaten barn, and a cluster of honeybee hives.

Although I am super sick of the road, going over the past month makes me so grateful to get to visit so many loved ones.

As far as settling down is concerned, none of the places we visited excited us as much as Birmingham.

**May 29, 1994**

The Hull's home is a 100-year-old farmhouse, painted white and peeling in spots, with a big front porch and a white picket fence. The interior, sure to be immortalized in one of our paintings, has a grandparent feel to it—traditional furniture interspersed with modern things and most surfaces covered with doilies and runners. The tiny kitchen is crowded with every baking tool necessary to prepare homemade treats often.

Ed and his sons, Tom and Doug, have been working tirelessly on Lucy's rear suspension problem. They are probably the best mechanics in the country (or world for that matter) for this particular job. Joe watches and asks questions, and I stay with the womenfolk, baking cookies and swapping near-death Ultra Van stories. The Hulls are a tight-knit, personable, bunch of people that Norman Rockwell would have loved to paint. (So will we).

As usual I'm writing at night. Joe's oversized limbs are presently protruding onto my area of the bed and disturbing my creative concentration. So I'll have to stop writing so I can get some good punching and kicking leverage.

**May 31, 1994**

Betsy told me that next week, after we've gone, she's having this old house renovated on the inside. I know all things have to change eventually, but it saddens me to think of this old stained wallpaper now infused with a century of stories, mishaps, and memories being washed a pastel peach. I have a hard time picturing carpet where the dark, sometimes splintered wood floor, is scattered with faded throw rugs. But of course I sympathize with the Hull's need for comfort. As Joe and have learned with dear Lucy, old things can look good and simultaneously be a pain in the butt.

**June 8, 1994   Milwaukee, Wisconsin**

I have lazy writing tendencies lately. I am like John Steinbeck in his *Travels with Charley*, when he had been on the road so long he didn't care to write much about traveling anymore. I am not like John Steinbeck in that I am an insignificant crumb of a writer compared to him.

Proof of lazy writing tendencies: ANOTHER UPDATE

1) The Hull's pronounced Lucy road-worthy. We paid them extra and were most thankful.

2) Pennsylvania ...Ohio ... Indiana ... freeways, tollbooths, fast-food, roadkill (lots and lots of deer!), singing, Frisbee games at gas stations and rest areas, Ultra Van gawkers, loud nights at rest stops—the usual.

3) Chicago. Typical bumper-to-bumper madness. Stayed at the Zamboni's during the mildly successful 57th Street Art festival. Felt much at home with them and ate Italian food beyond compare. Took a day in downtown Chicago for tourist activities: The Shedd Aquarium (They need to clean up their fish tanks and make the dolphins do more exciting tricks.), The Field Museum of Natural History (It's big.), Outdoor Fernando Bottero Sculpture Exhibit at the Chicago Institute of Art (Fabulous).

4) Drove to Milwaukee, where the Lakefront Festival of the Arts happens in two weeks. We are planted at the Wisconsin State Fairgrounds, in the RV park which is basically a blacktop parking lot with a few electrical hook-ups. We grabbed a spot near the only small tuft of grass in the lot, so we could be near nature.

## June 9, 1994  Wisconsin State Fairgrounds

It's hot. The locals say it's record-breaking hot. Low 100s in June. And we are situated on pavement. It's midnight, and I can't sleep due to the heat. I was just returning from the showers, a walk that requires me to pass by the pop-up camper of a rather wrinkly, overweight senior citizen couple. They are happily reading in their separate beds with the lights on, in nothing but their skimpy underwear, with no curtains on any of the wall-to-wall window screens.

Not that I blame them. I'm soaked with sweat at our combination dinner table/art studio table/business desk/driver seat, taking a break from the monotonous grind of cranking out paintings. My attitude sucks, I admit it, but it's late, and I'm hot. My feelings about art vary depending on how much food, sleep or attention I've received, on what time of the month it is, on how easily a painting is coming together, or the price we've been fetching, or how many compliments Joe has bestowed on my work up to that point. On rare occasions I'm in that wonderful state of perfect creative oneness; less frequently I'm thinking I am a sorry excuse for an artist. But mostly I'm somewhere in between, mildly enjoying myself and grateful not to have a boss.

If I had a home I would be happy every darn day, I'll bet.

**June 10, 1994**
It's our fifth wedding anniversary!! We made it! We celebrated it first by spending money on a new Wal-Mart oscillating fan with three settings. It's little defense against the onslaught of piercing sunrays bouncing off pavement (Lucy feels like she has a burner turned on under her) but it looks clean and new, unlike anything else we own.

For our finale on our big day, we went all out and ate Thai. We loved the food almost as much as the air conditioning.

Our evening ended very romantically in the back of the motor home.

**June 18, 1994**
MILWAUKEE:
Germans, dark corner taverns (everywhere), smell of hops in the air, blonde hair and blue eyes, homes of Americanized Old World architecture, people who keep to themselves, mostly.

**June 22, 1994**
Show's over. The Lakefront Festival was one of the most unpleasant experiences we've had on the circuit so far. The type of people who attended would surely have been more at home at a tractor pull or monster truck show. Like all cities, Milwaukee has a wealthy, art-buying crowd, but they must have all been out yachting this weekend, leaving us with 100,000 anti-art suburbanites. There were strollers—armies of strollers—which are a bad sign for the artists. We saw t-shirts by the scores, stamped with intelligent sayings such as, *24 cans of beer in a case, 24 hours in a day. Coincidence?* We saw beer guts and secretary butts. We received close to zero positive comments on our work, and a plethora of extremely negative ones. The butthole contest winners were:

1) A 10 year-old boy who saw our price tag and shouted at man-size volume, "Two thousand five hundred dollars!" and doubled over, laughing hysterically.

2) Two thirtyish tubby guys laughed at our work saying, "How'd you like to have that in your living room? Wo! Get me some sunglasses," referring to our bright colors.

We've never before left our booth unattended, for obvious reasons—mainly theft. But no Dori and Joseph originals were going to be heisted at this show, and the abuse we put up with most of the day became too much to bear.

After the show, we had dinner at one of the jillions of microbreweries in downtown Milwaukee, with Robin Maus' husband, Dave. He mentioned something in passing about "the OJ Simpson thing."

"What OJ Simpson thing?"

"What! You guys must be the only people in the world who haven't heard about it." He went on about the whole white Bronco, gruesome death thing.

"How long ago did this happen?"

"About a week or two ago. You guys are really in the dark."

I'd prefer to stay uninformed of the world's troubles, but this kind of thing is bound to reach us. Nothing is more important than football players and grizzly carnage.

## June 26, 1994  Gitchee Gumee Campground, Marquette, Michigan

We've chosen the Upper Peninsula of Michigan for our summer home, after last year's brief trip through the cool, green, and remote land. Marquette is situated equidistant from Cincinnati and Minneapolis, our next two shows, so we can take excursions from here.

When we arrived in Marquette, I called a few RV parks and weeded through the No Pets, Too Expensive, and Too Scummy ones. My final fateful call to Gitchee Gumee was as strange and ambiguous as it was hopeful.

Dori: Hello. Do you have any space at your RV park?

Man: Yes.

Dori: How much do you charge?

Man: That depends.

Dori: On what?

Silence.

Dori: On what?

Man: On how big your rig is, what space I give you, whether I like you or not.

Dori: How will you know that on the phone?

Man: I won't.

Dori: Can't you give me a ballpark price?

Man: Nope. I'll have to take a look at you.

Dori: So, what if we drive all the way out there and you don't like us?

Man: Oh, I probably will, but I've got to meet you first.

I hung up with resignation, and told Joe about the conversation. Joe was baffled but excited to meet the man, ready for another Cultural Experience.

Ten miles outside of Marquette, just across from a Lake Superior beach, we entered Gitchee Gumee. At the entrance was a great boulder adorned with a relief carving of the Edmond Fitzgerald sinking into the lake, and a hand-painted poster that read:

*Notice: Read! Read! Open only to Campers! Not open to General Public!! Entry Prohibited to: Sunday Drivers, Phone Users, Walk-ins from Beach, Sight Seers, Marquette People. "Looking": Back Out! Friends, Visitors, Semis: Back Out! U.P. Mosquitoes by Appointment Only. KEEP OUT or find out who I am. Ranger Jeff.*

We pulled up to the office and a lean, handsome fortyish man with dark hair and eyes sprinted out in nothing but running shorts.

"You the people that just called?"

"Yeah," Joe said.

"My name is Ranger Jeff. You can stay," he nodded, while looking at us and our camper and Ruby, "and I'll charge you $20 a night."

I gasped. "We're going to be staying a month, at least. Will that make our price any lower?"

"OK. $14 a night. That's as low as it gets around here. I charge the big 48-foot RVs $35 a night because I know they can afford it. One guy called my campground ' Gitcher Money'. I thought that was pretty funny. This place is worth it, though. Look over here. I've got a fudge shop, a movie theatre, a game room, the cleanest showers anywhere, and the roads are lined with my stone carvings. I did them myself. And I built every building here all by myself."

"Looks great. Do you mind if we get settled in before we look around?"

"Sure! I'll take you on a tour. Just stop by the office."

Ranger Jeff led us to our spot by running ahead of us. I love this guy.

## June 29, 1994

Ranger Jeff has been given a new name, behind his back only. I couldn't remember his official title and confused it with several of Joe's relatives, who we refer to as Cousin Kathy or

Cousin John. He's now Cousin Jeff. Cousin Jeff has become the topic of most of our conversations since we arrived, starting the morning after we set up camp when I walked over to the office to get more details about the place.

"Well, let's start with Mrs. Fudge. She's my wife, and sells homemade fudge from that little log store right there. I built that myself, you know. You can get fudge in the evenings from her. Oh! Did I tell you I'm a black belt in karate?" Cousin Jeff ran around the counter and promptly did the splits three feet in front of me on the concrete floor.

Joe and I now anxiously await Cousin Jeff encounters, for conversation fodder. Just this evening, Joe went down to the office to report a lawbreaker of the no campfire rule. Cousin Jeff, in the middle of a transaction with another camper, dropped everything, jumped over the chest-high counter, and sprinted (fast) straight to the delinquent campsite to warn them to stop their fire immediately. He helped dowse the flames and without a word, sprinted back to the office.

Here we are, in the middle of a pine forest, on the shores of majestic waters, with wildflowers and wild blueberries carpeting the ground, and all Joe and I can talk about is Cousin Jeff.

## June 30, 1994

We took a long walk along the piney shores of Lake Superior today, after painting. I tried singing Gordon Lightfoot's "Wreck of the Edmond Fitzgerald," but couldn't remember all the words. I think about that song all the time since we've been here. *Superior, they said, never gives up her dead when the gales of November come early.*

I could live here, if it wasn't as cold as Siberia in the winter.

## July 1, 1994

Today we finally took a full tour of the campground. We have taken breaks from painting, but we've always gone straight to the beach and ignored all the man-made wonders right around us. The many log structures that Cousin Jeff built are just the beginning of it all, he tells us. Each day he carts around logs with his backhoe and digs holes with his loader, building another log cabin. For what? He'll figure that out later. One cabin houses the big screen TV where movies are shown nightly. In it there are log couches and log tables to prop one's feet and a huge fireplace with a mini-library nearby for woodsy intellectuals. Near the door hangs a primitive drawing of Elizabeth Taylor done by Cousin Jeff, too.

Mrs. Fudge's hut stands in the middle of the giant Lincoln Log Town, and we still haven't caught a glimpse of her yet, but we are trying. The showers and bathrooms are housed in another log cabin, with the astonishing feature never before seen in a RV park—piped-in classical music. Joe and I have become accustomed to pretty pitiful conditions in showering facilities; Beethoven While Bathing is the height of luxury.

After the cabins, we inspected the huge granite stone carvings that lined the main dirt road of Cousin Jeff-ville. Each boulder, like the Wreck of the Edmond Fitzgerald Rock at the entrance, was meticulously carved and painted by Cousin Jeff. On one rock, the busts of John F. Kennedy and George Bush stand together in their business suits. Tammy Wynette looks quite regal in stone and hangs opposite the Harry Houdini rock that also includes the magician's real name, Ehrich Weiss. Recently he finished a life-size relief carving of Daniel Day Lewis in *The Last of the Mohicans*. Cousin Jeff is now completing the finishing touches on his Mount Rushmore rock, in between hauling logs and chasing down campers who start fires.

This place has renewed my interest in writing. Cousin Jeff is an inspiration.

NOTE: Painting has been getting very hard for me recently. My eyes water, I sneeze, I feel nauseous. I pray to heaven I'm not becoming allergic to making a living.

**July 5, 1994**

The weather is perfect here—always in the 70s, a constant cool breeze, sunny. We take to the beach for frequent walks and find the shells, rocks, glass, and wood pieces of the sort found nowhere else. The strangest and most deformed natural artifacts seem to wash up on the shores of Gitchee Gumee. Joe is mad with excitement and has unfortunately collected seven grocery bags full of the smelly stuff. My suggestion that we might not be able to take it all with us is unthinkable to him, so I don't' bring it up anymore.

**July 6, 1994**

We have a clever new way to get our paintings to dry faster. We set our oven on low heat and stick the paintings inside. The cooking fumes from oil paints probably aren't entirely healthful, but at least we don't have wet paintings lying around and getting in our way.

After all the ridiculous comments about the bright colors of our paintings at the Milwaukee show, we've been significantly neutralizing our colors. We don't want the wacky colors distracting from the narratives we're trying to portray. Our paintings have taken on a whole new reality. They seem to show more respect for the inhabitants of the homes by presenting their environment with more honesty.

## July 7, 1994

Last night we were watching *Ace Ventura, Pet Detective* on the big screen with two other camping families, laughing continuously like we did the two other times we've seen it, when a loud machine sound revved up somewhere outside the Log-O-Max cinema. The noise grew louder and louder, soon drowning out the movie. As we fellow campers looked at each other in bewilderment, a strange and hideous smell reached our noses. Beneath our feet, white smoke began billowing up from below the floorboards through the wide cracks. It didn't take long to recognize the familiar toxic stench of pesticides and realize we were being exterminated, along with the bugs. We all ran for the great log door and burst outside, coughing and spitting. Cousin Jeff waved at us from his death-machine rider mower, completely unaware that we would be affected by his murderous activities. Joe chased him down and asked him why he chose to spray the campground during the movie.

"The entire campground has to be sprayed daily and this is when I do it."

Joe smiled. "Well, these fumes aren't exactly good for breathing."

Cousin Jeff shrugged. "My wife walked behind the fumigator every night when she was pregnant and she never had a problem. Our kids turned out OK."

Joe didn't bother asking why a pregnant woman would chose to follow close behind a moving pesticide sprayer. We've learned with Cousin Jeff: that's the way things are. Ace Ventura was forgotten in favor of a much funnier Cousin Jeff discussion hour back at the camper.

**July 8, 1994**

We met Mrs. Fudge finally. She didn't show any signs of pesticide poisoning, or of having eaten one bite of fudge in her life. She is beautiful and slim, well-groomed, wears just the right amount of make-up, and dresses appropriately in Gap-style clothes. Cousin Jeff has been wearing nothing but those same running shorts since we met him, so we wondered about Mrs. Fudge. She seems quite the opposite of Cousin Jeff, really. She comes across as a perfectly normal human being. Except for one thing.

We met her at the Fudge Log Emporium where she was selling candy. When we had picked out our fudge of choice, she said, "You don't want to eat that stuff. It'll make you fat."

We laughed it off, saying, "That's OK with us," but she persisted with fat gram statistics and other ways to make us feel guilty for buying her fudge. We eventually wrangled ourselves some butter pecan fudge and left feeling guilty, wondering how she was able to sell anything.

SPECIAL NOTE: We leave in four days for the Cain Park Arts Festival in Cleveland, Ohio. I wonder if I'm pregnant. The oil fumes make me sick, my period is one day late, (I've been regular for seventeen years) and I remember feeling pretty fertile that night in Milwaukee on our fifth wedding anniversary. Feelings? I'm not granting myself feelings until we see the positive test results. I don't want to get my hopes up.

**June 9, 1994   HUGE NEWS**

We went to the Wal-Mart in Marquette, got the pregnancy test, and followed its directions in Lucy's bathroom in the parking lot.

The little blue line said YES, *most definitely you are pregnant!*

Joe was jumping around, rocking Lucy, hugging me while I repeated, "I knew I was, I knew I was." In the space of a few minutes, I went from doubt and nervousness to shock to supreme joy. Unfortunately, I didn't enjoy one of the happiest moments of my life as much as I deserved to. My jubilance would be tenfold if it weren't for our vagabond gypsy status. Suddenly, being on the road with no home has become an even more terrible thing. We have shows in Cleveland, Minneapolis, Sausalito, CA and Kansas City coming up—big shows that we must attend. We won't be able to settle down until late September, when I'll be over five months pregnant.

After much discussion back at Gitchee Gumee, we agreed that Birmingham, Alabama will be our new home for good unless we find some place we like more. The sudden news of a baby coming pushed us to make the decision final, and having a home to look forward to makes me a tiny bit more secure. Birmingham, Alabama. Our future home. I'll have to keep saying it out loud for a while.

Oh my gosh! A little baby is inside me right now!

## July 10, 1994

Mrs. Fudge was the first human to hear the good news. She was visibly thrilled for us, but lead right into the question; "Do you feel sick yet?" I told her no, and she looked relieved and told of her nine-month morning sickness nightmare. She looked worried for me. I'm confident I'll feel fine.

We leave tomorrow for Cleveland, a two-day drive in Lucy.

## July 12, 1994   Cain Park, Cleveland, Ohio

I'm lying in the back of Lucy while Joe attends to the hordes of humanity at the booth, just in front of the camper. I am writing to take my mind off how disgustingly ill I feel. Constant nausea has enveloped me and the stifling heat only fuels my misery. Back in lower areas of the Midwest, we are again subject to temperatures beyond human tolerance, and the lack of air movement and air conditioning is life threatening. (It's a pregnant woman's God-given right to complain and exaggerate.)

People keep coming over to Lucy to admire her, something I don't mind unless they are loud and disturb my rest. Some guy just peeped in the back window, saw my bare feet in his face and said to his friend, "Let's get outta here." Hopefully, it wasn't the smell that did it.

## July 15, 1994   Wal-Mart Parking Lot, Somewhere in Michigan

I'm sick as a dog. I can barely sit up. Joe doesn't realize how bad I feel. He had the audacity to ask me to help him buy supplies!

A recap of the Cain Park Festival:

Good sales. Nice people. Met artists Kate and Terry Cherry. They might come visit us at Gitchee Gumee!

The act of writing is making me feel like puking, only I can't puke.

### July 19, 1994   Back at Gitchee Gumee

I stayed in bed and watched Joe pick blueberries from the window near my head today. Joe is happier than I've ever seen him. Besides painting a lot, he takes long beach walks with Ruby, collects even more nature trinkets, picks blueberries (which I can't eat), and enjoys the cool weather and the quiet setting. It is especially quiet without me contributing my usual clever and meaningful conversations. All I can do is lie still. I think that's one of the main things he's happy about.

### July 25, 1994

Terry and Kate Cherry arrived to share the Gitchee Gumee experience with us!

### July 26, 1994

The Cherry's have joined us for Cousin Jeff discussion hour in the evenings. When they arrived at the campground for the first time, Cousin Jeff was going to charge them $20 a night to camp. When the Cherry's told him they knew we were being charged $14 a night, he gave them a discount. Thus began the Cherry's initiation into the land of Gitchee Gumee campground.

Cousin Jeff did not do the splits for them.

### July 27, 1994

I began puking today. I have designated an area behind Lucy, in the bushes, just for this purpose. At least four other campers have a clear view of my actions, but I don't care. When you're throwing up, you really don't care about much.

### July 29, 1994

Today we were awakened by the sound of an Indian call. Later this morning the Cherrys told us that they heard it, too, and when they peeked out their window to investigate, they saw Cousin Jeff sprinting down the road in his jogging shorts, yelling like an Indian brave.

Then, this afternoon, Terry reported the most incredible of all Cousin Jeff trivia. Terry made a comment to Cousin Jeff about how well this RV park must be doing to afford the constant improvements, to which Cousin Jeff replied, "You don't think I'm independently wealthy, do you? I barely make enough to cover expenses from these campers. No, I make money through lawsuits. I've already won five big lawsuits and have another one pending. This time I fell into a pothole in Marquette when I was riding my bike down the trail. So I sued the city."

Cousin Jeff Discussion Hour lasted longer than usual today.

I'm still puking, at least once every two hours. I had to make my designated area a little bigger in circumference.

## August 3, 1994

The end is near. I can confidently assert that the past two days have been the most horrible of our years on the road.

We were driving into Marquette in Lucy for one reason. I craved grapefruit. I absolutely had to get some grapefruit immediately. As we cruised at 50 mph up a hill just before getting into Marquette, I lay sideways on my seat cushion watching the treetops fly by and trying very hard not to throw up. Suddenly, it felt as if Lucy had completely collapsed in the rear on one side. We felt like we were riding a bicycle down railroad tracks, and it sounded like an airplane touching down without landing gear. And we were tipping sideways! Joe used every ounce of his strength to keep Lucy in a straight line, as the road was rather busy, but no shoulder was available. We finally stopped in the center of the right lane. Ruby looked as if she'd just been electrocuted.

As we got out to check the damage, all I could say was, "Oh Joe, why didn't you check the bearings last week? I told you to check the bearings last week. I knew those bearings were going to go." Joe took one look at the carnage and said solemnly, "Dori, I don't think it was the bearings."

Our axle was laying about 15 feet behind Lucy on the highway. The rear left wheel lay completely horizontal under Lucy's leaning hull. Barfing would have been the appropriate response, but somehow my state of shock kept my food down. A little cash register in my head was busy ringing up the fortunes it would cost to repair.

Joe stood staring for a minute until a car slowed down and called out, "You need some help?" Joe yelled yeah, and within seconds had climbed into the car for a ride into town to get help. I was told to lie down in the Ultra Van. I stepped into Lucy and found that our precious spice rack had fallen. I patted Ruby, then began sweeping the nutmeg and cumin and glass into a pile, sobbing and listening to the whoosh of cars flying by. I nearly peed my pants when a strange man poked his head into Lucy and yelled, "You better get out of here! You're going to be hit by a car any minute!" I stared wide-eyed at him, shaking by this time, from sickness, from the fright, and from embarrassment at being caught crying with abandon. The nice man, Jim, led me out of the camper by the hand, sat me on the guard rail, and explained that cars were coming up the hill at 60 mph and that our flashers were barely working. (This is always the case with Lucy.) He said he almost rammed into the back of us. "I'll sit with you until your husband comes back," he offered, and said he was on his way to a wedding. "They can wait," he assured me. I must have looked pretty pitiful.

Not five minutes after Jim had stopped, an old Subaru came up too fast, slammed on the brakes to stop, and rammed into the back of Jim's little pick-up, which was parked behind Lucy. Only minor damage appeared to have occurred. Jim and I watched as a thirtyish woman took a deep breath and slowly got out of the car. She was wearing a long braid, a batik skirt, and Birkenstocks. "I'm so sorry," she said in a pot-smokers' voice. I didn't realize the car wasn't moving at all." While she exchanged information with Jim, the woman noticed my green pallor and sad face. "Are you OK, woman?" she asked. Without thinking, I blurted out my morning sickness trauma, the horrible wreck, and our lack of money in a spewage of tears and sobs, probably frightening poor Jim to death. Alida, the woman, gave me a tight bear hug and said, "This is all going to come out fine." And then she left to deliver some flowers.

After I went to puke in the grass, my buddy Jim and I went back to sit on the guardrail.

We waited. I puked again. Then Joe arrived in the police car. I thanked Jim as he drove away, and the cop parked his car in the place of Jim's truck, with giant flashing red and blue lights whirling on top.

In the time that it took the officer to survey the damage and hear the story of Jim's truck getting hit, three new oblivious drivers almost rammed into the back of the police car. The exasperated cop said, "It's always this way. I don't know what these drivers are thinking or looking at, especially with a police car and flashing lights, but we get hit in the rear all the time in these situations. It doesn't surprise me a bit that your friend's truck got hit."

Finally a giant tow truck showed up and hooked Lucy up to be towed to "Superior Truck." There was no room in their tow truck cab, and the driver's weren't the least bit friendly, so we accepted a ride from the nice policeman. Just as we got into the car (Joe meanwhile biting his cuticles, Ruby shaking, and me sinking into nauseous oblivion), a domestic violence call came over the radio. The cop said to us, "Sorry, I gotta take this!" Before we could even look at each other, he started speeding down the road with us gripping the seat separator cage. In fast motion, he dropped us off at what I will now call The Extra Greasy Donut Shop, promising to return and give us that ride.

The Extra Greasy Donut Shop is the last place a woman of my constitution should hang out. Cigarette smoke hung in the air and mingled with a stale grease and sugar stench. Joe telephoned Superior Truck from the pay phone and got chewed out for not showing up at the garage. Joe came shuffling back, dejected, as I nibbled on a cold, previously cooked hamburger patty that I had tucked in my pocket back at the accident. At the time I packed it, I prayed that I wouldn't have to resort to eating it. I ate the whole thing, glad I had something to feed the baby, as donuts were no temptation whatsoever. We sat in silence and stared at the formica table until the policeman returned 45 minutes later. He gave us our ride to an old tin structure about 10 miles out of town. We thanked him, then went inside to discuss the repair situation with the mechanics.

Looming large in our minds were two questions: How much money and how much time? Our Minneapolis show was then only one week away, and we are nearly out of money again. The mechanics came up with an extremely low price compared to what we had imagined. We had pictured at least a $1,000 invoice, but after the quote was given we remembered we were in a small town in the boonies, where honest mechanics with big hearts for poor folks can often be found. We breathed a little easier until we realized that we'd be stuck living at this garage for at least three days. A motel, even at the practically free price offered in the Upper Peninsula, is simply not possible for us. Practically free does not equal actually free. So here I am, lying on our bed in Lucy, while the loud pounding of tools and sounds of twisting metal resonate right beneath me. We are parked in this dark garage with the smell

of diesel fuel-drenched dirt rising up from the floor. I have
been throwing up in the bushes ever since we arrived.

## August 5, 1994   Superior Truck, Marquette, Michigan

The nice mechanics are working vigorously to get us out of
here. I imagine they aren't used to having their customers living
in the vehicle they're fixing. We are out of food, so we've been
forced to walk a half-mile down the road to a greasy, smoky
diner for breakfast, lunch, and dinner. Thank God, it's cheap. I
don't enjoy anything I eat and most of it comes right back up
when I get back "home" to Superior Truck. The garage now
has a puker-designated area that surrounds the back half of the
building, in the weeds. There are no other homes or businesses
nearby so I have lost an audience, which I had grown
accustomed to at  Gitchee Gumee.

## August 8, 1994

This morning one of the mechanics brought two of their
children's bicycles from home so we could ride down to our
diner. Three times a day, drivers on the road get to witness two
sad-looking adults wobbling down the rocky shoulder of the
road, their knees bumping the handlebars of small children's
bikes. It has been five days since we were hauled into Superior
Truck.

I can't help but notice the beautiful countryside around
here. Joe, Ruby and I take short walks in the meadows across
the road; the fresh air and trees are probably saving my sanity.
This country reminds me so much of Steamboat. The terrain,
the climate, the foliage, although not exactly the same, have a
similar feel to them. Childhood memories surface often, even
the diesel fuel smell of the garage takes me back to when my
dad's business was small and he worked with my Grampa on
their equipment in a cramped, dark, smelly garage.

I keep thinking this breathtaking place would be a perfect
place to live, without the winters. I could settle for a summer
home here, when we get rich.

## August 10, 1994

We have just been informed that Lucy will not be finished
in time to drive to the Minneapolis show. We have reserved a
large van from Rent-a- Wreck, an expense that puts us
dangerously close to dead broke status again. The mechanics
say Lucy will be finished when we return. We are departing

now and I am waiting for Joe to finish packing while I lay across the back seat of the old van.

## August 11, 1994  Snelling Motel, Minneapolis, Minnesota

All day we drove and I saw nothing but the tops of trees whizzing by. Joe commented on the magnificence of the upper-Midwest—Michigan, Wisconsin, and Minnesota—and how much it is similar to the high country of Colorado. I wish I could have seen it.

Our lodging, the Snelling Motel, which was quickly renamed the Smelling Motel because it reeks as if twenty chain-smokers had camped here last night. There are no other rooms. We checked.

## August 13, 1994

Today's events: I watched TV and puked all day at the hotel while Joe worked the festival.

## August 14, 1994  Somewhere in Minnesota (or Wisconsin)

Joe gave his festival report this morning at the Smelling, over breakfast, after which I gave my television report. We made plenty of money to get us back to Colorado and then on to Sausalito, California, for our next show on Labor Day weekend. The best part was that *we won a Best of Show award!!* I thought winning the biggest award would finally satisfy Joe's competitive craving for glory, but no. Now he's even more glassy-eyed in his quest for fame.

"How can we win more?" he asked greedily.

"Who cares? Can't you just be happy with this one?"

"I am! It's great! But if we won these all the time, we'd make more money because of the cash awards, *and* we'd be invited for sure the following year, and we wouldn't have to worry about whether or not we get in all the time." He went on like this for some time, convinced we can eventually take home top awards like it's a steady paycheck.

Then he listened eagerly to my television report, the highlight being a *Charlie's Angels* rerun. He licked his chops and said, "You're so lucky."

## August 16, 1994  Marquette, Again

We're back at Superior Truck, ready to leave for Colorado tomorrow. Who knows if Lucy will get us anywhere? As I lay here in the camper (slip-on shoes next to my feet awaiting my next lightening-speed run for the bushes) our dreams of a house in Birmingham and a working vehicle and a healthy baby seem far away. Someone should make a TV show about our life called "I Hate Lucy."

### August 19, 1994   Somewhere, Nebraska

We made it to Nebraska. No problems at all, as far as Lucy is concerned. My morning sickness, however, has reached the dangerous stage. I can keep no food down.

While driving in traffic down the main street of a small town, one of my meals came back up. I dove for the kitchen sink, where several passengers of other cars witnessed my episode through our kitchen window. Their faces looked as if they were watching *The Night of the Living Dead*. I didn't care. Joe cleaned it up, but wouldn't speak to me for three hours. I can't say I blame him.

### August 21, 1994 Home of Joe's parents, Denver, Colorado

We just got here. My sister Debi and her boyfriend Bob have offered us a free place to stay for the next month up in Steamboat! Thanks to a trade they secured with some of their friends, we'll have our own condo for a month. We're going up there tomorrow.

I haven't kept one bite of food down for three days. I think I'm dying. I am going straight to our family doctor up in Steamboat, no matter what it costs.

### August 22, 1994   Our Condo, Steamboat Springs, Colorado

Wonderful sister Dana came down to Denver to give us a ride back to Steamboat. Rather than take Lucy up those mountain roads, we're leaving her in Deek and Nancy's driveway for a month. God bless them for babysitting that nutty machine.

I threw up four times on the way to Steamboat.
1) Dana couldn't stop the car in time, so I wretched in her cooler while she covered her ears and hummed. Joe is used to this noise by now.
2) One time I hurled behind a 7-Eleven while Joe washed out the cooler in a creek.
3) I made it out of the car door but threw up on my feet.
4) I don't remember and I don't care.

I gripped the door handle of Dana's car throughout the drive, chanting to myself, "Only three more hours until I see the doctor. Only two more hours until I see the doctor."

Dr. Dudley is my savior. I worship him. I give him thanks. I praise him for his glory. More than anyone, he felt supremely sorry for me. He understood the true nature of my suffering, and it showed in his face. He had the most sincere look of pity I have ever witnessed. Finally someone understands! He said that I have blah blah something or other, which means morning sickness, magnified about 50 times. I was dehydrated and my heart rate was far too high from hunger. I was put on an IV. The most wonderful feeling came over me when that juice reached my arm. I began to feel better, nourished, for the first time in weeks. As the bag drained, I became more confident, more relaxed, like a person again. I was given an anti-nausea drug to help keep my food down, which I am to take before meals. Normally, pregnant women should not take drugs, but in this case, the baby is in danger of being underfed, so we had to choose between the lesser-of-two-evils.

### August 23, 1994

I'm getting better! Still, I've lost 15 pounds, wear the same ugly pink flowered dress every day, and have dark circles under my eyes and gray skin. I lay on the couch of our typical ski-town condo and watch TV, mostly. Usually I wouldn't waste my time with TV, but when you're sick, it's a God-send.

Joe is painting like mad in anticipation of the Sausalito Arts Festival in a week. The paintings are improving dramatically, in our opinion. More drama, more depth, more detail, more contrast, more penetrating stories about the people whose homes we've visited. I know neither of us ever anticipated we'd become as skilled as we have. Thanks to art school I have underestimated skill for a long time.

Since I have zero capability of focusing on art, Joe is delving into it. I hope he doesn't leave me in the dust with all the extra practice he's getting.

### September 18, 1994  WEEKS LATER!!

Although the morning sickness has gradually lifted, I am still getting my strength back and trying to put on weight. I haven't had the energy to do more than watch television or take short shuffles to the apartment complex parking lot.

RECENT THRILLING EVENTS:

1) Joe was gone for eight days to the Sausalito Art Festival. We made tons of money; there was nothing left by the third day. We never dreamed in the beginning that we could make over $10,000! Joe said people were angry that we had no paintings left! This gives us enough money to put a down payment on a house when we get to Birmingham!

2) We won second place in painting!

3) While Joe was gone my family took care of me. Dad took me to the vintage car races; Derick had me over to his condo to throw the football and shoot cans with his BB gun; Mom and Dana keep me supplied with rented movies and conversation. Debi brought her dog Pete over. He walked into my apartment, lifted his leg and peed on my chair.

4) Without a rest after the California trip, Joe painted diligently by himself for two weeks in preparation for the Plaza Art Fair in Kansas City. He leaves in three days.

With so much time on my hands, I've been doing some thinking. I realized today that Joe and I are now completely comfortable with not being together. The change has been so gradual that I didn't notice it until now. During our first year on the road, we hated being apart even for a few minutes. Now I welcome the time to be by myself for a while—to decide what I want to eat without asking someone else, to use up the whole bed, or to listen to Neil Diamond. Like never before, I feel confident and self-sufficient whether we're together or not, and I know Joe is the same.

**September 19, 1992**

Eager to get paintings done as quickly as possible, Joe set a small painting of a bright red teapot in the oven and turned it up to 350 degrees so it would dry faster. Then he forgot about it.

Dinnertime came. We agreed upon Tombstone Pizza for dinner and, accordingly, turned the oven up to 425 degrees to preheat it.

"What's that smell?" I said after a few minutes.

"God. It smells like a toxic waste dump," Joe said.

"Yeah. On fire."

"It's burning my eyes."

"It's making me sick."

"Better look in the oven," Joe said, sniffing his way to the kitchen. "AAAAHHHHH!"

"What?" I screamed.

"Where's the hot-pad? Help!"

"Here. What's. . .Oh my God!" I said, as he pulled the charred picture out.

"Great," Joe said. "All that work."

"Well, who knows? Maybe someone will like a dark brown teapot."

## September 20, 1994

While Joe paints, I sit sufficiently away from the fumes and talk about getting to Birmingham, finding prenatal care, going over all the wonderful attributes of our new city (probably to convince us we've made the right decision). We'll find an apartment to rent for a few months, until we find a home to buy. How these things will come about, I am not sure, but planning ahead is not much of an option for us. Just knowing we'll be there soon is security enough.

## September 21, 1994

Joe left for Kansas City today. I take walks through the sagebrush near the condo and throw the Frisbee to Ruby. I also watch TV and perform small tasks such as remote clicking, or foot scratching. Occasionally I comb my hair.

## September 25, 1994

Joe returned late last night. The show completely sold out and we won Best In Show!! He was too excited to be exhausted.

SHOW REPORT:

Crowd: Friendly, wealthy, well-dressed, educated, enthusiastic.

Weather: Freezing cold. Joe had no winter clothes so he had to purchase a coat at the outlet stores on the way.

Food: Incredible corn-fed steaks. He ate steak for every meal, including breakfast.

Fad: Cigars. Everywhere.

Roads: One hell of a long drive in a day.

Interesting Fact: He titled the burnt painting *Red Hot Pot* and sold it.

He said it was strange driving a car and staying in a hotel, especially without me. Kind of lonely, but easier. In honor of our last festival while being homeless, and to keep himself occupied while he sat at the booth for three days without his one true love, Joe kept statistics of various crowd tendencies.

First, he kept stats of tennis shoe brands. The most popular brand was Reebok. Nike was a close second, and all other brands were far behind. Only New Balance and Saucony made a respectable showing in the less popular brands.

Next, he kept a record of the audience's questions and comments about our art and then a tally of how many times the comment was said.

THE RESULTS:
1) Do you use a magnifying glass? 27
2) This is the best art I've ever seen. 4
3) Amazing detail! 25
4) I could never work that closely with my spouse. We'd kill each other. 10
5) They look like photographs. 17
6) How long did they take you to paint? 21 (Joe did not reply, "Eat me.")
7  Are they oils? 20
8) Who does what? 22
9) Nice work/Beautiful work/Great! 163
10) You must be patient. 15

AND THE DREADED:
11) Are these 3D perspectives? 14
12) Are these miniatures? 6

GOOD SINGLE COMMENTS:
1) Oh! Itty Bitty pictures!
2) It takes a lot of guts to paint something so different, and a lot of money to buy.
3) This one looks boring. (And then when he saw Joe) Actually, it's kind of neat.
4) Small, aren't they?
5) Why would I want a picture of a TV when I already have a TV in my house?

BEST COMMENT OF ALL:
Ya got any cotton fields?

We stayed up until 2:00 in the morning, talking about how far we've come. All things are good. I'm weak, but over my morning sickness. We are having a baby! We are popular artists now! We are moving to a beautiful place! We have some money! (And Joe's favorite): We are winning awards often!

## September 27, 1994    Home of Joe's parents, Denver, Colorado

It's time to leave for Birmingham. Our life on the road is over. We've seen the country, had more than enough adventure, and have amazingly achieved our goal of making a living from our art (and then some). But since I got pregnant, a sedentary life could not have come soon enough.

Joe says he's relieved that the end of our life on the road is nearly over, but sad, too.

This morning held gloomy goodbyes to my family members in Steamboat. The realization that they won't see their grandchild/niece/nephew at birth makes me sorry. I still can't believe we're doing it. What do we really know about Birmingham, Alabama, anyway?

## September 28, 1994

UH OH.

Lucy will not make it to Alabama. During a short trip to the grocery store here in Denver, some part snapped in Lucy's rear end and she can't be driven faster than 35 mph. Joe has been pounding, screwing and shaking Lucy from underneath for three days; we have finally given up on her. We are switching to the recently invented Plan B, in which we put Lucy in storage here in Colorado, rent a moving truck, take all of our belongings out of storage, and move, Lucy-free. If we don't use Plan B, we will either run out of money or go crazy. It means, of course, that we'll have to A) Find a place to live in Birmingham in 2 days, B) Find new transportation quickly once we get there, and C) Say goodbye to our adorable, good-for-nothing friend, Lucy. It's too soon to know if we'll miss her and we're too busy to think about it anyway.

## October 3, 1994

We found an ad in the yellow pages for an RV storage space that costs only $25 a month. We rented a moving truck and Joe drove it, with me following behind in Lucy, to the other storage place where our belongings have been waiting for three years. The guy at the counter commented on how long we'd had our stuff there, how sad he was to see us go. I'll bet he was sad. He could buy a car with the money we've paid him.

We found our formerly shiny, bulletproof lock to be a rusted, crummy-looking thing but it had done its job. How funny that we thought we'd only be storing here for six months! Dust flew everywhere when we slid the door open. I moaned when I saw the 10-foot stack of heavy objects I knew my pregnant body couldn't lift. Slowly and emotionally we pulled the mountain apart, me moving pillows and pencils while Joe tackled the trunks and dressers. We had forgotten about many of the items, but there were none we regretted saving. We were especially excited about our Super Suck 2000 vacuum cleaner because it symbolizes a life with wall outlets and throw rugs and stability.

Looks of hatred were thrown at artwork of past unprofitable days, but we convinced ourselves that someday we might be glad that they are still around.

The moving truck was eventually packed and ready to lead Lucy to her new resting place.

We drove slowly to George's RV Storage to get Lucy her spot, only to find the place to be some redneck's backyard crammed with forty other beat-up RVs. Not wanting to pay double the money elsewhere, we sheepishly conceded, feeling guilty for leaving our special companion behind in this junkyard. She will probably feel right at home though, in this no-frills, weird and cheap place, much like most of our homes on the road.

We parked her tightly between a sun-bleached Winnebago and an old '60s flatbed truck. Joe rendered her storage-proof by pouring various potions into the gas and oil, while I made sure no light came in the tightly-closed gingham curtains. We locked her and walked away, neither of us looking back for fear of tears—whether sad or joyful. It's a good thing Ruby didn't realize what was going on. The only home she's ever known is now behind her.

Lucy has been so many things to us. She is a symbol of unpredictability, daring, hilarity, audacity, frustration, strangeness, toil, and hardship, and just as much warmth, safety, and tenderness. Mostly she's our icon of hope. She took us not only all over the map, put to uncharted places inside us that we never knew were there and would never have found without her. Just as it has been during each day of our life with Lucy, we have no idea what awaits us next.

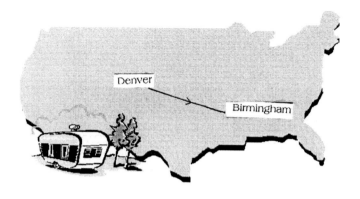

# EPILOGUE

Our familiar friend, the freeway, led us safely and uneventfully to Birmingham. Within two days we found an apartment to rent in the university neighborhood of Southside, where we were surrounded by the bizarre and eccentric characters we always seem to attract. We signed a six-month lease, hoping to find and buy a home within that time. Joe traveled alone for the next few months to outdoor festivals in Florida, while I ate and grew bigger.

In March of 1995, sweet Annabelle DeCamillis was born. While caring for a newborn, and continuing a rigorous festival schedule, we set out to find a house. Marie Lilla's prophecies came true on time—we had a child and bought our first gorgeous home within a year of her reading. Not long after, Marie's California forecast came about. One of the very art galleries that we used to worship in Los Angeles accepted our work for representation.

After four near sell-out shows in L.A., we continue to show there and at other galleries around the country. We've had museum shows here and abroad. We still participate in outdoor art festivals, but without financial pressure. To Joe's delight, we often take home top awards. Lucy is still on the road, used now for special projects and *short* camping trips. She still breaks down, and Joe still fixes her.

Ruby's getting old but still plays like a puppy.

From the day we moved here, we knew that Birmingham was the right place to be, and our love for the city still grows. We look back on our road years mostly with a smile; the breakdowns, uncertainties, discomforts, and even the carrots have blossomed into endearing recollections that we are grateful to have experienced. Those years changed us in ways that still affect us on a daily basis. There are a lot fewer things that we are afraid of. We have courage and boldness that allow us to try unusual and sometimes goofy things without much trepidation. We have no regrets. We never look back and wish we'd done more or tried something different. We don't have to ask ourselves if our life is going where we want it to. The road years helped us find the course for our career, home, and family that we still follow—not always serenely or faultlessly, but with determination, gratitude, and certainty that we are going to be all right no matter what swerves into our lane.

For a final update, my question regarding the mating habits of birds has finally been answered. Yes, birds do have penises. Our prediction about the Back Street Boys couldn't have been more wrong. And thanks to a freakish genetic anomaly, Annabelle loves carrots and eats them until her hands turn bright orange.

# *ACKNOWLEDGEMENTS*

Thank you to my friends who read earlier versions of the book and encouraged me: Linda Larson, Michael Burt, Annette Zablotsky, Sherry Frumkin, Kim DeCamillis, Dee Dee Leistenfeltz, Kent DeCardenas, Stephanie Shamsuddin, Becky Hairelson, and especially Joe.

Thanks to Robin Maus for her spectacular photo for the front cover, and to the amazing Charles Gaines for praise, editorial input, and for recommending it to others. Special thanks to my dear friend Joyce Maynard for moral support and advice, for writing the back cover, and for telling everyone she sees about us and our work.

# AUTHOR INFORMATION

If you wish to contact the author, comment about this book, or know more about the art of Dori and Joseph, visit www.doriandjoseph.com.

PHOTO CREDITS
Artist Portrait: Billy Brown
Cover Photo: Robin Maus